CHOPIN

THE MAN AND HIS MUSIC

Schuberth & Co., New York.

CHOPIN

THE MAN AND HIS MUSIC

BY

JAMES HUNEKER

NEW YORK
CHARLES SCRIBNER'S SONS

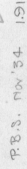

CONTENTS

PART I. — THE MAN.

PART II. — HIS MUSIC.

CONTENTS

PART 1
THE MAN

I

POLAND:—YOUTHFUL IDEALS

GUSTAVE FLAUBERT, pessimist and master of cadenced lyric prose, urged young writers to lead ascetic lives that in their art they might be violent. Chopin's violence was psychic, a travailing and groaning of the spirit; the bright roughness of adventure was missing from his quotidian existence. The tragedy was within. One recalls Maurice Maeterlinck: "Whereas most of our life is passed far from blood, cries and swords, and the tears of men have become silent, invisible and almost spiritual." Chopin went from Poland to France — from Warsaw to Paris — where, finally, he was borne to his grave in Père la Chaise. He lived, loved and died; and not for him were the perils, prizes and fascinations of a hero's career. He fought his battles within the walls of his soul — we may note and enjoy them in his music. His outward state was not niggardly of incident

3

though his inner life was richer, nourished as it was in the silence and the profound unrest of a being that irritably resented every intrusion. There were events that left ineradicable impressions upon his nature, upon his work: his early love, his sorrow at parting from parents and home, the shock of the Warsaw revolt, his passion for George Sand, the death of his father and of his friend Matuszyński, and the rupture with Madame Sand — these were crises of his history. All else was but an indeterminate factor in the scheme of his earthly sojourn. Chopin though not an anchorite resembled Flaubert, being both proud and timid; he led a detached life, hence his art was bold and violent. Unlike Liszt he seldom sought the glamor of the theatre, and was never in such public view as his maternal admirer, Sand. He was Frédéric François Chopin, composer, teacher of piano and a lyric genius of the highest range.

Recently the date of his birth has been again discussed by Natalie Janotha, the Polish pianist. Chopin was born in Zelazowa-Wola, six miles from Warsaw, March 1, 1809. This place is sometimes spelled Jeliasovaya-Volia. The medallion made for the tomb by Clésinger — the son-in-law of George Sand — and the watch given by the singer Catalani in 1820 with the inscription " Donné par Madame Catalani à Frédéric Chopin, âge de dix ans," have incited a conflict of authorities. Karasowski was informed by Chopin's sister that the correct year of his birth was 1809, and Szulc, Sowinski and Niecks agree with him. Szulc asserts that the memorial in the Holy Cross Church, Warsaw — where Chopin's heart is preserved — bears the date March 2, 1809. Chopin, so Henry T. Finck declares, was twenty-two years of age when he wrote to his teacher Elsner in 1831. Liszt told Niecks in 1878 that Karasowski had published the correct date in his biography. Now let us consider Janotha's arguments. According to her evidence the composer's natal day was February 22, 1810 and his christening occurred April 28 of the same year. The following baptismal certificate, originally in Latin and translated by Finck, is adduced. It is said to be from the church in which Chopin was christened: " I, the above, have performed the ceremony of baptizing in water a boy with the double name Frédéric François, on the 22d day of February, son of the musicians Nicolai Choppen, a

Frenchman, and Justina de Krzyzanowska
his legal spouse. God-parents: the musicians Franciscus Grembeki and Donna
Anna Skarbekowa, Countess of Zelazowa-
Wola." The wrong date was chiselled
upon the monument unveiled October 14,
1894, at Chopin's birthplace — erected practically through the efforts of Milia Balakireff the Russian composer. Janotha, whose
father founded the Warsaw Conservatory,
informed Finck that the later date has also
been put on other monuments in Poland.

Now Chopin's father was not a musician,
neither was his mother. I cannot trace
Grembeki, but we know that the Countess
Skarbek, mother of Chopin's namesake, was
not a musician; however, the title "musician" in the baptismal certificate may have
signified something eulogistic at that time.
Besides, the Polish clergy was not a particularly accurate class. But Janotha has
more testimony: in her controversy with
me in 1896 she quoted Father Bielawski,
the present curé of Bróchow parish church
of Zelazowa-Wola; this reverend person
consulted records and gave as his opinion
that 1810 is authentic. Nevertheless, the
biography of Wójcicki and the statement
of the Chopin family contradict him. And

so the case stands. Janotha continues firm in her belief although authorities do not justify her position.

All this petty pother arose since Niecks' comprehensive biography appeared. So sure was he of his facts that he disposed of the pseudo-date in one footnote. Perhaps the composer was to blame; artists, male as well as female, have been known to make themselves younger in years by conveniently forgetting their birthdate, or by attributing the error to carelessness in the registry of dates. Surely the Chopin family could not have been mistaken in such an important matter! Regarding Chopin's ancestry there is still a moiety of doubt. His father was born August 17, 1770 — the same year as Beethoven — at Nancy, Lorraine. Some claim that he had Polish blood in his veins. Szulc claims that he was the natural son of a Polish nobleman, who followed King Stanislas Leszcinski to Lorraine, dropping the Szopen, or Szop, for the more Gallic Chopin. When Frédéric went to Paris, he in turn changed the name from Szopen to Chopin, which is common in France.

Chopin's father emigrated to Warsaw in 1787 — enticed by the offer of a compatriot there in the tobacco business — and was the

7

traditional Frenchman of his time, well-bred, agreeable and more than usually cultivated.

He joined the national guard during the Kosciuszko revolution in 1794. When business stagnated he was forced to teach in the family of the Leszynskis; Mary of that name, one of his pupils, being beloved by Napoleon I. became the mother of Count Walewski, a minister of the second French empire. Drifting to Zelazowa-Wola, Nicholas Chopin lived in the house of the Countess Skarbek, acting as tutor to her son, Frédéric. There he made the acquaintance of Justina Krzyzanowska, born of "poor but noble parents." He married her in 1806 and she bore him four children: three girls, and the boy Frédéric François.

With a refined, scholarly French father, Polish in political sentiments, and an admirable Polish mother, patriotic to the extreme, Frédéric grew to be an intelligent, vivacious, home-loving lad. Never a hearty boy but never very delicate, he seemed to escape most of the disagreeable ills of childhood. The moonstruck, pale, sentimental calf of many biographers, he never was. Strong evidence exists that he was merry, pleasure-loving and fond of practical jokes. While his father was never rich, the family

after the removal to Warsaw lived at ease
The country was prosperous and Chopin
the elder became a professor in the Warsaw
Lyceum. His children were brought up in
an atmosphere of charming simplicity, love
and refinement. The mother was an ideal
mother, and, as George Sand declared, Chopin's "only love." But, as we shall discover later, Lélia was ever jealous — jealous
even of Chopin's past. His sisters were
gifted, gentle and disposed to pet him.
Niecks has killed all the pretty fairy tales
of his poverty and suffering.

Strong common sense ruled the actions of
Chopin's parents, and when his love for music
revealed itself at an early age they engaged
a teacher named Adalbert Zwyny, a Bohemian who played the violin and taught piano.
Julius Fontana, one of the first friends of the
boy — he committed suicide in Paris, December 31, 1869, — says that at the age of twelve
Chopin knew so much that he was left to
himself with the usual good and ill results.
He first played on February 24, 1818, a concerto by Gyrowetz and was so pleased with
his new collar that he naïvely told his mother,
"Everybody was looking at my collar." His
musical precocity, not as marked as Mozart's,
but phenomenal withal, brought him into in-

timacy with the Polish aristocracy and there his taste for fashionable society developed. The Czartoryskis, Radziwills, Skarbeks, Potockis, Lubeckis and the Grand Duke Constantine with his Princess Lowicka made life pleasant for the talented boy. Then came his lessons with Joseph Elsner in composition, lessons of great value. Elsner saw the material he had to mould, and so deftly did he teach that his pupil's individuality was never checked, never warped. For Elsner Chopin entertained love and reverence; to him he wrote from Paris asking his advice in the matter of studying with Kalkbrenner, and this advice he took seriously. "From Zwyny and Elsner even the greatest ass must learn something," he is quoted as having said.

Then there are the usual anecdotes — one is tempted to call them the stock stories of the boyhood of any great composer. In infancy Chopin could not hear music without crying. Mozart was morbidly sensitive to the tones of a trumpet. Later the Polish lad sported familiarly with his talents, for he is related to have sent to sleep and awakened a party of unruly boys at his father's school. Another story is his fooling of a Jew merchant. He had high spirits, perhaps too high, for his slender physique.

He was a facile mimic, and Liszt, Balzac, Bocage, Sand and others believed that he would have made an actor of ability. With his sister Emilia he wrote a little comedy. Altogether he was a clever, if not a brilliant lad. His letters show that he was not the latter, for while they are lively they do not reveal much literary ability. But their writer saw with open eyes, eyes that were disposed to caricature the peculiarities of others. This trait, much clarified and spiritualized in later life, became a distinct, ironic note in his character. Possibly it attracted Heine, although his irony was on a more intellectual plane.

His piano playing at this time was neat and finished, and he had already begun those experimentings in technique and tone that afterward revolutionized the world of music and the keyboard. He being sickly and his sister's health poor, the pair was sent in 1826 to Reinerz, a watering place in Prussian Silesia. This with a visit to his godmother, a titled lady named Wiesiolowska and a sister of Count Frédéric Skarbek, — the name does not tally with the one given heretofore, as noted by Janotha, — consumed this year. In 1827 he left his regular studies at the Lyceum and devoted his time to music. He was much in the country listening to the fiddling and singing of the peasants, thus laying the corner stone of his art as a national composer. In the fall of 1828 he went to Berlin, and this trip gave him a foretaste of the outer world.

Stephen Heller, who saw Chopin in 1830, described him as pale, of delicate health, and not destined, so they said in Warsaw, for a long life. This must have been during one of his depressed periods, for his stay in Berlin gives a record of unclouded spirits. However, his sister Emilia died young of pulmonary trouble and doubtless Frédéric was predisposed to lung complaint. He was constantly admonished by his relatives to keep his coat closed. Perhaps, as in Wagner's case, the uncontrollable gayety and hectic humors were but so many signs of a fatal disintegrating process. Wagner outlived them until the Scriptural age, but Chopin succumbed when grief, disappointment and intense feeling had undermined him. For the dissipations of the "average sensual man" he had an abiding contempt. He never smoked, in fact disliked it. His friend Sand differed greatly in this respect, and one of the saddest anecdotes related by De Lenz accuses her of calling for a match to light her cigar: "Frédéric, un fidibus," she commanded, and Frédéric obeyed. Mr. Philip Hale mentions a letter from Balzac to his Countess Hanska, dated March 15, 1841, which concludes: "George Sand did not leave Paris last year. She lives at Rue Pigalle, No. 16. . . . Chopin is always there. *Elle ne fume que des* CIGARETTES, *et pas autre chose.*" Mr. Hale states that the italics are in the letter. So much for De Lenz and his fidibus!

I am impelled here to quote from Mr. Earnest Newman's "Study of Wagner" because Chopin's exaltation of spirits, alternating with irritability and intense depression, were duplicated in Wagner. Mr. Newman writes of Wagner: "There have been few men in whom the torch of life has burned so fiercely. In his early days he seems to have had that gayety of temperament and that apparently boundless energy which men in his case, as in that of Heine, Nietzsche, Amiel and others, have wrongly assumed to be the outcome of harmonious physical and mental health. There is a pathetic exception in the outward lives of so many men of genius, the bloom being, to the instructed eye, only the indication of some subtle nervous derangement, only the forerunner of decay." The overmastering cerebral agitation that obsessed Wagner's life, was as with Chopin a symptom, not a sickness; but in the latter it had not yet assumed a sinister turn.

Chopin's fourteen days in Berlin, — he went there under the protection of his father's friend, Professor Jarocki, to attend the great scientific congress — were full of joy unrestrained. The pair left Warsaw September 9, 1828, and after five days travel in a diligence arrived at Berlin. This was a period of leisure travelling and living. Frédéric saw Spontini, Mendelssohn and Zelter at a distance and heard "Freischütz." He attended the congress and made sport of the scientists, Alexander von Humboldt included. On the way home they stopped at a place called Zullichau, and Chopin improvised on Polish airs so charmingly that the stage was delayed, "all hands turning in" to listen. This is another of the anecdotes of honorable antiquity. Count Tarnowski relates that "Chopin left Warsaw with a light heart, with a mind full of ideas, perhaps full of dreams of fame and happiness. 'I have only twenty kreuzers in my pockets,' he writes in his note-book, 'and it seems to me that I am richer than Arthur Potocki, whom I met only a moment ago;' besides this, witty conceptions, fun, showing a quiet and cheerful spirit; for example, ' May it be permitted to me to sign myself as belonging to the circle of your friends, — F. Chopin.' Or, ' A welcome moment in which I can express to you my friendship. — F. Chopin, office clerk.' Or again, ' Ah, my most lordly sir, I do not myself yet understand the joy which I feel on entering the circle of your real friends. — F. Chopin, penniless'!' "

These letters have a Micawber ring, but they indicate Chopin's love of jest. Sikorski tells a story of the lad's improvising in church so that the priest, choir and congregation were forgotten by him.

The travellers arrived at Warsaw October 6 after staying a few days in Posen where the Prince Radziwill lived; here Chopin played in private. This prince-composer, despite what Liszt wrote, did not contribute a penny to the youth's musical education, though he always treated him in a sympathetic manner.

Hummel and Paganini visited Warsaw in 1829. The former he met and admired, the latter he worshipped. This year may have seen the composition, if not the publication of the " Souvenir de Paganini," said to be in the key of A major and first published in the supplement of the " Warsaw Echo Mu-

zyczne." Niecks writes that he never saw a
copy of this rare composition. Paderewski
tells me he has the piece and that it is
weak, having historic interest only. I cannot find much about the Polish poet, Julius
Slowacki, who died the same year, 1849, as
Edgar Allan Poe. Tarnowski declares him
to have been Chopin's warmest friend and in
his poetry a starting point of inspiration for
the composer.

In July 1829, accompanied by two friends,
Chopin started for Vienna. Travelling in a
delightful, old-fashioned manner, the party
saw much of the country — Galicia, Upper
Silesia and Moravia — the Polish Switzerland.
On July 31 they arrived in the Austrian
capital. Then Chopin first began to enjoy
an artistic atmosphere, to live less parochially.
His home life, sweet and tranquil as it was,
could not fail to hurt him as artist; he was
flattered and coddled and doubtless the touch
of effeminacy in his person was fostered.
In Vienna the life was gayer, freer and infinitely more artistic than in Warsaw. He
met every one worth knowing in the artistic
world and his letters at that period are positively brimming over with gossip and pen
pictures of the people he knew. The little
drop of malice he injects into his descriptions

of the personages he encounters is harm-
less enough and proves that the young man
had considerable wit. Count Gallenberg, the
lessee of the famous Kärnthnerthor Theatre,
was kind to him, and the publisher Haslinger
treated him politely. He had brought with
him his variations on " La ci darem la mano ";
altogether the times seemed propitious and
much more so when he was urged to give
a concert. Persuaded to overcome a natural
timidity, he made his Vienna début at this
theatre August 11, 1829, playing on a Stein
piano his Variations, opus 2. His Krakowiak
Rondo had been announced, but the parts
were not legible, so instead he improvised.
He had success, being recalled, and his improvisation on the Polish tune called " Chmiel '
and a theme from " La Dame Blanche "
stirred up much enthusiasm in which a grumbling orchestra joined. The press was favorable, though Chopin's playing was considered
rather light in weight. His style was admired and voted original — here the critics
could see through the millstone — while a lady
remarked " It's a pity his appearance is so
insignificant." This reached the composer's
ear and caused him an evil quarter of an hour
for he was morbidly sensitive; but being, like
most Poles, secretive, managed to hide it

August 18, encouraged by his triumph, Chopin gave a second concert on the same stage. This time he played the Krakowiak and his talent for composition was discussed by the newspapers. " He plays very quietly, without the daring élan which distinguishes the artist from the amateur," said one; " his defect is the non-observance of the indication of accent at the beginning of musical phrases." What was then admired in Vienna was explosive accentuations and piano drumming. The article continues: " As in his playing he was like a beautiful young tree that stands free and full of fragrant blossoms and ripening fruits, so he manifested as much estimable individuality in his compositions where new figures and passages, new forms unfolded themselves." This rather acute critique, translated by Dr. Niecks, is from the Wiener "Theaterzeitung" of August 20, 1829. The writer of it cannot be accused of misoneism, that hardening of the faculties of curiousness and prophecy — that semi-paralysis of the organs of hearing which afflicts critics of music so early in life and evokes rancor and dislike to novelties. Chopin derived no money from either of his concerts.

By this time he was accustomed to being

18

reminded of the lightness and exquisite delicacy of his touch and the originality of his style. It elated him to be no longer mistaken for a pupil and he writes home that " my manner of playing pleases the ladies so very much." This manner never lost its hold over female hearts, and the airs, caprices and little struttings of Frédéric are to blame for the widely circulated legend of his effeminate ways. The legend soon absorbed his music, and so it has come to pass that this fiction, begotten of half fact and half mental indolence, has taken root, like the noxious weed it is. When Rubinstein, Tausig and Liszt played Chopin in passional phrases, the public and critics were aghast. This was a transformed Chopin indeed, a Chopin transposed to the key of manliness. Yet it is the true Chopin. The young man's manners were a trifle feminine but his brain was masculine, electric, and his soul courageous. His Polonaises, Ballades, Scherzi and Études need a mighty grip, a grip mental and physical.

Chopin met Czerny. " He is a good man, but nothing more," he said of him. Czerny admired the young pianist with the elastic hand and on his second visit to Vienna, characteristically inquired, " Are you still industrious?" Czerny's brain was a tireless incubator of piano exercises, while Chopin so fused the technical problem with the poetic idea, that such a nature as the old pedagogue's must have been unattractive to him. He knew Franz, Lachner and other celebrities and seems to have enjoyed a mild flirtation with Leopoldine Blahetka, a popular young pianist, for he wrote of his sorrow at parting from her. On August 19 he left with friends for Bohemia, arriving at Prague two days later. There he saw everything and met Klengel, of canon fame, a still greater canon-eer than the redoubtable Jadassohn of Leipzig. Chopin and Klengel liked each other. Three days later the party proceeded to Teplitz and Chopin played in aristocratic company. He reached Dresden August 26, heard Spohr's "Faust" and met capellmeister Morlacchi — that same Morlacchi whom Wagner succeeded as a conductor January 10, 1843 — vide Finck's "Wagner." By September 12, after a brief sojourn in Breslau, Chopin was again safe at home in Warsaw.

About this time he fell in love with Constantia Gladowska, a singer and pupil of the Warsaw Conservatory. Niecks dwells gingerly upon his fervor in love and friend-

ship — "a passion with him" and thinks
that it gives the key to his life. Of his
romantic friendship for Titus Woyciechowski and John Matuszyński — his "Johnnie"
— there are abundant evidences in the
letters. They are like the letters of a
love-sick maiden. But Chopin's purity of
character was marked; he shrank from
coarseness of all sorts, and the Fates only
know what he must have suffered at times
from George Sand and her gallant band
of retainers. To this impressionable man,
Parisian badinage — not to call it anything
stronger — was positively antipathetical.
Of him we might indeed say in Laf-
cadio Hearn's words, "Every mortal man
has been many million times a woman."
And was it the Goncourts who dared to
assert that, "there are no women of genius :
women of genius are men"? Chopin needed
an outlet for his sentimentalism. His piano
was but a sieve for some, and we are rather
amused than otherwise on reading the romantic nonsense of his boyish letters.

After the Vienna trip his spirits and his
health flagged. He was overwrought and
Warsaw became hateful to him, for he loved
but had not the courage to tell it to the
beloved one. He put it on paper, he played

it, but speak it he could not. Here is a point that reveals Chopin's native indecision, his inability to make up his mind. He recalls to me the Frédéric Moreau of Flaubert's "L'Éducation Sentimentale." There is an atrophy of the will, for Chopin can neither propose nor fly from Warsaw. He writes letters that are full of self-reproaches, letters that must have both bored and irritated his friends. Like many other men of genius he suffered all his life from folie de doute, indeed his was what specialists call "a beautiful case." This halting and irresolution was a stumbling block in his career and is faithfully mirrored in his art.

Chopin went to Posen in October, 1829, and at the Radziwills was attracted by the beauty and talent of the Princess Elisa, who died young. George Sand has noted Chopin's emotional versatility in the matter of falling in and out of love. He could accomplish both of an evening and a crumpled roseleaf was sufficient cause to induce frowns and capricious flights — decidedly a young man très difficile. He played at the "Ressource" in November, 1829, the Variations, opus 2. On March 17, 1830, he gave his first concert in Warsaw, and

22

selected the adagio and rondo of his first
concerto, the one in F minor, and the Pot-
pourri on Polish airs. His playing was
criticised for being too delicate — an old
complaint — but the musicians, Elsner, Kurpinski and the rest were pleased. Edouard
Wolff said they had no idea in Warsaw of
"the real greatness of Chopin." He was
Polish, this the public appreciated, but of
Chopin the individual they missed entirely
the flavor. A week later, spurred by adverse
and favorable criticism, he gave a second
concert, playing the same excerpts from this
concerto — the slow movement is Constance
Gladowska musically idealized — the Krakowiak and an improvisation. The affair
was a success. From these concerts he
cleared six hundred dollars, not a small sum
in those days for an unknown virtuoso.
A sonnet was printed in his honor, champagne was offered him by an enthusiastic
Paris bred, but not born, pianist named
Dunst, who for this act will live in all chron-
icles of piano playing. Worse still, Orlowski
served up the themes of his concerto into
mazurkas and had the impudence to publish
them.

Then came the last blow: he was asked by a
music seller for his portrait, which he refused,

having no desire, he said with a shiver, to see his face on cheese and butter wrappers Some of the criticisms were glowing, others absurd as criticisms occasionally are. Chopin wrote to Titus the same rhapsodical protestations and finally declared in meticulous peevishness, "I will no longer read what people write about me." This has the familiar ring of the true artist who cares nothing for the newspapers but reads them religiously after his own and his rivals' concerts.

Chopin heard Henrietta Sontag with great joy; he was ever a lover and a connoisseur of singing. He advised young pianists to listen carefully and often to great singers. Mdlle. de Belleville the pianist and Lipinski the violinist were admired, and he could write a sound criticism when he chose. But the Gladowska is worrying him. "Unbearable longing" is driving him to exile. He attends her début as Agnese in Paer's opera of that title and writes a complete description of the important function to Titus, who is at his country seat where Chopin visits him betimes. Agitated, he thinks of going to Berlin or Vienna, but after much philandering remains in Warsaw. On October 11, 1830, following many preparations and much emotional shilly-shallying, Chopin gave his third

and last Warsaw concert. He played the
E minor concerto for the first time in public
but not in sequence. The first and last two
movements were separated by an aria, such
being the custom of those days. Later
he gave the Fantasia on Polish airs. Best
of all for him, Miss Gladowska sang a
Rossini air, "wore a white dress and roses
in her hair, and was charmingly beautiful." Thus Chopin; and the details have
all the relevancy of a male besieged by Dan
Cupid. Chopin must have played well. He
said so himself, and he was always a cautious
self-critic despite his pride. His vanity and
girlishness peep out in his recital by the response to a quartet of recalls: "I believe I
did it yesterday with a certain grace, for
Brandt had taught me how to do it properly."
He is not speaking of his poetic performance,
but of his bow to the public. As he formerly
spoke to his mother of his pretty collar, so
as young man he makes much of his deport-
ment. But it is all quite in the rôle; scratch
an artist and you surprise a child.

Of course, Constantia sang wonderfully.
"Her low B came out so magnificently that
Zieliński declared it alone was worth a thou-
sand ducats." Ah, these enamored ones!
Chopin left Warsaw November 1, 1830, for

Vienna and without declaring his love. Or
was he a rejected suitor? History is dumb.
He never saw his Gladowska again, for he
did not return to Warsaw. The lady was
married in 1832 — preferring a solid certainty
to nebulous genius — to Joseph Grabowski, a
merchant at Warsaw. Her husband, so saith
a romantic biographer, Count Wodzinski, became blind; perhaps even a blind country
gentleman was preferable to a lachrymose
pianist. Chopin must have heard of the
attachment in 1831. Her name almost dis-
appears from his correspondence. Time as
well as other nails drove from his memory
her image. If she was fickle, he was inconstant, and so let us waste no pity on this
episode, over which lakes of tears have been
shed and rivers of ink have been spilt.

Chopin was accompanied by Elsner and a
party of friends as far as Wola, a short distance from Warsaw. There the pupils of the
Conservatory sang a cantata by Elsner, and
after a banquet he was given a silver goblet
filled with Polish earth, being adjured, so
Karasowski relates, never to forget his country or his friends wherever he might wander.
Chopin, his heart full of sorrow, left home,
parents, friends, and " ideal," severed with his
youth, and went forth in the world with the

keyboard and a brain full of beautiful music as his only weapons.

At Kaliz he was joined by the faithful Titus, and the two went to Breslau, where they spent four days, going to the theatre and listening to music. Chopin played quite impromptu two movements of his E minor concerto, supplanting a tremulous amateur. In Dresden where they arrived November 10, they enjoyed themselves with music. Chopin went to a soirée at Dr. Kreyssig's and was overwhelmed at the sight of a circle of dames armed with knitting needles which they used during the intervals of music-making in the most formidable manner. He heard Auber and Rossini operas and Rolla, the Italian violinist, and listened with delight to Dotzauer and Kummer the violoncellists — the 'cello being an instrument for which he had a consuming affection. Rubini, the brother of the great tenor, he met, and was promised important letters of introduction if he desired to visit Italy. He saw Klengel again, who told the young Pole, thereby pleasing him very much, that his playing was like John Field's. Prague was also visited, and he arrived at Vienna in November. There he confidently expected a repetition of his former successes, but was disappointed.

Haslinger received him coldly and refused to print his variations or concerto unless he got them for nothing. Chopin's first brush with the hated tribe of publishers begins here, and he adopts as his motto the pleasing device, " Pay, thou animal," a motto he strictly adhered to; in money matters Chopin was very particular. The bulk of his extant correspondence is devoted to the exposure of the ways and wiles of music publishers. " Animal " is the mildest term he applies to them, " Jew " the most frequent objurgation. After all Chopin was very Polish.

He missed his friends the Blahetkas, who had gone to Stuttgart, and altogether did not find things so promising as formerly. No profitable engagements could be secured, and, to cap his misery, Titus, his other self, left him to join the revolutionists in Poland November 30. His letters reflect his mental agitation and terror over his parents' safety. A thousand times he thought of renouncing his artistic ambitions and rushing to Poland to fight for his country. He never did, and his indecision — it was not cowardice — is our gain. Chopin put his patriotism, his wrath and his heroism into his Polonaises. That is why we have them now, instead of Chopin having been the target of some black-browed Russian. Chopin was psychically brave; let us not cavil at the almost miraculous delicacy of his organization. He wrote letters to his parents and to Matuszyński, but they are not despairing — at least not to the former. He pretended gayety and had great hopes for the future, for he was living entirely on means supplied him by his father. News of Constantia gladdened him, and he decided to go to Italy, but the revolution early in 1831 decided him for France. Dr. Malfatti was good to him and cheered him, and he managed to accomplish much social visiting. The letters of this period are most interesting. He heard Sarah Heinefetter sing, and listened to Thalberg's playing of a movement of his own concerto. Thalberg was three years younger than Chopin and already famous. Chopin did not admire him: "Thalberg plays famously, but he is not my man. . . . He plays forte and piano with the pedals but not with the hand; takes tenths as easily as I do octaves, and wears studs with diamonds." Thalberg was not only too much of a technician for Chopin, but he was also a Jew and a successful one. In consequence, both poet and Pole revolted.

Hummel called on Frédéric, but we hear

nothing of his opinion of the elder man and his music; this is all the more strange, considering how much Chopin built on Hummel's style. Perhaps that is the cause of the silence, just as Wagner's dislike for Meyerbeer was the result of his obligations to the composer of "Les Huguenots." He heard Aloys Schmitt play, and uttered the very Heinesque witticism that "he is already over forty years old, and composes eighty years old music." This in a letter to Elsner. Our Chopin could be amazingly sarcastic on occasion. He knew Slavik the violin virtuoso, Merk the 'cellist, and all the music publishers. At a concert given by Madame Garzia-Vestris, in April, 1831, he appeared, and in June gave a concert of his own, at which he must have played the E minor concerto, because of a passing mention in a musical paper. He studied much, and it was July 20, 1831, before he left Vienna after a second, last, and thoroughly discouraging visit.

Chopin got a passport viséd for London, "passant par Paris à Londres," and had permission from the Russian Ambassador to go as far as Munich. Then the cholera gave him some bother, as he had to secure a clean bill of health, but he finally got away. The romantic story of "I am only passing through Paris," which he is reported to have said in after years, has been ruthlessly shorn of its sentiment. At Munich he played his second concerto and pleased greatly. But he did not remain in the Bavarian capital, hastening to Stuttgart, where he heard of the capture of Warsaw by the Russians, September 8, 1831. This news, it is said, was the genesis of the great C minor étude in opus 10, sometimes called the "Revolutionary." Chopin exclaimed in a letter dated December 16, 1831, "All this caused me much pain — who could have foreseen it!" and in another letter he wrote, "How glad my mamma will be that I did not go back." Count Tarnowski in his recollections prints some extracts from a diary said to have been kept by Chopin. According to this his agitation must have been terrible. Here are several examples :

" My poor father ! My dearest ones ! Perhaps they hunger? Maybe he has not anything to buy bread for mother? Perhaps my sisters have fallen victims to the fury of the Muscovite soldiers? Oh, father, is this the consolation of your old age? Mother, poor suffering mother, is it for this you outlived your daughter? "

" And I here unoccupied ! And I am here with empty hands ! Sometimes I groan, suffer and despair at the piano! O God, move the earth, that it may swallow the humanity of this century! May the most cruel fortune fall upon the French, that they did not come to our aid." All this sounds a trifle melodramatic and quite unlike Chopin.

He did not go to Warsaw, but started for France at the end of September, arriving early in October, 1831. Poland's downfall had aroused him from his apathy, even if it sent him further from her. This journey, as Liszt declares, "settled his fate." Chopin was twenty-two years old when he reached Paris.

PARIS:— IN THE MAËLSTROM

Here, according to Niecks, is the itinerary of Chopin's life for the next eighteen years: In Paris, 27 Boulevard Poisonnière, to 5 and 38 Chaussée d'Antin, to Aix-la-Chapelle, Carlsbad, Leipzig, Heidelberg, Marienbad, and London, to Majorca, to 5 Rue Tronchet, 16 Rue Pigalle, and 9 Square d'Orléans, to England and Scotland, to 9 Square d'Orléans once more, Rue Chaillot and 12 Place Vendôme, and then — Père la Chaise, the last resting-place. It may be seen that Chopin was a restless, though not roving nature. In later years his inability to remain settled in one place bore a pathological impress, — consumptives are often so.

The Paris of 1831, the Paris of arts and letters, was one of the most delightful cities in the world for the culture-loving. The molten tide of passion and decorative extravagance that swept over intellectual Europe three score years and ten ago, bore on its foaming crest Victor Hugo, prince of romanticists. Near by was Henri Heine, — he left

3

Heinrich across the Rhine, — Heine, who dipped his pen in honey and gall, who sneered and wept in the same couplet. The star of classicism had seemingly set. In the rich conflict of genius were Gautier, Schumann, and the rest. All was romance, fantasy, and passion, and the young men heard the moon sing silvery — you remember De Musset! — and the leaves rustle rhythms to the heart-beats of lovers. "Away with the gray-beards," cried he of the scarlet waistcoat, and all France applauded "Ernani." Pity it was that the romantic infant had to die of intellectual anæmia, leaving as a legacy the memories and work of one of the most marvellous groupings of genius since the Athens of Pericles. The revolution of 1848 called from the mud the sewermen. Flaubert, his face to the past, gazed sorrowfully at Carthage and wrote an epic of the French bourgeois. Zola and his crowd delved into a moral morass, and the world grew weary of them. And then the faint, fading flowers of romanticism were put into albums where their purple harmonies and subtle sayings are pressed into sweet twilight forgetfulness. Berlioz, mad Hector of the flaming locks, whose orchestral ozone vivified the scores of Wagner and Liszt, began to sound garishly empty,

brilliantly superficial; "the colossal night-
ingale" is difficult to classify even to-day.
A romantic by temperament he unquestionably was. But then his music, all color,
nuance, and brilliancy, was not genuinely
romantic in its themes. Compare him with
Schumann, and the genuine romanticist tops
the virtuoso. Berlioz, I suspect, was a mag-
nified virtuoso. His orchestral technique is
supreme, but his music fails to force its way
into my soul. It pricks the nerves, it pleases
the sense of the gigantic, the strange, the
formless, but there is something uncanny
about it all, like some huge, prehistoric bird,
an awful Pterodactyl with goggle eyes, horrid
snout and scream. Berlioz, like Baudelaire,
has the power of evoking the shudder. But
as John Addington Symonds wrote: "The
shams of the classicists, the spasms of the
romanticists have alike to be abandoned.
Neither on a mock Parnassus nor on a paste-
board Blocksberg can the poet of the age
now worship. The artist walks the world at
large beneath the light of natural day." All
this was before the Polish charmer distilled
his sugared wormwood, his sweet, exasperated
poison, for thirsty souls in morbid Paris.

Think of the men and women with whom
the new comer associated — for his genius

was quickly divined: Hugo, Lamartine,
Père Lamenais, — ah! what balm for those
troubled days was in his " Paroles d'un Croy-
ant,"—Chateaubriand, Saint-Simon, Mérimée,
Gautier, Liszt, Victor Cousin, Baudelaire, Ary
Scheffer, Berlioz, Heine, — who asked the
Pole news of his muse the " laughing nymph,"
— " If she still continued to drape her silvery
veil around the flowing locks of her green
hair, with a coquetry so enticing; if the old
sea god with the long white beard still pur-
sued this mischievous maid with his ridicu-
lous love?" — De Musset, De Vigny, Rossini,
Meyerbeer, Auber, Sainte-Beuve, Adolphe
Nourrit, Ferdinand Hiller, Balzac, Dumas,
Heller, Delacroix, — the Hugo of painters,
— Michelet, Guizot, Thiers, Niemcevicz and
Mickiewicz the Polish bards, and George
Sand: the quintessence of the Paris of art
and literature.

The most eloquent page in Liszt's
" Chopin " is the narrative of an evening in
the Chaussée d'Antin, for it demonstrates the
Hungarian's literary gifts and feeling for the
right phrase. This description of Chopin's
apartment " invaded by surprise " has a hyp-
notizing effect on me. The very furnishings
of the chamber seem vocal under Liszt's
fanciful pen. In more doubtful taste is his

statement that "the glace which covers the grace of the élite, as it does the fruit of their desserts, . . . could not have been satisfactory to Chopin"! Liszt, despite his tendency to idealize Chopin after his death, is our most trustworthy witness at this period. Chopin was an ideal to Liszt though he has not left us a record of his defects. The Pole was ombrageux and easily offended; he disliked democracies, in fact mankind in the bulk stunned him. This is one reason, combined with a frail physique, of his inability to conquer the larger public. Thalberg could do it; his aristocratic tournure, imperturbability, beautiful touch and polished mechanism won the suffrage of his audiences. Liszt never stooped to cajole. He came, he played, he overwhelmed. Chopin knew all this, knew his weaknesses, and fought to overcome them but failed. Another crumpled roseleaf for this man of excessive sensibility.

Since told of Liszt and first related by him, is the anecdote of Chopin refusing to play, on being incautiously pressed, after dinner, giving as a reason "Ah, sir, I have eaten so little!" Even though his host was gauche it cannot be denied that the retort was rude.

Chopin met Osborne, Mendelssohn — who rather patronized him with his "Chopinetto."

— Baillot the violinist and Franchomme the
'cellist. With the latter he contracted a last-
ing friendship, often playing duos with him
and dedicating to him his G minor 'cello
Sonata. He called on Kalkbrenner, then
the first pianist of his day, who was puzzled
by the prodigious novelty of the young Pole's
playing. Having heard Herz and Hiller,
Chopin did not fear to perform his E minor
concerto for him. He tells all about the
interview in a letter to Titus: " Are you a
pupil of Field's?" was asked by Kalkbrenner,
who remarked that Chopin had the style of
Cramer and the touch of Field. Not having
a standard by which to gauge the new phenomenon, Kalkbrenner was forced to fall back
on the playing of men he knew. He then
begged Chopin to study three years with
him — only three ! — but Elsner in an earnest
letter dissuaded his pupil from making any
experiments that might hurt his originality
of style. Chopin actually attended the class
of Kalkbrenner but soon quit, for he had
nothing to learn of the pompous, penurious
pianist. The Hiller story of how Mendelssohn, Chopin, Liszt and Heller teased this
grouty old gentleman on the Boulevard des
Italiens is capital reading, if not absolutely
true. Yet Chopin admired Kalkbrenner's

finished technique despite his platitudinous manner. Heine said — or rather quoted Koreff — that Kalkbrenner looked like a bonbon that had been in the mud. Niecks thinks Chopin might have learned of Kalkbrenner on the mechanical side. Chopin, in public, was modest about his attainments, looking upon himself as self-taught. " I cannot create a new school, because I do not even know the old," he said. It is this very absence of scholasticism that is both the power and weakness of his music. In reality his true technical ancestor was Hummel.

He played the E minor concerto first in Paris, February 26, 1832, and some smaller pieces. Although Kalkbrenner, Baillot and others participated, Chopin was the hero of the evening. The affair was a financial failure, the audience consisting mostly of distinguished and aristocratic Poles. Mendelssohn, who disliked Kalkbrenner and was angered at his arrogance in asking Chopin to study with him, " applauded furiously." " After this," Hiller writes, " nothing more was heard of Chopin's lack of technique." The criticisms were favorable. On May 20, 1832, Chopin appeared at a charity concert organized by Prince de la Moskowa. He was lionized in society and he wrote to

Titus that his heart beat in syncopation, so exciting was all this adulation, social excitement and rapid gait of living. But he still sentimentalizes to Titus and wishes him in Paris.

A flirtation of no moment, with Francilla Pixis, the adopted daughter of Pixis the hunchback pianist — cruelly mimicked by Chopin — aroused the jealousy of the elder artist. Chopin was delighted, for he was malicious in a dainty way. "What do you think of this?" he writes. "I, a dangerous séducteur!" The Paris letters to his parents were unluckily destroyed, as Karasowski relates, by Russian soldiers in Warsaw, September 19, 1863, and with them were burned his portrait by Ary Scheffer and his first piano. The loss of the letters is irremediable. Karasowski who saw some of them says they were tinged with melancholy. Despite his artistic success Chopin needed money and began to consider again his projected trip to America. Luckily he met Prince Valentine Radziwill on the street, so it is said, and was persuaded to play at a Rothschild soirée. From that moment his prospects brightened, for he secured paying pupils. Niecks, the iconoclast, has run this story to earth and finds it built on airy, romantic foundations. Liszt,

Hiller, Franchomme and Sowinski never heard of it although it was a stock anecdote of Chopin.

Chopin must have broadened mentally as well as musically in this congenial, artistic environment. He went about, hobnobbed with princesses, and of the effect of this upon his compositions there can be no doubt. If he became more cosmopolitan he also became more artificial and for a time the salon with its perfumed, elegant atmosphere threatened to drug his talent into forgetfulness of loftier aims. Luckily the master-sculptor Life intervened and real troubles chiselled his character on tragic, broader and more passionate lines. He played frequently in public during 1832–1833 with Hiller, Liszt, Herz and Osborne, and much in private. There was some rivalry in this parterre of pianists. Liszt, Chopin and Hiller indulged in friendly contests and Chopin always came off winner when Polish music was essayed. He delighted in imitating his colleagues, Thalberg especially. Adolphe Brisson tells of a meeting of Sand, Chopin and Thalberg, where, as Mathias says, the lady " chattered like a magpie " and Thalberg, after being congratulated by Chopin on his magnificent virtuosity, reeled off polite phrases in return; doubtless

ne valued the Pole's compliments for what
they were worth. The moment his back
was presented, Chopin at the keyboard was
mocking him. It was then Chopin told
Sand of his pupil, Georges Mathias, " c'est
une bonne caboche." Thalberg took his re-
venge whenever he could. After a concert
by Chopin he astonished Hiller by shouting
on the way home. In reply to questions he
slily answered that he needed a forte as he
had heard nothing but pianissimo the entire
evening!

Chopin was never a hearty partisan of the
Romantic movement. Its extravagance, misplaced enthusiasm, turbulence, attacks on
church, state and tradition disturbed the
finical Pole while noise, réclame and boister-
ousness chilled and repulsed him. He
wished to be the Uhland of Poland, but
he objected to smashing idols and refused
to wade in gutters to reach his ideal. He
was not a fighter, yet as one reviews the
past half century it is his still small voice
that has emerged from the din, the golden
voice of a poet and not the roar of the
artistic demagogues of his day. Liszt's
influence was stimulating, but what did not
Chopin do for Liszt? Read Schumann. He
managed in 1834 to go to Aix-la-Chapelle

to attend the Lower Rhenish Music Festival
There he met Hiller and Mendelssohn at
the painter Schadow's and improvised marvellously, so Hiller writes. He visited
Coblenz with Hiller before returning home.

Professor Niecks has a deep spring of personal humor which he taps at rare intervals.
He remarks that "the coming to Paris and
settlement there of his friend Matuszyński
must have been very gratifying to Chopin,
who felt so much the want of one with whom
to sigh." This slanting allusion is matched
by his treatment of George Sand. After
literally ratting her in a separate chapter, he
winds up his work with the solemn assurance
that he abstains "from pronouncing judgment because the complete evidence did not
seem to me to warrant my doing so." This
is positively delicious. When I met this
biographer at Bayreuth in 1896, I told him
how much I had enjoyed his work, adding that
I found it indispensable in the re-construc-
tion of Chopin. Professor Niecks gazed at me
blandly — he is most amiable and scholarly-
looking — and remarked, "You are not
the only one." He was probably thinking
of the many who have had recourse to his
human documents of Chopin. But Niecks,
in 1888, built on Karasowski, Liszt, Schu-

mann, Sand and others, so the process is bound to continue. Since 1888 much has been written of Chopin, much surmised.

With Matuszyśnki the composer was happier. He devoutly loved his country and despite his sarcasm was fond of his countrymen. Never an extravagant man, he invariably assisted the Poles. After 1834-5, Chopin's activity as a public pianist began to wane. He was not always understood and was not so warmly welcomed as he deserved to be; on one occasion when he played the Larghetto of his F minor concerto in a Conservatoire concert, its frigid reception annoyed him very much. Nevertheless he appeared at a benefit concert at Habeneck's, April 26, 1835. The papers praised, but his irritability increased with every public performance. About this time he became acquainted with Bellini, for whose sensuous melodies he had a peculiar predilection.

In July, 1835, Chopin met his father at Carlsbad. Then he went to Dresden and later to Leipzig, playing privately for Schumann, Clara Wieck, Wenzel and Mendelssohn. Schumann gushes over Chopin, but this friendliness was never reciprocated. On his return to Paris Chopin visited Heidelberg, where he saw the father of his pupil, Adolphe Gutmann, and reached the capital of the civilized world the middle of October.

Meanwhile a love affair had occupied his attention in Dresden. In September, 1835, Chopin met his old school friends, the Wodzinskis, former pupils at his father's school. He fell in love with their sister Marie and they became engaged. He spoke to his father about the matter, and for the time Paris and his ambitions were forgotten. He enjoyed a brief dream of marrying and of settling near Warsaw, teaching and composing — the occasional dream that tempts most active artists, soothing them with the notion that there is really a haven of rest from the world's buffets. Again the gods intervened in the interest of music. The father of the girl objected on the score of Chopin's means and his social position — artists were not Paderewskis in those days — although the mother favored the romance. The Wodzinskis were noble and wealthy. In the summer of 1836, at Marienbad, Chopin met Marie again. In 1837, the engagement was broken and the following year the inconstant beauty married the son of Chopin's godfather, Count Frédéric Skarbek. As the

marriage did not prove a success — perhaps
the lady played too much Chopin — a divorce
ensued and later she married a gentleman
by the name of Orpiszewski. Count Wodzinski wrote " Les Trois Romans de Frédéric
Chopin," in which he asserts that his sister
rejected Chopin at Marienbad in 1836. But
Chopin survived the shock. He went back
to Paris, and in July 1837, accompanied by
Camille Pleyel and Stanislas Kózmian, visited
England for the first time. His stay was
short, only eleven days, and his chest trouble
dates from this time. He played at the house
of James Broadwood, the piano manufacturer,
being introduced by Pleyel as M. Fritz; but
his performance betrayed his identity. His
music was already admired by amateurs
but the critics with a few exceptions were
unfavorable to him.

Now sounds for the first time the sinister
motif of the George Sand affair. In defer-
ence to Mr. Hadow I shall not call it a liai-
son. It was not, in the vulgar sense. Chopin
might have been petty — a common failing
of artistic men — but he was never vulgar in
word or deed. He disliked "the woman with
the sombre eye" before he had met her.
Her reputation was not good, no matter if
George Eliot, Matthew Arnold, Elizabeth

46

Barrett Browning and others believed her an injured saint. Mr. Hadow indignantly repudiates anything that savors of irregularity in the relations of Chopin and Aurore Dudevant. If he honestly believes that their contemporaries flagrantly lied and that the woman's words are to be credited, why by all means let us leave the critic in his Utopia. Mary, Queen of Scots, has her Meline; why should not Sand boast of at least one apologist for her life — besides herself? I do not say this with cynical intent. Nor do I propose to discuss the details of the affair which has been dwelt upon ad nauseam by every twanger of the romantic string. The idealists will always see a union of souls, the realists — and there were plenty of them in Paris taking notes from 1837 to 1847 — view the alliance as a matter for gossip. The truth lies midway.

Chopin, a neurotic being, met the polyandrous Sand, a trampler on all the social and ethical conventions, albeit a woman of great gifts; repelled at first he gave way before the ardent passion she manifested toward him. She was his elder, so could veil the situation with the maternal mask, and she was the stronger intellect, more celebrated — Chopin was but a pianist in the eyes of the many —

and so won by her magnetism the man she
desired. Paris, artistic Paris, was full of such
situations. Liszt protected the Countess
d'Agoult, who bore him children, Cosima
Von Bülow-Wagner among the rest. Balzac
— Balzac, that magnificent combination of
Bonaparte and Byron, pirate and poet —
was apparently leading the life of a saint,
but his most careful student, Viscount Spelboerch de Lovenjoul — whose name is
veritably Balzac-ian — tells us some different
stories; even Gustave Flaubert, the ascetic
giant of Rouen, had a romance with Madame
Louise Colet, a mediocre writer and imitator
of Sand, — as was Countess d'Agoult, the
Frankfort Jewess better known as "Daniel
Stern," — that lasted from 1846 to 1854, according to Émile Faguet. Here then was a
medium which was the other side of good
and evil, a new transvaluation of morals, as
Nietzsche would say. Frédéric deplored the
union for he was theoretically a Catholic.
Did he not once resent the visit of Liszt and
a companion to his apartments when he was
absent? Indeed he may be fairly called a
moralist. Carefully reared in the Roman
Catholic religion he died confessing that
faith. With the exception of the Sand episode, his life was not an irregular one.

He abhorred the vulgar and tried to conceal this infatuation from his parents.

This intimacy, however, did the pair no harm artistically, notwithstanding the inevitable sorrow and heart burnings at the close. Chopin had some one to look after him — he needed it — and in the society of this brilliant Frenchwoman he throve amazingly: his best work may be traced to Nohant and Majorca. She on her side profited also. After the bitterness of her separation from Alfred de Musset about 1833 she had been lonely, for the Pagello intermezzo was of short duration. The De Musset-Sand story was not known in its entirety until 1896. Again M. Spelboerch de Lovenjoul must be consulted, as he possessed a bundle of letters that were written by George Sand and M. Buloz, the editor of " La Revue des Deux Mondes," in 1858.

De Musset went to Venice with Sand in the fall of 1833. They had the maternal sanction and means supplied by Madame de Musset. The story gives forth the true Gallic resonance on being critically tapped. De Musset returned alone, sick in body and soul, and thenceforth absinthe was his constant solace. There had been references, vague and disquieting, of a Dr. Pagello for whom

Sand had suddenly manifested one of her extraordinary fancies. This she denied, but De Musset's brother plainly intimated that the aggravating cause of his brother's illness had been the unexpected vision of Sand coquetting with the young medical man called in to prescribe for Alfred. Dr. Pagello in 1896 was interviewed by Dr. Cabanes of the Paris "Figaro" and here is his story of what had happened in 1833. This story will explain the later behavior of "la merle blanche" toward Chopin.

"One night George Sand, after writing three pages of prose full of poetry and inspiration, took an unaddressed envelope, placed therein the poetic declaration, and handed it to Dr. Pagello. He, seeing no address, did not, or feigned not, to understand for whom the letter was intended, and asked George Sand what he should do with it. Snatching the letter from his hands, she wrote upon the envelope: 'To the Stupid Pagello.' Some days afterward George Sand frankly told De Musset that henceforth she could be to him only a friend."

De Musset died in 1857 and after his death Sand startled Paris with "Elle et Lui," an obvious answer to "Confessions of a Child of the Age," De Musset's version — an un complimentary one to himself — of their separation. The poet's brother Paul rallied to his memory with "Lui et Elle," and even Louisa Colet ventured into the fracas with a trashy novel called "Lui." During all this mud-throwing the cause of the trouble calmly lived in the little Italian town of Belluno. It was Dr. Giuseppe Pagello who will go down in literary history as the one man that played Joseph to George Sand.

Now do you ask why I believe that Sand left Chopin when she was bored with him? The words "some days afterwards" are significant. I print the Pagello story not only because it is new, but as a reminder that George Sand in her love affairs was always the man. She treated Chopin as a child, a toy, used him for literary copy — pace Mr. Hadow! — and threw him over after she had wrung out all the emotional possibilities of the problem. She was true to herself even when she attempted to palliate her want of heart. Beware of the woman who punctuates the pages of her life with " heart " and " maternal feelings." " If I do not believe any more in tears it is because I saw thee crying! " exclaimed Chopin. Sand was the product of abnormal forces, she herself was abnormal, and her mental activity, while it created no permanent types in literary fiction, was also abnormal. She dominated Chopin, as she had dominated Jules Sandeau, Calmatta the mezzotinter, De Musset, Franz Liszt, Delacroix, Michel de Bourges — I have not the exact chronological order — and later Flaubert. The most lovable event in the life of this much loved woman was her old age affair — purely platonic — with Gustave Flaubert. The correspondence shows her to have been "maternal" to the last.

In the recently published "Lettres à l'Étrangère" of Honoré de Balzac, this about Sand is very apropos. A visit paid to George Sand at Nohant, in March 1838, brought the following to Madame Hanska:

It was rather well that I saw her, for we exchanged confidences regarding Sandeau. I, who blamed her to the last for deserting him, now feel only a deep compassion for her, as you will have for me, when you learn with whom we have had relations, she of love, I of friendship.

But she has been even more unhappy with Musset. So here she is, in retreat, denouncing both marriage and love, because in both she has found nothing but delusion.

I will tell you of her immense and secret devotion to these two men, and you will agree that there is nothing in common between angels and

devils. All the follies she has committed are
claims to glory in the eyes of great and beautiful
souls. She has been the dupe of la Dorval,
Bocage, Lamenais, etc.; through the same sentiment she is the dupe of Liszt and Madame
d'Agoult.

So let us accept without too much questioning as did Balzac, a reader of souls, the
Sand-Chopin partnership and follow its sin-
uous course until 1847.

Chopin met Sand at a musical matinée in
1837. Niecks throttles every romantic yarn
about the pair that has been spoken or
printed. He got his facts viva voce from
Franchomme. Sand was antipathetic to
Chopin but her technique for overcoming
masculine coyness was as remarkable in its
particular fashion as Chopin's proficiency at
the keyboard. They were soon seen together,
and everywhere. She was not musical, not
a trained musician, but her appreciation for
all art forms was highly sympathetic. Not
a beautiful woman, being swarthy and rather
heavy-set in figure, this is what she was, as
seen by Édouard Grenier: —

She was short and stout, but her face attracted
all my attention, the eyes especially. They were
wonderful eyes, a little too close together, it may

be, large, with full eyelids, and black, very black, but by no means lustrous; they reminded me or unpolished marble, or rather of velvet, and this gave a strange, dull, even cold expression to her countenance. Her fine eyebrows and these great placid eyes gave her an air of strength and dignity which was not borne out by the lower part of her face. Her nose was rather thick and not over shapely. Her mouth was also rather coarse and her chin small. She spoke with great simplicity, and her manners were very quiet.

But she attracted with imperious power all that she met. Liszt felt this attraction at one time — and it is whispered that Chopin was jealous of him. Pouf! the woman who could conquer Franz Liszt in his youth must have been a sorceress. He, too, was versatile.

In 1838, Sand's boy Maurice being ill, she proposed a visit to Majorca. Chopin went with the party in November and full accounts of the Mediterranean trip, Chopin's illness, the bad weather, discomforts and all the rest may be found in the "Histoire de Ma Vie" by Sand. It was a time of torment. "Chopin is a detestable invalid," said Sand, and so they returned to Nohant in June 1839. They saw Genoa for a few days in May, but that is as far as Chopin ever penetrated into the promised land — Italy, at one time a passion with him. Sand enjoyed the subtle and truly feminine pleasure of again entering the city which six years before she had visited in company with another man, the former lover of Rachel.

Chopin's health in 1839 was a source of alarm to himself and his friends. He had been dangerously ill at Majorca and Marseilles. Fever and severe coughing proved to be the dread forerunners of the disease that killed him ten years later. He was forced to be very careful in his habits, resting more, giving fewer lessons, playing but little in private or public, and becoming frugal of his emotions. Now Sand began to cool, though her lively imagination never ceased making graceful, touching pictures of herself in the rôles of sister of mercy, mother, and discreet friend, all merged into one sentimental composite. Her invalid was her one thought, and for an active mind and body like hers, it must have been irksome to submit to the caprices of a moody, ailing man. He composed at Nohant, and she has told us all about it; how he groaned, wrote and re-wrote and tore to pieces draft after draft of his work. This brings to memory another martyr to style, Gustave Flaubert, who for

forty years in a room at Croisset, near
Rouen, wrestled with the devils of syntax
and epithet. Chopin was of an impatient,
nervous disposition. All the more remarkable then his capacity for taking infinite
pains. Like Balzac he was never pleased
with the final "revise" of his work, he
must needs aim at finishing touches. His
letters at this period are interesting for the
Chopinist but for the most part they consist of requests made to his pupils, Fontana,
Gutmann and others, to jog the publishers,
to get him new apartments, to buy him
many things. Wagner was not more impor-
tunate or minatory than this Pole, who de-
pended on others for the material comforts
and necessities of his existence. Nor is his
abuse of friends and patrons, the Leos and
others, indicative of an altogether frank,
sincere nature. He did not hesitate to lump
them all as "pigs" and "Jews" if anything
happened to jar his nerves. Money, money,
is the leading theme of the Paris and Mal-
lorcan letters. Sand was a spendthrift and
Chopin had often to put his hands in his
pocket for her. He charged twenty francs
a lesson, but was not a machine and for at
least four months of the year he earned
nothing. Hence his anxiety to get all he

could for his compositions. Heaven-born geniuses are sometimes very keen in financial transactions, and indeed why should they not be?

In 1839 Chopin met Moscheles. They appeared together at St. Cloud, playing for the royal family. Chopin received a gold cup, Moscheles a travelling case. " The King gave him this," said the amiable Frédéric, " to get the sooner rid of him." There were two public concerts in 1841 and 1842, the first on April 26 at Pleyel's rooms, the second on February 20 at the same hall. Niecks devotes an engrossing chapter to the public accounts and the general style of Chopin's playing; of this more hereafter. From 1843 to 1847 Chopin taught, and spent the vacations at Nohant, to which charming retreat Liszt, Matthew Arnold, Delacroix, Charles Rollinat and many others came. His life was apparently happy. He composed and amused himself with Maurice and Solange, the " terrible children " of this Bohemian household. There, according to reports, Chopin and Liszt were in friendly rivalry — are two pianists ever friendly? — Liszt imitating Chopin's style, and once in the dark they exchanged places and fooled their listeners. Liszt denied this. Another

story is of one or the other working the
pedal rods — the pedals being broken. This
too has been laughed to scorn by Liszt.
Nor could he recall having played while
Viardot-Garcia sang out on the terrace of
the château. Garcia's memory is also short
about this event. Rollinat, Delacroix and
Sand have written abundant souvenirs
of Nohant and its distinguished gatherings,
so let us not attempt to impugn the details
of the Chopin legend, that legend which
coughs deprecatingly as it points to its
aureoled alabaster brow. De Lenz should
be consulted for an account of this period;
he will add the finishing touches of unreality
that may be missing.

Chopin knew every one of note in Paris.
The best salons were open to him. Some
of his confrères have not hesitated to describe him as a bit snobbish, for during the
last ten years of his life he was generally inaccessible. But consider his retiring
nature, his suspicious Slavic temperament,
above all his delicate health! Where one
accuses him of indifference and selfishness
there are ten who praise his unfaltering
kindness, generosity and forbearance. He
was as a rule a kind and patient teacher,
and where talent was displayed his interest

58

trebled. Can you fancy this Ariel of the piano giving lessons to hum-drum pupils! Playing in a charmed and bewitching circle of countesses, surrounded by the luxury and the praise that kills, Chopin is a much more natural figure, yet he gave lessons regularly and appeared to relish them. He had not much taste for literature. He liked Voltaire though he read but little that was not Polish — did he really enjoy Sand's novels? — and when asked why he did not compose symphonies or operas, answered that his métier was the piano, and to it he would stick. He spoke French though with a Polish accent, and also German, but did not care much for German music except Bach and Mozart. Beethoven — save in the C sharp minor and several other sonatas — was not sympathetic. Schubert he found rough, Weber, in his piano music, too operatic and Schumann he dismissed without a word. He told Heller that the "Carneval" was really not music at all. This remark is one of the curiosities of musical anecdotage.

But he had his gay moments when he would gossip, chatter, imitate every one, cut up all manner of tricks and, like Wagner, stand on his head. Perhaps it was feverish, agitated gayety, yet somehow it seemed more human than that eternal Thaddeus of War saw melancholy and regret for the vanished greatness and happiness of Poland — a greatness and happiness that never had existed. Chopin disliked letter writing and would go miles to answer one in person. He did not hate any one in particular, being rather indifferent to every one and to political events — except where Poland was concerned. Theoretically he hated Jews and Russians, yet associated with both. He was, like his music, a bundle of unreconciled affirmations and evasions and never could have been contented anywhere or with any one. Of himself he said that " he was in this world like the E string of a violin on a contrabass." This " divine dissatisfaction " led him to extremes : to the flouting of friends for fancied affronts, to the snubbing of artists who sometimes visited him. He grew suspicious of Liszt and for ten years was not on terms of intimacy with him although they never openly quarrelled.

The breach which had been very perceptibly widening became hopeless in 1847, when Sand and Chopin parted forever. A literature has grown up on the subject. Chopin never had much to say but Sand did; so did Chopin's pupils, who were quite virulent in their assertions that she killed their master. The break had to come. It was the inevitable end of such a friendship. The dynamics of free-love have yet to be formulated. This much we know: two such natures could never entirely cohere. When the novelty wore off the stronger of the two — the one least in love — took the initial step. It was George Sand who took it with Chopin. He would never have had the courage nor the will.

The final causes are not very interesting. Niecks has sifted all the evidence before the court and jury of scandal-mongers. The main quarrel was about the marriage of Solange Sand with Clésinger the sculptor. Her mother did not oppose the match, but later she resented Clésinger's actions. He was coarse and violent, she said, with the true mother-in-law spirit — and when Chopin received the young woman and her husband after a terrible scene at Nohant, she broke with him. It was a good excuse. He had ennuiéd her for several years, and as he had completed his artistic work on this planet and there was nothing more to be studied, — the psychological portrait was supposedly painted — Madame George got rid of him. The dark stories of maternal jealousy, of

Chopin's preference for Solange, the visit to
Chopin of the concierge's wife to complain
of her mistress' behavior with her husband,
all these rakings I leave to others. It was
a triste affair and I do not doubt in the least
that it undermined Chopin's feeble health.
Why not! Animals die of broken hearts,
and this emotional product of Poland, de-
prived of affection, home and careful attention, may well, as De Lenz swears, have died
of heart-break. Recent gossip declares that
Sand was jealous of Chopin's friendships —
this is silly.

Mr. A. B. Walkley, the English dramatic
critic, after declaring that he would rather
have lived during the Balzac epoch in Paris,
continues in this entertaining vein:

And then one might have had a chance of seeing George Sand in the thick of her amorisms.
For my part I would certainly rather have met her
than Pontius Pilate. The people who saw her
in her old age — Flaubert, Gautier, the Goncourts
— have left us copious records of her odd appearance, her perpetual cigarette smoking, and
her whimsical life at Nohant. But then she was
only an " extinct volcano ; " she must have been
much more interesting in full eruption. Of her
earlier career — the period of Musset and Pagello
— she herself told us something in " Elle et Lui,"

PARIS:— IN THE MAËLSTROM

and correspondence published a year or so ago in the " Revue de Paris " told us more. But, to my mind, the most fascinating chapter in this part of her history is the Chopin chapter, covering the next decade, or, roughly speaking, the 'forties. She has revealed something of this time — naturally from her own point of view — in " Lucrezia Floriana " (1847). For it is, of course, one of the most notorious characteristics of George Sand that she invariably turned her loves into "copy." The mixture of passion and printer's ink in this lady's composition is surely one of the most curious blends ever offered to the palate of the epicure.

But it was a blend which gave the lady an unfair advantage for posterity. We hear too much of her side of the matter. This one feels especially as regards her affair with Chopin. With Musset she had to reckon a writer like herself; and against her " Elle et Lui " we can set his " Confession d'un enfant du siècle." But poor Chopin, being a musician, was not good at " copy." The emotions she gave him he had to pour out in music, which, delightful as sound, is unfortunately vague as a literary " document." How one longs to have his full, true, and particular account of the six months he spent with George Sand in Majorca ! M. Pierre Mille, who has just published in the " Revue Bleue " some letters of Chopin (first printed, it seems, in a Warsaw

63

newspaper), would have us believe that the lady was really the masculine partner. We are to understand that it was Chopin who did the weeping, and pouting, and "scene"-making while George Sand did the consoling, the pooh-poohing, and the protecting. Liszt had already given us a characteristic anecdote of this Majorca period. We see George Sand, in sheer exuberance of health and animal spirits, wandering out into the storm, while Chopin stays at home, to have an attack of "nerves," to give vent to his anxiety (oh, "artistic temperament"!) by composing a prelude, and to fall fainting at the lady's feet when she returns safe and sound. There is no doubt that the lady had enough of the masculine temper in her to be the first to get tired. And as poor Chopin was coughing and swooning most of the time, this is scarcely surprising. But she did not leave him forthwith. She kept up the pretence of loving him, in a maternal, protecting sort of way, out of pity, as it were, for a sick child.

So much the published letters clearly show. Many of them are dated from Nohant. But in themselves the letters are dull enough. Chopin composed with the keyboard of a piano; with ink and paper he could do little. Probably his love letters were wooden productions, and George Sand, we know, was a fastidious critic in that matter. She had received and written so many!

But any rate, Chopin did not write whining recriminations like Musset. His real view of her we shall never know — and, if you like, you may say it is no business of ours. She once uttered a truth about that (though not apropos of Chopin), "There are so many things between two lovers of which they alone can be the judges."

Chopin gave his last concert in Paris, February 16, 1848, at Pleyel's. He was ill but played beautifully. Oscar Commettant said he fainted in the artist's room. Sand and Chopin met but once again. She took his hand, which was "trembling and cold," but he escaped without saying a word. He permitted himself in a letter to Grzymala from London dated November 17–18, 1848, to speak of Sand. "I have never cursed any one, but now I am so weary of life that I am near cursing Lucrezia. But she suffers too, and suffers more because she grows older in wickedness. What a pity about Soli! Alas! everything goes wrong with the world!" I wonder what Mr. Hadow thinks of this reference to Sand!

"Soli" is Solange Sand, who was forced to leave her husband because of ill-treatment. As her mother once boxed Clésinger's ears at Nohant, she followed the example. In

5   65

trying to settle the affair Sand quarrelled
hopelessly with her daughter. That energetic descendant of "emancipated woman"
formed a partnership, literary of course, with
the Marquis Alfieri, the nephew of the Italian poet. Her salon was as much in vogue
as her mother's, but her tastes were inclined
to politics, revolutionary politics preferred.
She had for associates Gambetta, Jules Ferry,
Floquet, Taine, Hervé, Weiss, the critic of the
"Débats," Henri Fouquier and many others.
She had the "curved Hebraic nose of her
mother and hair coal-black." She died in
her château at Montgivray and was buried
March 20, 1899, at Nohant where, as my
informant says, "her mother died of over-
much cigarette smoking." She was a clever
woman and wrote a book "Masks and
Buffoons." Maurice Sand died in 1883.
He was the son of his mother, who was
gathered to her heterogeneous ancestors
June 8, 1876.

In literature George Sand is a feminine
pendant to Jean Jacques Rousseau, full of
ill-digested, troubled, fermenting, social, po
litical, philosophical and religious specula-
tions and theories. She wrote picturesque
French, smooth, flowing and full of color
The sketches of nature, of country life, have

positive value, but where has vanished her gallery of Byronic passion-pursued women? Where are the Lelias, the Indianas, the Rudolstadts? She had not, as Mr. Henry James points out, a faculty for characterization. As Flaubert wrote her: "In spite of your great Sphinx eyes you have always seen the world as through a golden mist." She dealt in vague, vast figures, and so her Prince Karol in "Lucrezia Floriana," unquestionably intended for Chopin, is a burlesque — little wonder he was angered when the precious children asked him "Cher M. Chopin, have you read 'Lucrezia'? Mamma has put you in it." Of all persons Sand was pre-elected to give to the world a true, a sympathetic picture of her friend. She understood him, but she had not the power of putting him between the covers of a book. If Flaubert, or better still, Pierre Loti, could have known Chopin so intimately we should possess a memoir in which every vibration of emotion would be recorded, every shade noted, and all pinned with the precise adjective, the phrase exquisite.

III

ENGLAND, SCOTLAND AND PÈRE LA CHAISE.

THE remaining years of Chopin's life were lonely. His father died in 1844 of chest and heart complaint, his sister Emilia died of consumption — ill-omens these! — and shortly after, John Matuszyński died. Titus Woyciechowski was in far-off Poland on his estates and Chopin had but Grzymala and Fontana to confide in; they being Polish he preferred them, although he was diplomatic enough not to let others see this. Both Franchomme and Gutmann whispered to Niecks at different times that each was the particular soul, the alter ego, of Chopin. He appeared to give himself to his friends but it was usually surface affection. He had coaxing, coquettish ways, playful ways that cost him nothing when in good spirits. So he was "more loved than loving." This is another trait of the man, which, allied with his fastidiousness and spiritual brusquerie, made him difficult to decipher. The loss of Sand completed his misery and we find him in poor health when he arrived in London, for the second and last time, April 21, 1848.

Mr. A. J. Hipkins is the chief authority on the details of Chopin's visit to England. To this amiable gentleman and learned writer on pianos, Franz Hueffer, Joseph Bennett and Niecks are indebted for the most of their facts. From them the curious may learn all there is to learn. The story is not especially noteworthy, being in the main a record of ill-health, complainings, lamentations and not one signal artistic success.

War was declared upon Chopin by a part of the musical world. The criticism was compounded of pure malice and stupidity. Chopin was angered but little for he was too sick to care now. He went to an evening party but missed the Macready dinner where he was to have met Thackeray, Berlioz, Mrs. Procter and Sir Julius Benedict. With Benedict he played a Mozart duet at the Duchess of Sutherland's. Whether he played at court the Queen can tell; Niecks cannot. He met Jenny Lind-Goldschmidt and liked her exceedingly — as did all who had the honor of knowing her. She sided with him, womanlike, in the Sand affair — echoes of which had floated across the channel — and visited

him in Paris in 1849. Chopin gave two
matinées at the houses of Adelaide Kem-
ble and Lord Falmouth — June 23 and
July 7. They were very recherché, so it
appears. Viardot-Garcia sang. The composer's face and frame were wasted by illness
and Mr. Solomon spoke of his "long attenuated fingers." He made money and that
was useful to him, for doctors' bills and living
had taken up his savings. There was talk
of his settling in London, but the climate,
not to speak of the unmusical atmosphere,
would have been fatal to him. Wagner
succumbed to both, sturdy fighter that
he was.

Chopin left for Scotland in August and
stopped at the house of his pupil, Miss
Stirling. Her name is familiar to Chopin
students, for the two nocturnes, opus 55, are
dedicated to her. He was nearly killed with
kindness but continually bemoaned his existence. At the house of Dr. Lyschinski, a
Pole, he lodged in Edinburgh and was so
weak that he had to be carried up and down
stairs. To the doctor's good wife he replied
in answer to the question "George Sand is
your particular friend?" "Not even George
Sand." And is he to be blamed for evad-
ing tiresome reminders of the past? He con-

fessed that his excessive thinness had caused Sand to address him as " My Dear Corpse." Charming, is it not? Miss Stirling was doubtless in love with him and Princess Czartoryska followed him to Scotland to see if his health was better. So he was not altogether deserted by the women — indeed he could not live without their little flatteries and agreeable attentions. It is safe to say that a woman was always within call of Chopin.

He played at Manchester on the 28th of August, but his friend Mr. Osborne, who was present, says " his playing was too delicate to create enthusiasm and I felt truly sorry for him." On his return to Scotland he stayed with Mr. and Mrs. Salis Schwabe.

Mr. J. Cuthbert Hadden wrote several years ago in the Glasgow " Herald" of Chopin's visit to Scotland in 1848. The tone-poet was in the poorest health, but with characteristic tenacity played at concerts and paid visits to his admirers. Mr. Hadden found the following notice in the back files of the Glasgow " Courier":

Monsieur Chopin has the honour to announce that his matinée musicale will take place on Wednesday, the 27th September, in the Merchant

Hall, Glasgow. To commence at half-past two
o'clock. Tickets, limited in number, half-a-guinea
each, and full particulars to be had from Mr. Muir
Wood, 42, Buchanan street.

He continues:

The net profits of this concert are said to have
been exactly £60 — a ridiculously low sum when
we compare it with the earnings of later day virtuosi; nay, still more ridiculously low when we
recall the circumstance that for two concerts in
Glasgow sixteen years before this Paganini had
£1,400. Muir Wood, who has since died, said:
"I was then a comparative stranger in Glasgow,
but I was told that so many private carriages had
never been seen at any concert in the town. In
fact, it was the county people who turned out,
with a few of the élite of Glasgow society. Being
a morning concert, the citizens were busy otherwise, and half a guinea was considered too high a
sum for their wives and daughters."

The late Dr. James Hedderwick, of Glasgow,
tells in his reminiscences that on entering the hall
he found it about one-third full. It was obvious
that a number of the audience were personal
friends of Chopin. Dr. Hedderwick recognized
the composer at once as " a little, fragile-looking
man, in pale gray suit, including frock coat of
identical tint and texture, moving about among
the company, conversing with different groups,

and occasionally consulting his watch," which seemed to be " no bigger than an agate stone on the forefinger of an alderman." Whiskerless, beardless, fair of hair, and pale and thin of face, his appearance was "interesting and conspicuous," and when, "after a final glance at his miniature horologe, he ascended the platform and placed himself at the instrument, he at once commanded attention." Dr. Hedderwick says it was a drawing-room entertainment, more piano than forte, though not without occasional episodes of both strength and grandeur. It was perfectly clear to him that Chopin was marked for an early grave.

So far as can be ascertained, there are now living only two members of that Glasgow audience of 1848. One of the two is Julius Seligmann, the veteran president of the Glasgow Society of Musicians, who, in response to some inquiries on the subject, writes as follows :

" Several weeks before the concert Chopin lived with different friends or pupils on their invitations, in the surrounding counties. I think his pupil Miss Jane Stirling had something to do with all the general arrangements. Muir Wood managed the special arrangements of the concert, and I distinctly remember him telling me that he never had so much difficulty in arranging a concert as on this occasion. Chopin constantly changed his mind. Wood had to visit him several times at the house of Admiral Napier, at Milliken Park, near

Johnstone, but scarcely had he returned to Glasgow when he was summoned back to alter something. The concert was given in the Merchant Hall, Hutcheson street, now the County Buildings. The hall was about three-quarters filled. Between Chopin's playing Madame Adelasio de Margueritte, daughter of a well-known London physician, sang, and Mr. Muir accompanied her. Chopin was evidently very ill. His touch was very feeble, and while the finish, grace, elegance and delicacy of his performances were greatly admired by the audience, the want of power made his playing somewhat monotonous. I do not remember the whole programme, but he was encored for his well-known mazurka in B flat (op. 7, No. 1), which he repeated with quite different nuances from those of the first time. The audience was very aristocratic, consisting mostly of ladies, among whom were the then Duchess of Argyll and her sister, Lady Blantyre."

The other survivor is George Russell Alexander, son of the proprietor of the Theatre Royal, Dunlop street, who in a letter to the writer remarks especially upon Chopin's pale, cadaverous appearance. "My emotion," he says, "was so great that two or three times I was compelled to retire from the room to recover myself. I have heard all the best and most celebrated stars of the musical firmament, but never one has left such an impress on my mind."

Chopin played October 4 in Edinburgh, and returned to London in November after various visits. We read of a Polish ball and concert at which he played, but the affair was not a success. He left England in January 1849 and heartily glad he was to go. " Do you see the cattle in this meadow? " he asked, en route for Paris: " Ça a plus d'intelligence que des Anglais," which was not nice of him. Perhaps M. Niedzwiecki, to whom he made the remark took as earnest a pure bit of non-sense, and perhaps — ! He certainly disliked England and the English.

Now the curtain prepares to fall on the last dreary finale of Chopin's life, a life not for a moment heroic, yet lived according to his lights and free from the sordid and the soil of vulgarity. Jules Janin said: " He lived ten miraculous years with a breath ready to fly away," and we know that his servant Daniel had always to carry him to bed. For ten years he had suffered from so much illness that a relapse was not noticed by the world. His very death was at first received with incredulity, for, as Stephen Heller said, he had been reported dead so often that the real news was doubted. In 1847 his legs began to bother him by swell-ing, and M. Mathias described him as " a painful spectacle, the picture of exhaustion, the back bent, head bowed — but always amiable and full of distinction." His purse was empty, and his lodgings in the Rue Chaillot were represented to the proud man as being just half their cost, — the balance being paid by the Countess Obreskoff, a Russian lady. Like a romance is the sending, by Miss Stirling, of twenty-five thousand francs, but it is nevertheless true. The noble-hearted Scotchwoman heard of Chopin's needs through Madame Rubio, a pupil, and the money was raised. That packet containing it was mislaid or lost by the portress of Chopin's house, but found after the woman had been taxed with keeping it.

Chopin, his future assured, moved to Place Vendôme, No. 12. There he died. His sister Louise was sent for, and came from Poland to Paris. In the early days of October he could no longer sit upright without support. Gutmann and the Countess Delphine Potocka, his sister, and M. Gavard, were constantly with him. It was Turgenev who spoke of the half hundred countesses in Europe who claimed to have held the dying Chopin in their arms. In reality he died in Gutmann's, raising that pupil's hand to his mouth and murmuring " cher ami " as he expired. Solange Sand was there, but not her mother, who called and was not admitted — so they say. Gutmann denies having refused her admittance. On the other hand, if she had called, Chopin's friends would have kept her away from him, from the man who told Franchomme two days before his death, "She said to me that I would die in no arms but hers." Surely — unless she was monstrous in her egotism, and she was not — George Sand did not hear this sad speech without tears and boundless regrets. Alas! all things come too late for those who wait.

Tarnowski relates that Chopin gave his last orders in perfect consciousness. He begged his sister to burn all his inferior compositions. "I owe it to the public," he said, "and to myself to publish only good things. I kept to this resolution all my life; I wish to keep to it now." This wish has not been respected. The posthumous publications are for the most part feeble stuff.

Chopin died, October 17, 1849, between three and four in the morning, after having been shrived by the Abbé Jelowicki. His last word, according to Gavard, was "Plus," on being asked if he suffered. Regarding the touching and slightly melodramatic death bed scene on the day previous, when Delphine Potocka sang Stradella and Mozart — or was it Marcello? — Liszt, Karasowski, and Gutmann disagree.

The following authentic account of the last hours of Chopin appears here for the first time in English, translated by Mr. Hugh Craig. In Liszt's well-known work on Chopin, second edition, 1879, mention is made of a conversation that he had held with the Abbé Jelowicki respecting Chopin's death; and in Niecks' biography of Chopin some sentences from letters by the Abbé are quoted. These letters, written in French, have been translated and published in the "Allgemeine Musik Zeitung," to which they were given by the Princess Marie Hohenlohe, the daughter of Princess Caroline Sayn Wittgenstein, Liszt's universal legatee and executor, who died in 1887.

For many years [so runs the document] the life of Chopin was but a breath. His frail, weak body was visibly unfitted for the strength and force of his genius. It was a wonder how in such a weak state, he could live at all, and occasionally act with the greatest energy. His body was almost diaphanous; his eyes were almost shadowed by a cloud from which, from time to time, the lightnings of his glance flashed. Gentle, kind, bubbling with

humor, and every way charming, he seemed no
'onger to belong to earth, while, unfortunately, he
had not yet thought of heaven. He had good
friends, but many bad friends. These bad friends
were his flatterers, that is, his enemies, men and
women without principles, or rather with bad
principles. Even his unrivalled success, so much
more subtle and thus so much more stimulating
than that of all other artists, carried the war into
his soul and checked the expression of faith and
of prayer. The teachings of the fondest, most
pious mother became to him a recollection of his
childhood's love. In the place of faith, doubt had
stepped in, and only that decency innate in every
generous heart hindered him from indulging in
sarcasm and mockery over holy things and the
consolations of religion.

While he was in this spiritual condition he was
attacked by the pulmonary disease that was soon
to carry him away from us. The knowledge of
this cruel sickness reached me on my return from
Rome. With beating heart I hurried to him, to
see once more the friend of my youth, whose soul
was infinitely dearer to me than all his talent. I
found him, not thinner, for that was impossible,
but weaker. His strength sank, his life faded visibly. He embraced me with affection and with
tears in his eyes, thinking not of his own pain but
of mine; he spoke of my poor friend Eduard
Worte, whom I had just lost, you know how.

CHOPIN

(He was shot, a martyr of liberty, at Vienna, November 10, 1848.)

I availed myself of his softened mood to speak to him about his soul. I recalled his thoughts to the piety of his childhood and of his beloved mother. "Yes," he said, " in order not to offend my mother I would not die without the sacraments, but for my part I do not regard them in the sense that you desire. I understand the blessing of confession in so far as it is the unburdening of a heavy heart into a friendly hand, but not as a sacrament. I am ready to confess to you if you wish it, because I love you, not because I hold it necessary." Enough: a crowd of anti-religious speeches filled me with terror and care for this elect soul, and I feared nothing more than to be called to be his confessor.

Several months passed with similar conversations, so painful to me, the priest and the sincere friend. Yet I clung to the conviction that the grace of God would obtain the victory over this rebellious soul, even if I knew not how. After all my exertions, prayer remained my only refuge.

On the evening of October 12 I had with my brethren retired to pray for a change in Chopin's mind, when I was summoned by orders of the physician, in fear that he would not live through the night. I hastened to him. He pressed my hand, but bade me at once to depart, while he assured me he loved me much, but did not wish to speak to me.

Imagine, if you can, what a night I passed! Next day was the 13th, the day of St. Edward, the patron of my poor brother. I said mass for the repose of his soul and prayed for Chopin's soul. "My God," I cried, "if the soul of my brother Edward is pleasing to thee, give me, this day, the soul of Frédéric."

In double distress I then went to the melancholy abode of our poor sick man.

I found him at breakfast, which was served as carefully as ever, and after he had asked me to partake I said: "My friend, to-day is the name day of my poor brother." "Oh, do not let us speak of it!" he cried. "Dearest friend," I continued, "you must give me something for my brother's name day." "What shall I give you?" "Your soul." "Ah! I understand. Here it is; take it!"

At these words unspeakable joy and anguish seized me. What should I say to him? What should I do to restore his faith, how not to lose instead of saving this beloved soul? How should I begin to bring it back to God? I flung myself on my knees, and after a moment of collecting my thoughts I cried in the depths of my heart, "Draw it to Thee, Thyself, my God!"

Without saying a word I held out to our dear invalid the crucifix. Rays of divine light, flames of divine fire, streamed, I might say, visibly from the figure of the crucified Saviour, and at once illumined the soul and kindled the heart of Chopin. Burning tears streamed from his eyes. His faith was once more revived, and with unspeakable fervor he made his confession and received the Holy Supper. After the blessed Viaticum, penetrated by the heavenly consecration which the sacraments pour forth on pious souls, he asked for Extreme Unction. He wished to pay lavishly the sacristan who accompanied me, and when I remarked that the sum presented by him was twenty times too much he replied, "Oh, no, for what I have received is beyond price."

From this hour he was a saint. The death struggle began and lasted four days. Patience, trust in God, even joyful confidence, never left him, in spite of all his sufferings, till the last breath. He was really happy, and called himself happy. In the midst of the sharpest sufferings he expressed only ecstatic joy, touching love of God, thankfulness that I had led him back to God, contempt of the world and its good, and a wish for a speedy death.

He blessed his friends, and when, after an apparently last crisis, he saw himself surrounded by the crowd that day and night filled his chamber, he asked me, "Why do they not pray?" At these words all fell on their knees, and even the

Protestants joined in the litanies and prayers for the dying.

Day and night he held my hand, and would not let me leave him. "No, you will not leave me at the last moment," he said, and leaned on my breast as a little child in a moment of danger hides itself in its mother's breast.

Soon he called upon Jesus and Mary, with a fervor that reached to heaven ; soon he kissed the crucifix in an excess of faith, hope and love. He made the most touching utterances. "I love God and man," he said. "I am happy so to die ; do not weep, my sister. My friends, do not weep. I am happy. I feel that I am dying. Farewell, pray for me !"

Exhausted by deathly convulsions he said to the physicians, "Let me die. Do not keep me longer in this world of exile. Let me die ; why do you prolong my life when I have renounced all things and God has enlightened my soul? God calls me ; why do you keep me back?"

Another time he said, "O lovely science, that only lets one suffer longer ! Could it give me back my strength, qualify me to do any good, to make any sacrifice — but a life of fainting, of grief, of pain to all who love me, to prolong such a life — O lovely science !"

Then he said again : "You let me suffer cruelly. Perhaps you have erred about my sickness. But God errs not. He punishes me, and I bless him

therefor. Oh, how good is God to punish me
here below! Oh, how good God is!"

His usual language was always elegant, with well
chosen words, but at last to express all his thankfulness and, at the same time, all the misery of
those who die unreconciled to God, he cried,
"Without you I should have croaked (krepiren)
like a pig."

While dying he still called on the names of
Jesus, Mary, Joseph, kissed the crucifix and
pressed it to his heart with the cry "Now I am at
the source of Blessedness!"

Thus died Chopin, and in truth, his death was
the most beautiful concerto of all his life.

The worthy abbé must have had a phenomenal memory. I hope that it was an
exact one. His story is given in its entirety
because of its novelty. The only thing that
makes me feel in the least sceptical is that
La Mara, — the pen name of a writer on
musical subjects, — translated these letters
into German. But every one agrees that
Chopin's end was serene; indeed it is one
of the musical death-beds of history, another was Mozart's. His face was beautiful and young in the flower-covered coffin,
says Liszt. He was buried from the Madeleine, October 30, with the ceremony befit-
ting a man of genius. The B flat minor

Funeral march, orchestrated by Henri Reber was given, and during the ceremony Lefé-bure-Wely played on the organ the E and B minor Preludes. The pall-bearers were distinguished men, Meyerbeer, Delacroix, Pleyel and Franchomme — at least Théophile Gautier so reported it for his journal. Even at his grave in Père la Chaise no two persons could agree about Chopin. This contro-versy is quite characteristic of Chopin who was always the calm centre of argument.

He was buried in evening clothes, his concert dress, but not at his own request. Kwiatowski the portrait painter told this to Niecks. It is a Polish custom for the dying to select their grave clothes, yet Lombroso writes that Chopin " in his will directed that he should be buried in a white tie, small shoes and short breeches," adducing this as an evidence of his insanity. He further adds " he abandoned the woman whom he tenderly loved because she offered a chair to some one else before giving the same invitation to himself." Here we have a Sand story raised to the dignity of a diagnosed symptom. It is like the other nonsense.

IV

THE ARTIST

CHOPIN'S personality was a pleasant, persuasive one without being so striking or so dramatic as Liszt's. As a youth his nose was too large, his lips thin, the lower one protruding. Later, Moscheles said that he looked like his music. Delicacy and a certain aristrocratic bearing, a harmonious ensemble, produced a most agreeable sensation. "He was of slim frame, middle height; fragile but wonderfully flexible limbs, delicately formed hands, very small feet, an oval, softly outlined head, a pale transparent complexion, long silken hair of a light chestnut color, parted on one side, tender brown eyes, intelligent rather than dreamy, a finely-curved aquiline nose, a sweet subtle smile, graceful and varied gestures." This precise description is by Niecks. Liszt said he had blue eyes, but he has been overruled. Chopin was fond of elegant, costly attire, and was very correct in the matter of studs, walking sticks and cravats. Not the ideal musician we read of, but a gentleman. Berlioz told Legouvé to see Chopin, " for he is something which you have never seen — and some one you will never forget." An orchidaceous individuality this.

With such personal refinement he was a man punctual and precise in his habits. Associating constantly with fashionable folk his naturally dignified behavior was increased. He was an aristocrat — there is no other word — and he did not care to be hail-fellow-well-met with the musicians. A certain primness and asperity did not make him popular. While teaching, his manner warmed, the earnest artist came to life, all halting of speech and polite insincerities were abandoned. His pupils adored him. Here at least the sentiment was one of solidarity. De Lenz is his most censorious critic and did not really love Chopin. The dislike was returned, for the Pole suspected that his pupil was sent by Liszt to spy on his methods. This I heard in Paris.

Chopin was a remarkable teacher. He never taught but one genius, little Filtsch, the Hungarian lad of whom Liszt said, " When he starts playing I will shut up shop." The boy died in 1845, aged fifteen; Paul Gunsberg, who died the same year, was also very talented. Once after delivering in a lovely way the master's E minor concerto Filtsch was taken by Chopin to a music store and presented with the score of Beethoven's "Fidelio." He was much affected by the talents of this youthful pupil. Lindsay Sloper and Brinley Richards studied with Chopin. Caroline Hartmann, Gutmann, Lysberg, Georges Mathias, Mlle. O'Meara, many Polish ladies of rank, Delphine Potocka among the rest, Madame Streicher, Carl Mikuli, Madame Rubio, Madame Peruzzi, Thomas Tellefsen, Casimir Wernik, Gustav Schumann, Werner Steinbrecher, and many others became excellent pianists. Was the American pianist, Louis Moreau Gottschalk, ever his pupil? His friends say so, but Niecks does not mention him. Ernst Pauer questions it. We know that Gottschalk studied in Paris with Camille Stamaty, and made his first appearance there in 1847. This was shortly before Chopin's death when his interest in music had abated greatly. No doubt Gottschalk played for Chopin for he was the first to introduce the Pole's music in America.

Chopin was very particular about the formation of the touch, giving Clementi's Preludes at first. "Is that a dog barking?" was

his sudden exclamation at a rough attack
He taught the scales staccato and legato
beginning with E major. Ductility, ease,
gracefulness were his aim; stiffness, harshness annoyed him. He gave Clementi, Moscheles and Bach. Before playing in concert
he shut himself up and played, not Chopin
but Bach, always Bach. Absolute finger
independence and touch discrimination and
color are to be gained by playing the preludes and fugues of Bach. Chopin started a
method but it was never finished and his
sister gave it to the Princess Czartoryska
after his death. It is a mere fragment.
Janotha has translated it. One point is
worth quoting. He wrote:

No one notices inequality in the power of the
notes of a scale when it is played very fast and
equally, as regards time. In a good mechanism
the aim is not to play everything with an equal
sound, but to acquire a beautiful quality of touch
and a perfect shading. For a long time players
have acted against nature in seeking to give equal
power to each finger. On the contrary, each finger should have an appropriate part assigned it.
The thumb has the greatest power, being the
thickest finger and the freest. Then comes the
little finger, at the other extremity of the hand.
The middle finger is the main support of the

hand, and is assisted by the first. Finally comes
the third, the weakest one. As to this Siamese
twin of the middle finger, some players try to force
it with all their might to become independent.
A thing impossible, and most likely unnecessary.
There are, then, many different qualities of sound,
just as there are several fingers. The point is to
utilize the differences; and this, in other words,
is the art of fingering.

Here, it seems to me, is one of the most
practical truths ever uttered by a teacher.
Pianists spend thousands of hours trying to
subjugate impossible muscles. Chopin, who
found out most things for himself, saw the
waste of time and force. I recommend his
advice. He was ever particular about fingering, but his innovations horrified the purists.
"Play as you feel," was his motto, a rather
dangerous precept for beginners. He gave
to his pupils the concertos and sonatas — all
carefully graded — of Mozart, Scarlatti, Field,
Dussek, Hummel, Beethoven, Mendelssohn,
Weber and Hiller and, of Schubert, the four-
hand pieces and dances. Liszt he did not
favor, which is natural, Liszt having written
nothing but brilliant paraphrases in those
days. The music of the later Liszt is quite
another thing.

Chopin's genius for the pedal, his utilization of its capacity for the vibration of related strings, the overtones, I refer to later. Rubinstein said:

The piano bard, the piano rhapsodist, the piano mind, the piano soul is Chopin. . . . Tragic, romantic, lyric, heroic, dramatic, fantastic, soulful, sweet, dreamy, brilliant, grand, simple ; all possible expressions are found in his compositions and all are sung by him upon his instrument.

Chopin is dead only fifty years, but his fame has traversed the half century with ease, and bids fair to build securely in the loves of our great-grandchildren. The six letters that comprise his name pursue every piano that is made. Chopin and modern piano playing are inseparable, and it is a strain upon homely prophecy to predict a time when the two shall be put asunder. Chopin was the greatest interpreter of Chopin, and following him came those giants of other days, Liszt, Tausig, and Rubinstein.

While he never had the pupils to mould as had Liszt, Chopin made some excellent piano artists. They all had, or have — the old guard dies bravely — his tradition, but exactly what the Chopin tradition is no man may dare to say. Anton Rubinstein, when I last heard him, played Chopin inimitably. Never shall I forget the Ballades, the two Polonaises in F sharp minor and A flat major, the B flat minor Prelude, the A minor "Winter Wind" the two C minor studies, and the F minor Fantasie. Yet the Chopin pupils, assembled in judgment at Paris when he gave his Historical Recitals, refused to accept him as an interpreter. His touch was too rich and full, his tone too big. Chopin did not care for Liszt's reading of his music, though he trembled when he heard him thunder in the Eroica Polonaise. I doubt if even Karl Tausig, impeccable artist, unapproachable Chopin player, would have pleased the composer. Chopin played as his moods prompted, and his playing was the despair and delight of his hearers. Rubinstein did all sorts of wonderful things with the coda of the Barcarolle — such a page! — but Sir Charles Hallé said that it was "clever but not Chopinesque." Yet Hallé heard Chopin at his last Paris concert, February, 1848, play the two forte passages in the Barcarolle "pianissimo and with all sorts of dynamic finesse." This is precisely what Rubinstein did, and his pianissimo was a whisper. Von Bülow was too much of a martinet to reveal the poetic quality, though he appreciated Chopin on the intellectual side; his touch was not beautiful enough. The Slavic and Magyar races are your only true Chopin interpreters. Witness Liszt the magnificent, Rubinstein a passionate genius, Tausig who united in his person all the elements of greatness, Essipowa fascinating and feminine, the poetic Paderewski, de Pachmann the fantastic, subtle Joseffy, and Rosenthal a phenomenon.

A world-great pianist was this Frédéric François Chopin. He played as he composed: uniquely. All testimony is emphatic as to this. Scales that were pearls, a touch rich, sweet, supple and singing and a technique that knew no difficulties, these were part of Chopin's equipment as a pianist. He spiritualized the timbre of his instrument until it became transformed into something strange, something remote from its original nature. His pianissimo was an enchanting whisper, his forte seemed powerful by contrast so numberless were the gradations, so widely varied his dynamics. The fairylike quality of his play, his diaphanous harmonies, his liquid tone, his pedalling — all were the work of a genius and a lifetime; and the appealing humanity he infused into his touch, gave his listeners a delight that bordered on the supernatural. So the accounts, critical, professional and personal read. There must have been a hypnotic quality in his performances that transported his audience wherever the poet willed. Indeed the stories told wear an air of enthusiasm that borders on the exaggerated, on the fantastic. Crystalline pearls falling on red hot velvet—or did Scudo write this of Liszt?—infinite nuance and the mingling of silvery bells,—these are a few of the least exuberant notices. Was it not Heine who called "Thalberg a king, Liszt a prophet, Chopin a poet, Herz an advocate, Kalkbrenner a minstrel, Madame Pleyel a sibyl, and Doehler—a pianist"? The limpidity, the smoothness and ease of Chopin's playing were, after all, on the physical plane. It was the poetic melancholy, the grandeur, above all the imaginative lift, that were more in evidence than mere sensuous sweetness. Chopin had, we know, his salon side when he played with elegance, brilliancy and coquetry. But he had dark moments when the keyboard was too small, his ideas too big for utterance. Then he astounded, thrilled his auditors. They were rare moments. His mood-versatility was reproduced in his endless colorings and capricious rhythms. The instrument vibrated with these new, nameless effects like the violin in Paganini's hands. It was ravishing. He was called the Ariel, the Undine of the piano. There was something imponderable, fluid, vaporous, evanescent in his music that eluded analysis and illuded all but hardheaded critics. This novelty was the reason why he has been classed as a " gifted amateur " and even to-day is he regarded by many musicians as a skilful inventor of piano passages and patterned figures instead of what he really is — one of the most daring harmonists since Bach.

Chopin's elastic hand, small, thin, with lightly articulated fingers, was capable of stretching tenths with ease. Examine his first study for confirmation of this. His wrist was very supple. Stephen Heller said that " it was a wonderful sight to see Chopin's small hands expand and cover a third of the keyboard. It was like the opening of the mouth of a serpent about to swallow a rabbit whole." He played the octaves in the A flat Polonaise with infinite ease but pianissimo. Now where is the "tradition" when confronted by the mighty crashing of Rosenthal in this particular part of the Polonaise? Of Karl Tausig, Weitzmann said that " he relieved the romantically sentimental Chopin of his Weltschmerz and showed him in his pristine creative vigor and wealth of imagination." In Chopin's music there are many pianists, many styles and all are correct if they are poetically musical, logical and individually sincere. Of his rubato I treat in the chapter devoted to the Mazurkas, making also an attempt to define the "żal" of his playing and music.

When Chopin was strong he used a Pleyel piano, when he was ill an Erard — a nice fable of Liszt's! He said that he liked the Erard but he really preferred the Pleyel with its veiled sonority. What could not he have accomplished with the modern grand piano?

In the artist's room of the Maison Pleyel there stands the piano at which Chopin composed the Preludes, the G minor nocturne, the Funeral March, the three supplementary Études, the A minor Mazurka, the Tarantelle, the F minor Fantasie and the B minor Scherzo. A brass tablet on the inside lid notes this. The piano is still in good condition as regards tone and action.

Mikuli asserted that Chopin brought out an "immense" tone in cantabiles. He had not a small tone, but it was not the orchestral tone of our day. Indeed how could it be, with the light action and tone of the French pianos built in the first half of the century? After all it was quality, not quantity that Chopin sought. Each one of his ten fingers was a delicately differentiated voice, and these ten voices could sing at times like the morning stars.

Rubinstein declared that all the pedal marks are wrong in Chopin. I doubt if any edition can ever give them as they should be, for here again the individual equation comes into play. Apart from certain fundamental rules for managing the pedals, no pedagogic regulations should ever be made for the more refined nuanciren.

The portraits of Chopin differ widely. There is the Ary Scheffer, the Vigneron — praised by Mathias — the Bovy medallion, the Duval drawing, and the head by Kwiatowski. Delacroix tried his powerful hand at transfixing in oil the fleeting expressions of Chopin. Felix Barrias, Franz Winterhalter, and Albert Graefle are others who tried with more or less success. Anthony Kolberg painted Chopin in 1848–49. Kleczynski reproduces it; it is mature in expression. The Clésinger head I have seen at Père la Chaise. It is mediocre and lifeless. Kwiatowski has caught

some of the Chopin spirit in the etching that
may be found in volume one of Niecks' biography. The Winterhalter portrait in Mr.
Hadow's volume is too Hebraic, and the
Graefle is a trifle ghastly. It is the dead
Chopin, but the nose is that of a predaceous
bird, painfully aquiline. The " Echo Muzy-
czne" Warsaw, of October 1899 — in Polish
" 17 Pazdźiernika " — printed a picture of
the composer at the age of seventeen. It
is that of a thoughtful, poetic, but not hand-
some lad, his hair waving over a fine forehead, a feminine mouth, large, aquiline nose,
the nostrils delicately cut, and about his slender neck a Byronic collar. Altogether a
novel likeness. Like the Chopin interpretation, a satisfactory Chopin portrait is extremely rare.

As some difficulty was experienced in dis-
covering the identity of Countess Delphine
Potocka, I applied in 1899 to Mr. Jaraslow
de Zielinski, a pianist of Buffalo, New York,
for assistance; he is an authority on Polish
and Russian music and musicians. Here are
the facts he kindly transmitted : " In 1830
three beautiful Polish women came to Nice to
pass the winter. They were the daughters of
Count Komar, the business manager of the
wealthy Count Potocki. They were singu-

larly accomplished; they spoke half the
languages of Europe, drew well, and sang to
perfection. All they needed was money to
make them queens of society; this they soon
obtained, and with it high rank. Their graceful manners and loveliness won the hearts of
three of the greatest of noblemen. Marie
married the Prince de Beauvau-Craon; Delphine became Countess Potocka, and Natha-
lie, Marchioness Medici Spada. The last
named died young, a victim to the zeal in
favor of the cholera-stricken of Rome. The
other two sisters went to live in Paris, and
became famous for their brilliant elegance.
Their sumptuous 'hotels' or palaces were
thrown open to the most prominent men of
genius of their time, and hither came Chopin, to meet not only with the homage due
to his genius, but with a tender and sisterly
friendship, which proved one of the greatest
consolations of his life. To the amiable
Princess de Beauvau he dedicated his famous
Polonaise in F sharp minor, op. 44, written in
the brilliant bravura style for pianists of the
first force. To Delphine, Countess Potocka,
he dedicated the loveliest of his valses, op.
64, No. 1, so well transcribed by Joseffy into
a study in thirds."

Therefore the picture of the Gräfin Potocka

in the Berlin gallery is not that of Chopin's devoted friend.

Here is another Count Tarnowski story. It touches on a Potocka episode. "Chopin liked and knew how to express individual characteristics on the piano. Just as there formerly was a rather widely-known fashion of describing dispositions and characters in so-called 'portraits,' which gave to ready wits a scope for parading their knowledge of people and their sharpness of observation; so he often amused himself by playing such musical portraits. Without saying whom he had in his thoughts, he illustrated the characters of a few or of several people present in the room, and illustrated them so clearly and so delicately that the listeners could always guess correctly who was intended, and admired the resemblance of the portrait. One little anecdote is related in connection with this which throws some light on his wit, and a little pinch of sarcasm in it.

"During the time of Chopin's greatest brilliancy and popularity, in the year 1835, he once played his musical portraits in a certain Polish salon, where the three daughters of the house were the stars of the evening. After a few portraits had been extemporized, one of these ladies wished to have hers — Mme.

Delphine Potocka. Chopin, in reply, drew
her shawl from her shoulders, threw it on the
keyboard and began to play, implying in this
two things; first, that he knew the character
of the brilliant and famous queen of fashion
so well, that by heart and in the dark he was
able to depict it; secondly, that this character and this soul is hidden under habits, or-
namentations and decorations of an elegant
worldly life, through the symbol of elegance
and fashion of that day, as the tones of the
piano through the shawl."

Because Chopin did not label his works
with any but general titles, Ballades, Scherzi,
Studies, Preludes and the like, his music
sounds all the better: the listener is not
pinned down to any precise mood, the music
being allowed to work its particular charm
without the aid of literary crutches for unim-
aginative minds. Dr. Niecks gives specimens
of what the ingenious publisher, without a
sense of humor, did with some of Chopin's
compositions: Adieu à Varsovie, so was
named the Rondo, op. 1; Hommage à Mozart, the Variations, op. 2; La Gaité, Introduction and Polonaise, op. 3 for piano and
'cello; La Posiana — what a name! — the
Rondo à la Mazur, op. 5; Murmures de la
Seine, Nocturnes op. 9; Les Zéphirs, Noc-

turnes, op. 15; Invitation à la Valse, Valse, op. 18; Souvenir d'Andalousie, Bolero, op. 19 — a bolero which sounds Polish! — Le Banquet Infernal, the First Scherzo, op. 20 — what a misnomer! — Ballade ohne Worte, the G minor Ballade — there is a polyglot mess for you! — Les Plaintives, Nocturnes, op. 27; La Méditation, Second Scherzo, B flat minor — meditation it is not! — Il Lamento é la Consolazione, Nocturnes, op. 32 ; Les Soupirs, Nocturnes, op. 37, and Les Favorites, Polonaises, op. 40. The C minor Polonaise of this opus was never, is not now, a favorite. The mazurkas generally received the title of Souvenir de la Pologne.

In commemoration of the fiftieth anniversary of the death of Chopin, October 17, 1899, a medal was struck at Warsaw, bearing on one side an artistically executed profile of the Polish composer. On the reverse, the design represents a lyre, surrounded by a laurel branch, and having engraved upon it the opening bars of the Mazurka in A flat major. The name of the great composer with the dates of his birth and death, are given in the margin. Paderewski is heading a movement to remove from Paris to Warsaw the ashes of the pianist, but it is doubtful if it can be managed. Paris will certainly object to losing the bones of such a genius.

Chopin's acoustic parallelisms are not so concrete, so vivid as Wagner's. Nor are they so theatrical, so obvious. It does not, however, require much fancy to conjure up "the drums and tramplings of three conquests" in the Eroica Polonaise or the F sharp major Impromptu. The rhythms of the Cradle Song and the Barcarolle are suggestive enough and if you please there are dew-drops in his cadenzas and there is the whistling of the wind in the last A minor Study. Of the A flat Study Chopin said: "Imagine a little shepherd who takes refuge in a peaceful grotto from an approaching storm. In the distance rushes the wind and the rain, while the shepherd gently plays a melody on his flute." This is quoted by Kleczynski. There are word-whisperings in the next study in F minor, whilst the symbolism of the dance — the Valse, Mazurka, Polonaise, Menuetto, Bolero, Schottische, Krakowiak and Tarantella — is admirably indicated in all of them. The bells of the Funeral March, the will o' wisp character of the last movement of the B flat minor Sonata, the dainty Butterfly Study in G flat, opus 25, the æolian murmurs of the E flat Study, in opus 10, the tiny prancing silvery hoofs in the F major Study, opus 25, the flickering flame-like C major Study No. 7, opus 10, the spinning in the D flat Valse and the cyclonic rush of chromatic double notes in the E flat minor Scherzo — these are not studied imitations but spontaneous transpositions to the ideal plane of primary, natural phenomena.

Chopin's system — if it be a system — of cadenzas, fioriture embellishment and ornamentation is perhaps traceable to the East. In his "Folk Music Studies," Mr. H. E. Krehbiel quotes the description of "a rhapsodical embellishment, called 'alap,' which after going through a variety of ad libitum passages, rejoins the melody with as much grace as if it had never been disunited, the musical accompaniment all the while keeping time. These passages are not reckoned essential to the melody, but are considered only as grace notes introduced according to the fancy of the singer, when the only limitations by which the performer is bound are the notes peculiar to that particular melody and a strict regard to time."

Chopin founded no school, although the possibilities of the piano were canalized by him. In playing, as in composition, only the broad trend of his discoveries may be followed, for his was a manner not a method He has had for followers Liszt, Rubinstein Mikuli, Zarembski, Nowakowski, Xaver Scharwenka, Saint-Saens, Scholtz, Heller, Nicodé, Moriz Moszkowski, Paderewski, Stojowski, Arenski, Leschetizki, the two Wieniawskis, and a whole group of the younger Russians Liadoff, Scriàbine and the rest. Even Brahms — in his F sharp major Sonata and E flat minor Scherzo — shows Chopin's influence. Indeed but for Chopin much modern music would not exist.

But a genuine school exists not. Henselt was only a German who fell asleep and dreamed of Chopin. To a Thalberg-ian euphony he has added a technical figuration not unlike Chopin's, and a spirit quite Teutonic in its sentimentality. Rubinstein calls Chopin the exhalation of the third epoch in art. He certainly closed one. With a less strong rhythmic impulse and formal sense Chopin's music would have degenerated into mere overperfumed impressionism. The French piano school of his day, indeed of to-day, is entirely drowned by its devotion to cold decoration, to unemotional ornamentation. Mannerisms he had — what great artist has not? — but the Greek in him, as in Heine, kept him from formlessness. He is seldom a landscapist, but he can handle his brush deftly before nature if he must. He paints atmosphere, the open air at eventide, with consummate skill, and for playing fantastic tricks on your nerves in the depiction of the superhuman he has a peculiar faculty. Remember that in Chopin's early days the Byronic pose, the grandiose and the horrible prevailed — witness the pictures of Ingres and Delacroix — and Richter wrote with his heart-strings saturated in moonshine and tears. Chopin did not altogether escape the artistic vices of his generation. As a man he was a bit of poseur — the little whisker grown on one side of his face, the side which he turned to his audience, is a note of foppery — but was ever a detester of the sham-artistic. He was sincere, and his survival, when nearly all of Mendelssohn, much of Schumann and half of Berlioz have suffered an eclipse, is proof positive of his vitality. The fruit of his experimentings in tonality we see in the whole latter-day school of piano, dramatic and orchestral composers. That Chopin may lead to the development and adoption of the new enharmonic scales, the " Homotonic scales," I do not know. For these M. A. de Bertha claimed the future of music. He wrote :

106

" Now vaporously illumined by the crepus
cular light of a magical sky on the boundaries of the major and minor modes, now
seeming to spring from the bowels of the
earth with sepulchral inflexions, melody
moves with ease on the serried degrees of
the enharmonic scales. Lively or slow she
always assumed in them the accents of a
fatalist impossibility, for the laws of arith-
metic have preceded her, and there still
remains, as it were, an atmosphere of proud
rigidity. Melancholy or passionate she preserves the reflected lines of a primitive rus-
ticity, which clings to the homotones in
despite of their artificial origin." But all
this will be in the days to come when the
flat keyboard will be superseded by a Janko
many-banked clavier contrivance, when Mr.
Krehbiel's oriental srootis are in use and Mr.
Apthorp's nullitonic order, no key at all, is
invented. Then too a new Chopin may be
born, but I doubt it.

Despite his idiomatic treatment of the
piano it must be remembered that Chopin
under Sontag's and Paganini's influence imitated both voice and violin on the keyboard.
His lyricism is most human, while the porta-
mento, the slides, trills and indescribably
subtle turns — are they not of the violin?

CHOPIN

Wagner said to Mr. Dannreuther — see Finck's "Wagner and his Works" — that "Mozart's music and Mozart's orchestra are a perfect match; an equally perfect balance exists between Palestrina's choir and Palestrina's counterpoint, and I find a similar correspondence between Chopin's piano and some of his Études and Preludes — I do not care for the Ladies' Chopin; there is too much of the Parisian salon in that, but he has given us many things which are above the salon." Which latter statement is slightly condescending. Recollect, however, Chopin's calm depreciation of Schumann. Mr. John F. Runciman, the English critic, asserts that "Chopin thought in terms of the piano, and only the piano. So when we see Chopin's orchestral music or Wagner's music for the piano we realize that neither is talking his native tongue — the tongue which nature fitted him to speak." Speaking of "Chopin and the Sick Men" Mr. Runciman is most pertinent:

"These inheritors of rickets and exhausted physical frames made some of the most wonderful music of the century for us. Schubert was the most wonderful of them all, but Chopin runs him very close. . . . He wrote less, far less than Schubert wrote; but, for

tne quantity he did write, its finish is miraculous. It may be feverish, merely mournful,
cadavre, or tranquil, and entirely beautiful;
but there is not a phrase that is not polished
as far as a phrase will bear polishing. It is
marvellous music; but, all the same, it is
sick, unhealthy music."

"Liszt's estimate of the technical importance of Chopin's works," writes Mr. W. J.
Henderson, "is not too large. It was Chopin
who systematized the art of pedalling and
showed us how to use both pedals in combination to produce those wonderful effects
of color which are so necessary in the performance of his music. . . . The harmonic
schemes of the simplest of Chopin's works
are marvels of originality and musical loveliness, and I make bold to say that his treatment of the passing note did much toward
showing later writers how to produce the
restless and endless complexity of the harmony in contemporaneous orchestral music."

Heinrich Pudor in his strictures on German music is hardly complimentary to Chopin:
"Wagner is a thorough-going decadent, an
off-shoot, an epigonus, not a progonus. His
cheeks are hollow and pale — but the Germans have the full red cheeks. Equally
decadent is Liszt. Liszt is a Hungarian

and the Hungarians are confessedly a completely disorganized, self-outlived, dying people. No less decadent is Chopin, whose figure comes before one as flesh without bones, this morbid, womanly, womanish, slip-slop, powerless, sickly, bleached, sweet-caramel Pole!" This has a ring of Nietzsche — Nietzsche who boasted of his Polish origin.

Now listen to the fatidical Pole Przyby-szewski: "In the beginning there was sex, out of sex there was nothing and in it everything was. And sex made itself brain whence was the birth of the soul." And then, as Mr. Vance Thompson, who first Englished this "Mass of the Dead" — wrote: "He pictures largely in great cosmic symbols, decorated with passionate and mystic fervors, the singular combat between the growing soul and the sex from which it fain would be free." Arno Holz thus parodies Przyby-szewski: "In our soul there is surging and singing a song of the victorious bacteria. Our blood lacks the white corpuscles. On the sounding board of our consciousness there echoes along the frightful symphony of the flesh. It becomes objective in Chopin; he alone, the modern primeval man, puts our brains on the green meadows, he alone thinks in hyper-European dimensions. He alone rebuilds the shattered Jerusalem of our souls." All of which shows to what comically delirious lengths this sort of deleterious soul-probing may go.

It would be well to consider this word "decadent" and its morbid implications. There is a fashion just now in criticism to over-accentuate the physical and moral weaknesses of the artist. Lombroso started the fashion, Nordau carried it to its logical absurdity, yet it is nothing new. In Hazlitt's day he complains, that genius is called mad by foolish folk. Mr. Newman writes in his Wagner, that "art in general, and music in particular, ought not to be condemned merely in terms of the physical degeneration or abnormality of the artist. Some of the finest work in art and literature, indeed, has been produced by men who could not, from any standpoint, be pronounced normal. In the case of Flaubert, of De Maupassant, of Dostoievsky, of Poe, and a score of others, though the organic system was more or less flawed, the work remains touched with that universal quality that gives artistic permanence even to perceptions born of the abnormal." Mr. Newman might have added other names to his list, those of Michael Angelo and Beethoven and Swinburne. Really, is any great genius quite sane according to philistine standards? The answer must be negative. The old enemy has merely changed his mode of attack: instead of charging genius with madness, the abnormal used in an abnormal sense is lugged in and though these imputations of degeneracy, moral and physical, have in some cases proven true, the genius of the accused one can in no wise be denied. But then as Mr. Philip Hale asks: Why this timidity at being called decadent? What's in the name?

Havelock Ellis in his masterly study of Joris Karl Huysmans, considers the much misunderstood phenomenon in art called decadence. "Technically a decadent style is only such in relation to a classic style. It is simply a further development of a classic style, a further specialization, the homogeneous in Spencerian phraseology having become heterogeneous. The first is beautiful because the parts are subordinated to the whole; the second is beautiful because the whole is subordinated to the parts." Then he proceeds to show in literature that Sir Thomas Browne, Emerson, Pater, Carlyle, Poe, Hawthorne and Whitman are decadents — not in any invidious sense — but simply in " the breaking up of the whole for the benefit of its parts." Nietzsche is quoted to the effect that "in the period of corruption in the evolution of societies we are apt to overlook the fact that the energy which in more primitive times marked the operations of a community as a whole has now simply been transferred to the individuals themselves, and this aggrandizement of the individual really produces an even greater amount of energy." And further, Ellis: " All art is the rising and falling of the slopes of a rhythmic curve between these two classic and decadent extremes. Decadence suggests to us going down, falling, decay. If we walk down a real hill we do not feel that we commit a more wicked act than when we walked up it. . . . Roman architecture is classic to become in its Byzantine developments completely decadent, and St. Mark's is the perfected type of decadence in art. . . . We have to recognize that decadence is an æsthetic and not a moral conception. The power of words is great but they need not befool us. . . . We are not called upon to air our moral indignation over the bass end of the musical clef." I recommend the entire chapter to such men as Lombroso Levi,

Max Nordau and Heinrich Pudor, who have
yet to learn that "all confusion of intellectual substances is foolish."

Oscar Bie states the Chopin case most
excellently : —

Chopin is a poet. It has become a very bad
habit to place this poet in the hands of our youth.
The concertos and polonaises being put aside, no
one lends himself worse to youthful instruction
than Chopin. Because his delicate touches in-
evitably seem perverse to the youthful mind, he
has gained the name of a morbid genius. The
grown man who understands how to play Chopin,
whose music begins where that of another leaves
off, whose tones show the supremest mastery in
the tongue of music — such a man will discover
nothing morbid in him. Chopin, a Pole, strikes
sorrowful chords, which do not occur frequently
to healthy normal persons. But why is a Pole to
receive less justice than a German? We know
that the extreme of culture is closely allied to
decay ; for perfect ripeness is but the foreboding
of corruption. Children, of course, do not know
this. And Chopin himself would have been much
too noble ever to lay bare his mental sickness to
the world. And his greatness lies precisely in
this : that he preserves the mean between im-
maturity and decay. His greatness is his aristocracy. He stands among musicians in his faultless

vesture, a noble from head to foot. The sublim-
est emotions toward whose refinement whole gen-
rations had tended, the last things in our soul,
whose foreboding is interwoven with the mystery
of Judgment Day, have in his music found their
form.

Further on I shall attempt — I write the
word with a patibulary gesture — in a sort
of a Chopin variorum, to analyze the salient
aspects, technical and æsthetic, of his music.
To translate into prose, into any language
no matter how poetical, the images aroused
by his music, is impossible. I am forced to
employ the technical terminology of other arts,
but against my judgment. Read Mr. W. F.
Apthorp's disheartening dictum in "By the
Way." "The entrancing phantasmagoria of
picture and incident which we think we see
rising from the billowing sea of music is in
reality nothing more than an enchanting fata
morgana, visible at no other angle than that
of our own eye. The true gist of music it
never can be; it can never truly translate
what is most essential and characteristic in
its expression. It is but something that we
have half unconsciously imputed to music;
nothing that really exists in music."

The shadowy miming of Chopin's soul has
nevertheless a significance for this generation.

CHOPIN

It is now the reign of the brutal, the realistic, the impossible in music. Formal excellence is neglected and programme-music has reduced art to the level of an anecdote. Chopin neither preaches nor paints, yet his art is decorative and dramatic — though in the climate of the ideal. He touches earth and its emotional issues in Poland only; otherwise his music is a pure æsthetic delight, an artistic enchantment, freighted with no ethical or theatric messages. It is poetry made audible, the " soul written in sound." All that I can faintly indicate is the way it affects me, this music with the petals of a glowing rose and the heart of gray ashes. Its analogies to Poe, Verlaine, Shelley, Keats, Heine and Mickiewicz are but critical sign-posts, for Chopin is incomparable, Chopin is unique. " Our interval," writes Walter Pater, " is brief." Few pass it recollectedly and with full understanding of its larger rhythms and more urgent colors. Many endure it in frivol and violence, the majority in bored, sullen submission. Chopin, the New Chopin, is a foe to ennui and the spirit that denies; in his exquisite soul-sorrow, sweet world-pain, we may find rich impersonal relief.

V

POET AND PSYCHOLOGIST

I

MUSIC is an order of mystic, sensuous mathematics. A sounding mirror, an aural mode of motion, it addresses itself on the formal side to the intellect, in its content of expression it appeals to the emotions. Ribot, admirable psychologist, does not hesitate to proclaim music as the most emotional of the arts. "It acts like a burn, like heat, cold or a caressing contact, and is the most dependent on physiological conditions."

Music then, the most vague of the arts in the matter of representing the concrete, is the swiftest, surest agent for attacking the sensibilities. The *cry* made manifest, as Wagner asserts, it is a cry that takes on fanciful shapes, each soul interpreting it in an individual fashion. Music and beauty are synonymous, just as their form and substance are indivisible.

Havelock Ellis is not the only æsthetician who sees the marriage of music and sex.

"No other art tells us such old forgotten secrets about ourselves. . . . It is in the mightiest of all instincts, the primitive sex traditions of the race before man was, that music is rooted. . . . Beauty is the child of love." Dante Gabriel Rossetti has imprisoned in a sonnet the almost intangible feeling aroused by music, the feeling of having pursued in the immemorial past the "route of evanescence."

Is it this sky's vast
vault or ocean's
sound,
That is Life's self
  and draws my life from me,
And by instinct ineffable decree
Holds my breath
Quailing on the bitter bound?
Nay, is it Life or Death, thus thunder-crown'd,
That 'mid the tide of all emergency
Now notes my separate wave, and to what
sea
Its difficult eddies labor in the ground?
Oh! what is this that knows the road
I came,
The flame turned cloud, the cloud returned to
flame,
The lifted, shifted steeps and all the way?
That draws around me at last this wind-
warm space,
And in regenerate rapture turns my face
Upon the devious coverts of dismay?

This "azure psychology" gives music its power, it steers straight for the soul through the cortical cells.

During the last half of the nineteenth century two men became rulers of musical emotion, Richard Wagner and Frédéric François Chopin. The music of the latter is the most ravishing gesture that art has yet made. Wagner and Chopin, the macrocosm and the microcosm! "Wagner has made the largest impersonal synthesis attainable of the personal influences that thrill our lives," cries Havelock Ellis. Chopin, a young man slight of frame, furiously playing out upon the keyboard his soul, the soul of his nation, the soul of his time, is the most individual composer that has ever set humming the looms of our dreams. Wagner and Chopin have a motor element in their music that is fiercer, intenser and more fugacious than that of all other composers. For them is not the Buddhistic void, in which shapes slowly form and fade; their psychical tempo is devouring. They voiced their age, they moulded their age and we listen eagerly to them, to these vibrile prophetic voices, so sweetly corrosive, bardic and appealing. Chopin being nearer the soil in the selection of forms, his style and structure are more naïve, more original than Wagner's, while his medium, less artificial, is easier filled than the vast empty frame of the theatre. Through their intensity of conception and of life, both men touch issues, though widely dissimilar in all else. Chopin had greater melodic and as great harmonic genius as Wagner; he made more themes, he was, as Rubinstein wrote, the last of the original composers, but his scope was not scenic, he preferred the stage of his soul to the windy spaces of the music-drama. His is the interior play, the eternal conflict between body and soul. He viewed music through his temperament and it often becomes so imponderable, so bodiless as to suggest a fourth dimension in the art. Space is obliterated. With Chopin one does not get, as from Beethoven, the sense of spiritual vastness, of the overarching sublime. There is the pathos of spiritual distance, but it is pathos, not sublimity. " His soul was a star and dwelt apart," though not in the Miltonic or Wordsworthian sense. A Shelley-like tenuity at times wings his thought, and he is the creator of a new thrill within the thrill. The charm of the dying fall, the unspeakable cadence of regret for the love that is dead, is in his music; like John Keats he sometimes sees: —

POET AND PSYCHOLOGIST

Charm'd magic casements, opening on the foam
Of perilous seas, in faëry lands forlorn.

Chopin, " subtle-souled psychologist," is more kin to Keats than Shelley, he is a greater artist than a thinker. His philosophy is of the beautiful, as was Keats', and while he lingers by the river's edge to catch the song of the reeds, his gaze is oftener fixed on the quiring planets. He is nature's most exquisite sounding-board and vibrates to her with intensity, color and vivacity that have no parallel. Stained with melancholy, his joy is never that of the strong man rejoicing in his muscles. Yet his very tenderness is tonic and his cry is ever restrained by an Attic sense of proportion. Like Alfred De Vigny, he dwelt in a " tour d'ivoire " that faced the west and for him the sunrise was not, but O! the miraculous moons he discovered, the sunsets and cloud-shine! His notes cast great rich shadows, these chains of blown-roses drenched in the dew of beauty. Pompeian colors are too restricted and flat; he divulges a world of half-tones, some " enfolding sunny spots of greenery," or singing in silvery shade the song of chromatic ecstasy, others "huge fragments vaulted like rebounding hail" and black upon black. Chopin is the color genius of the piano, his

CHOPIN

eye was attuned to hues the most fragile and attenuated; he can weave harmonies that are as ghostly as a lunar rainbow. And lunar-like in their libration are some of his melodies — glimpses, mysterious and vast, as of a strange world.

His utterances are always dynamic, and he emerges betimes, as if from Goya's tomb, and etches with sardonic finger Nada in dust. But this spirit of denial is not an abiding mood; Chopin throws a net of tone over souls wearied with rancors and revolts, bridges " salty, estranged seas " of misery and presently we are viewing a mirrored, a fabulous universe wherein Death is dead, and Love reigns Lord of all.

II

Heine said that " every epoch is a sphinx which plunges into the abyss as soon as its problem is solved." Born in the very upheaval of the Romantic revolution — a revolution evoked by the intensity of its emotion, rather than by the power of its ideas — Chopin was not altogether one of the insurgents of art. Just when his individual soul germinated, who may tell? In his early music are discovered the roots and fibres of **Hummel** and Field. His growth, involuntary, inevitable, put forth strange sprouts, and he saw in the piano, an instrument of two dimensions, a third, and so his music deepened and took on stranger colors. The keyboard had never sung so before; he forged its formula. A new apocalyptic seal of melody and harmony was let fall upon it. Sounding scrolls, delicious arabesques gorgeous in tint, martial, lyric, " a resonance of emerald," a sobbing of fountains — as that Chopin of the Gutter, Paul Verlaine, has it — the tear crystallized midway, an arrested pearl, were overheard in his music, and Europe felt a new shudder of sheer delight.

The literary quality is absent and so is the ethical — Chopin may prophesy but he never flames into the divers tongues of the upper heaven. Compared with his passionate abandonment to the dance, Brahms is the Lao-tsze of music, the great infant born with gray hair and with the slow smile of childhood. Chopin seldom smiles, and while some of his music is young, he does not raise in the mind pictures of the fatuous romance of youth. His passion is mature, self-sustained and never at a loss for the mot propre. And with what marvellous vibration he gamuts the passions, festooning them with carnations and great white tuberoses, but the dark dramatic motive is never lost in the decorative wiles of this magician. As the man grew he laid aside his pretty garlands and his line became sterner, its traceries more gothic; he made Bach his chief god and within the woven walls of his strange harmonies he sings the history of a soul, a soul convulsed by antique madness, by the memory of awful things, a soul lured by Beauty to secret glades wherein sacrificial rites are performed to the solemn sounds of unearthly music. Like Maurice de Guérin, Chopin perpetually strove to decipher Beauty's enigma and passionately demanded of the sphinx that defies:

"Upon the shores of what oceans have they rolled the stone that hides them, O Macareus?"

His name was as the stroke of a bell to the Romancists; he remained aloof from them though in a sympathetic attitude. The classic is but the Romantic dead, said an acute critic. Chopin was a classic without knowing it; he compassed for the dances of his land what Bach did for the older forms. With Heine he led the spirit of revolt, but enclosed his note of agitation in a frame beautiful. The color, the "lithe perpetual escape" from the formal de-

ceived his critics, Schumann among the rest.
Chopin, like Flaubert, was the last of the
idealists, the first of the realists. The new-
ness of his form, his linear counterpoint,
misled the critics, who accused him of the
lack of it. Schumann's formal deficiency de-
tracts from much of his music, and because
of their formal genius Wagner and Chopin
will live.

To Chopin might be addressed Sar Mero-
dack Peladan's words:

"When your hand writes a perfect line
the Cherubim descend to find pleasure
therein as in a mirror." Chopin wrote many
perfect lines; he is, above all, the faultless
lyrist, the Swinburne, the master of fiery,
many rhythms, the chanter of songs before
sunrise, of the burden of the flesh, the sting
of desire and large-moulded lays of passionate freedom. His music is, to quote
Thoreau, "a proud sweet satire on the mean-
ness of our life." He had no feeling for the
epic, his genius was too concentrated, and
though he could be furiously dramatic the
sustained majesty of blank verse was denied
him. With musical ideas he was ever gravid
but their intensity is parent to their brevity.
And it must not be forgotten that with Chopin the form was conditioned by the idea.

He took up the dancing patterns of Poland because they suited his vivid inner life; he transformed them, idealized them, attaining to more prolonged phraseology and denser architecture in his Ballades and Scherzi — but these periods are passionate, never philosophical.

All artists are androgynous; in Chopin the feminine often prevails, but it must be noted that this quality is a distinguishing sign of masculine lyric genius, for when he unbends, coquets and makes graceful confessions or whimpers in lyric loveliness at fate, then his mother's sex peeps out, a picture of the capricious, beautiful tyrannical Polish woman. When he stiffens his soul, when Russia gets into his nostrils, then the smoke and flame of his Polonaises, the tantalizing despair of his Mazurkas are testimony to the strong man-soul in rebellion. But it is often a psychical masquerade. The sag of melancholy is soon felt, and the old Chopin, the subjective Chopin, wails afresh in melodic moodiness.

That he could attempt far flights one may see in his B flat minor Sonata, in his Scherzi, in several of the Ballades, above all in the F minor Fantasie. In this great work the technical invention keeps pace with the inspiration. It coheres, there is not a flaw in the

reverberating marble, not a rift in the idea.
If Chopin, diseased to death's door, could
erect such a Palace of Dreams, what might
not he have dared had he been healthy? But
forth from his misery came sweetness and
strength, like honey from the lion. He grew
amazingly the last ten years of his existence,
grew with a promise that recalls Keats, Shelley, Mozart, Schubert and the rest of the
early slaughtered angelic crew. His flame-
like spirit waxed and waned in the gusty surprises of a disappointed life. To the earth
for consolation he bent his ear and caught
echoes of the cosmic comedy, the far-off
laughter of the hills, the lament of the sea
and the mutterings of its depths. These
things with tales of sombre clouds and shining skies and whisperings of strange creatures
dancing timidly in pavonine twilights, he
traced upon the ivory keys of his instrument
and the world was richer for a poet. Chopin
is not only the poet of the piano, he is also
the poet of music, the most poetic of composers. Compared with him Bach seems a
maker of solid polyphonic prose, Beethoven a
scooper of stars, a master of growling storms,
Mozart a weaver of gay tapestries, Schumann
a divine stammerer. Schubert, alone of all the
composers, resembles him in his lyric prodi-

gality. Both were masters of melody, but Chopin was the master-workman of the two and polished, after bending and beating, his theme fresh from the fire of his forge. He knew that to complete his "wailing Iliads" the strong hand of the reviser was necessary, and he also realized that nothing is more difficult for the genius than to retain his gift. Of all natures the most prone to pessimism, procrastination and vanity, the artist is most apt to become ennuied. It is not easy to flame always at the focus, to burn fiercely with the central fire. Chopin knew this and cultivated his ego. He saw too that the love of beauty for beauty's sake was fascinating but led to the way called madness. So he rooted his art, gave it the earth of Poland and its deliquescence is put off to the day when a new system of musical æstheticism will have routed the old, when the Ugly shall be king and Melody the handmaiden of science. But until that most grievous and undesired time he will catch the music of our souls and give it cry and flesh.

III

Chopin is the open door in music. Besides having been a poet and giving vibratory expression to the concrete, he was something else — he was a pioneer. Pioneer because in

youth he had bowed to the tyranny of the diatonic scale and savored the illicit joys of the
chromatic. It is briefly curious that Chopin
is regarded purely as a poet among musicians
and not as a practical musician. They will
swear him a phenomenal virtuoso, but your
musician, orchestral and theoretical, raises
the eyebrow of the supercilious if Chopin is
called creative. A cunning finger-smith, a
moulder of decorative patterns, a master at
making new figures, all this is granted, but
speak of Chopin as path-breaker in the harmonic forest — that true "forest of numbers" — as the forger of a melodic metal, the
sweetest, purest in temper, and lo! you are
regarded as one mentally askew. Chopin
invented many new harmonic devices, he
untied the chord that was restrained within
the octave, leading it into the dangerous but
delectable land of extended harmonies. And
how he chromaticized the prudish, rigid garden of German harmony, how he moistened
it with flashing changeful waters until it grew
bold and brilliant with promise! A French
theorist, Albert Lavignac, calls Chopin a
product of the German Romantic school.
This is hitching the star to the wagon. Chopin influenced Schumann; it can be proven
a hundred times. And Schumann under

stood Chopin else he could not have written the "Chopin" of the Carneval, which quite out-Chopins Chopin.

Chopin is the musical soul of Poland; he incarnates its political passion. First a Slav, by adoption a Parisian, he is the open door because he admitted into the West, Eastern musical ideas, Eastern tonalities, rhythms, in fine the Slavic, all that is objectionable, decadent and dangerous. He inducted Europe into the mysteries and seductions of the Orient. His music lies wavering between the East and the West. A neurotic man, his tissues trembling, his sensibilities aflame, the offspring of a nation doomed to pain and partition, it was quite natural for him to go to France — Poland had ever been her historical client — the France that overheated all Europe. Chopin, born after two revolutions, the true child of insurrection, chose Paris for his second home. Revolt sat easily upon his inherited aristocratic instincts — no proletarian is quite so thorough a revolutionist as the born aristocrat, witness Nietzsche — and Chopin, in the bloodless battle of the Romantics, in the silent warring of Slav against Teuton, Gaul and Anglo-Saxon, will ever stand as the protagonist of the artistic drama.

130

All that followed, the breaking up of the old hard-and-fast boundaries on the musical map is due to Chopin. A pioneer, he has been rewarded as such by a polite ignorement or bland condescension. He smashed the portals of the convention that forbade a man baring his soul to the multitude. The psychology of music is the gainer thereby. Chopin, like Velasquez, could paint single figures perfectly, but to great massed effects he was a stranger. Wagner did not fail to profit by his marvellously drawn soul-portraits. Chopin taught his century the pathos of patriotism, and showed Grieg the value of national ore. He practically re-created the harmonic charts, he gave voice to the individual, himself a product of a nation dissolved by overwrought individualism. As Schumann assures us, his is "the proudest and most poetic spirit of his time." Chopin, subdued by his familiar demon, was a true specimen of Nietzsche's Übermensch, — which is but Emerson's Oversoul shorn of her wings. Chopin's transcendental scheme of technics is the image of a supernormal lift in composition. He sometimes robs music of its corporeal vesture and his transcendentalism lies not alone in his striving after strange tonalities and rhythms, but in seeking the emotionally recondite

Self-tormented, ever " a dweller on the threshold " he saw visions that outshone the glories of Hasheesh and his nerve-swept soul ground in its mills exceeding fine music. His vision is of beauty; he persistently groped at the hem of her robe, but never sought to transpose or to tone the commonplace of life. For this he reproved Schubert. Such intensity cannot be purchased but at the cost of breadth, of sanity, and his picture of life is not so high, wide, sublime, or awful as Beethoven's. Yet is it just as inevitable, sincere and as tragically poignant.

Stanislaw Przybyszewski in his "Zur Psychologie des Individuums" approaches the morbid Chopin — the Chopin who threw open to the world the East, who waved his chromatic wand to Liszt, Tschaikowsky, Saint-Saëns, Goldmark, Rubinstein, Richard Strauss, Dvórák and all Russia with its consonantal composers. This Polish psychologist — a fulgurant expounder of Nietzsche — finds in Chopin faith and mania, the true stigma of the mad individualist, the individual "who in the first instance is naught but an oxidation apparatus." Nietzsche and Chopin are the most outspoken individualities of the age — he forgets Wagner — Chopin himself the finest flowering of a morbid

and rare culture. His music is a series of
psychoses — he has the sehnsucht of a marvellously constituted nature — and the shrill
dissonance of his nerves, as seen in the physiological outbursts of the B minor Scherzo, is
the agony of a tortured soul. The piece is
Chopin's Iliad; in it are the ghosts that lurk
near the hidden alleys of the soul, but here
come out to leer and exult.

Horla! the Horla of Guy de Maupassant,
the sinister Doppelgänger of mankind, which
races with him to the goal of eternity, perhaps to outstrip and master him in the next
evolutionary cycle, master as does man, the
brute creation. This Horla, according to
Przybyszewski, conquered Chopin and became vocal in his music — this Horla has
mastered Nietzsche, who, quite mad, gave
the world that Bible of the Übermensch,
that dancing lyric prose-poem, " Also Sprach
Zarathustra."

Nietzsche's disciple is half right. Chopin's
moods are often morbid, his music often
pathological; Beethoven too is morbid, but
in his kingdom, so vast, so varied, the mood
is lost or lightly felt, while in Chopin's province, it looms a maleficent upas-tree, with
flowers of evil and its leaves glistering with
sensuousness. But so keen for symmetry

133

for all the term formal beauty implies, is Chopin, that seldom does his morbidity madden, his voluptuousness poison. His music has its morass, but also its upland where the gale blows strong and true. Perhaps all art is, as the incorrigible Nordau declares, a slight deviation from the normal, though Ribot scoffs at the existence of any standard of normality. The butcher and the candlestick-maker have their Horla, their secret soul convulsions, which they set down to taxation, the vapors, or weather.

Chopin has surprised the musical malady of the century. He is its chief spokesman. After the vague, mad, noble dreams of Byron, Shelley and Napoleon, the awakening found those disillusioned souls, Wagner, Nietzsche and Chopin. Wagner sought in the epical rehabilitation of a vanished Valhalla a surcease from the world-pain. He consciously selected his anodyne and in "Die Meistersinger" touched a consoling earth. Chopin and Nietzsche, temperamentally finer and more sensitive than Wagner — the one musically, the other intellectually — sang themselves in music and philosophy, because they were so constituted. Their nerves rode them to their death. Neither found the serenity and repose of Wagner, for neither was as

sane and both suffered mortally from hyper-
æsthesia, the penalty of all sick genius.

Chopin's music is the æsthetic symbol of
a personality nurtured on patriotism, pride
and love; that it is better expressed by the
piano is because of that instrument's idiosyn-
crasies of evanescent tone, sensitive touch
and wide range in dynamics. It was Chopin's lyre, the "orchestra of his heart," from
it he extorted music the most intimate
since Sappho. Among lyric moderns Heine
closely resembles the Pole. Both sang because they suffered, sang ineffable and ironic
melodies; both will endure because of their
brave sincerity, their surpassing art. The
musical, the psychical history of the nineteenth century would be incomplete without
the name of Frédéric François Chopin.
Wagner externalized its dramatic soul; in
Chopin the mad lyricism of the Time-spirit
is made eloquent. Into his music modulated
the poesy of his age; he is one of its heroes,
a hero of whom Swinburne might have sung:

> O strong-winged soul with prophetic
> Lips hot with the blood-beats of song;
> With tremor of heart-strings magnetic,
> With thoughts as thunder in throng;
> With consonant ardor of chords
> That pierce men's souls as with swords
> And hale them hearing along.

PART II
HIS MUSIC

VI

THE STUDIES:— TITANIC EXPERIMENTS

I

OCTOBER 20, 1829, Frédéric Chopin, aged twenty, wrote to his friend Titus Woycie-chowski, from Warsaw: "I have composed a study in my own manner;" and November 14, the same year: "I have written some studies; in your presence I would play them well."

Thus, quite simply and without booming of cannon or brazen proclamation by bell, did the great Polish composer announce an event of supreme interest and importance to the piano-playing world. Niecks thinks these studies were published in the summer of 1833, July or August, and were numbered op. 10. Another set of studies, op. 25, did not find a publisher until 1837, although some of them were composed at the same time as the previous work; a Polish musi-cian who visited the French capital in 1834 heard Chopin play the studies contained in op. 25. The C minor study, op. 10, No. 12, commonly known as the Revolutionary, was born at Stuttgart, September, 1831, " while under the excitement caused by the news of the taking of Warsaw by the Russians, on September 8, 1831." These dates are given so as to rout effectually any dilatory suspicion that Liszt influenced Chopin in the production of his masterpieces. Lina Ramann, in her exhaustive biography of Franz Liszt, openly declares that Nos. 9 and 12 of op. 10 and Nos. 11 and 12 of op. 25 reveal the influence of the Hungarian virtuoso. Figures prove the fallacy of her assertion. The influence was the other way, as Liszt's three concert studies show — not to mention other compositions. When Chopin arrived in Paris his style had been formed, he was the creator of a new piano technique.

The three studies known as Trois Nouvelles Études, which appeared in 1840 in Moscheles and Fétis Method of Methods were published separately afterward. Their date of composition we do not know.

Many are the editions of Chopin's studies, but after going over the ground, one finds only about a dozen worthy of study and consultation. Karasowski gives the date of the first complete edition of the Chopin works as 1846, with Gebethner & Wolff, Warsaw, as publishers. Then, according to Niecks, followed Tellefsen, Klindworth — Bote & Bock — Scholtz — Peters — Breitkopf & Härtel, Mikuli, Schuberth, Kahnt, Steingraber — better known as Mertke's — and Schlesinger, edited by the great pedagogue Theodor Kullak. Xaver Scharwenka has edited Klindworth for the London edition of Augener & Co. Mikuli criticised the Tellefsen edition, yet both men had been Chopin pupils. This is a significant fact and shows that little reliance can be placed on the brave talk about tradition. Yet Mikuli had the assistance of a half dozen of Chopin's "favorite" pupils, and, in addition, Ferdinand Hiller. Herman Scholtz, who edited the works for Peters, based his results on careful inspection of original French, German and English editions, besides consulting M. Georges Mathias, a pupil of Chopin. If Fontana, Wolff, Gutmann, Mikuli and Tellefsen, who copied from the original Chopin manuscripts under the supervision of the composer, cannot agree, then upon what foundation are reared the structures of the modern critical editions? The early French, German and Polish editions are faulty, indeed useless, because of misprints and errata of all kinds. Every succeeding edition has cleared away some of

these errors, but only in Karl Klindworth has
Chopin found a worthy, though not faultless,
editor. His edition is a work of genius and
was called by Von Bülow "the only model
edition." In a few sections others, such as
Kullak, Dr. Hugo Riemann and Hans von
Bülow, may have outstripped him, but as a
whole his editing is amazing for its exacti-
tude, scholarship, fertility in novel fingerings
and sympathetic insight in phrasing. This
edition appeared at Moscow from 1873 to
1876.

The twenty-seven studies of Chopin have
been separately edited by Riemann and Von
Bülow.

Let us narrow our investigations and critical comparisons to Klindworth, Von Bülow,
Kullak and Riemann. Carl Reinecke's edition of the studies in Breitkopf & Härtel's collection offers nothing new, neither do Mertke,
Scholtz and Mikuli. The latter one should
keep at hand because of the possible freedom from impurities in his text, but of phrasing or fingering he contributes little. It must
be remembered that with the studies, while
they completely exhibit the entire range of
Chopin's genius, the play's the thing after
all. The poetry, the passion of the Ballades
and Scherzi wind throughout these technical

problems like a flaming skein. With the modern avidity for exterior as well as interior analysis, Mikuli, Reinecke, Mertke and Scholtz evidence little sympathy. It is then from the masterly editing of Kullak, Von Bülow, Riemann and Klindworth that I shall draw copiously. They have, in their various ways, given us a clue to their musical individuality, as well as their precise scholarship. Klindworth is the most genially intellectual, Von Bülow the most pedagogic, and Kullak is poetic, while Riemann is scholarly; the latter gives more attention to phrasing than to fingering. The Chopin studies are poems fit for Parnassus, yet they also serve a very useful purpose in pedagogy. Both aspects, the material and the spiritual, should be studied, and with four such guides the student need not go astray.

In the first study of the first book, op. 10, dedicated to Liszt, Chopin at a leap reached new land. Extended chords had been sparingly used by Hummel and Clementi, but to take a dispersed harmony and transform it into an epical study, to raise the chord of the tenth to heroic stature — that could have been accomplished by Chopin only. And this first study in C is heroic. Theodore Kullak writes of it: " Above a ground bass proudly and boldly striding along, flow mighty waves of sound. The étude — whose technical end is the rapid execution of widely extended chord figurations exceeding the span of an octave — is to be played on the basis of forte throughout. With sharply dissonant harmonies the forte is to be increased to fortissimo, diminishing again with consonant ones. Pithy accents! Their effect is enhanced when combined with an elastic recoil of the hand."

The irregular, black, ascending and descending staircases of notes strike the neophyte with terror. Like Piranesi's marvellous aerial architectural dreams, these dizzy acclivities and descents of Chopin exercise a charm, hypnotic, if you will, for eye as well as ear. Here is the new technique in all its nakedness, new in the sense of figure, design, pattern, web, new in a harmonic way. The old order was horrified at the modulatory harshness, the young sprigs of the new, fascinated and a little frightened. A man who could explode a mine that assailed the stars must be reckoned with. The nub of modern piano music is in the study, the most formally reckless Chopin ever penned. Kullak gives Chopin's favorite metronome sign, 176 to the quarter, but this editor rightly believes that "the majestic grandeur is impaired," and suggests 152 instead. The gain is at once apparent. Indeed Kullak, a man of moderate pulse, is quite right in his strictures on the Chopin tempi, tempi that sprang from the expressively light mechanism of the prevailing pianos of Chopin's day. Von Bülow declares that "the requisite suppleness of the hand in gradual extension and rapid contraction will be most quickly attained if the player does not disdain first of all to impress on the individual fingers the chord which is the foundation of each arpeggio;" a sound pedagogic point. He also inveighs against the disposition to play the octave basses arpeggio. In fact, those basses are the argument of the play; they must be granitic, ponderable and powerful. The same authority calls attention to a misprint C, which he makes B flat, the last note treble in the twenty-ninth bar. Von Bülow gives the Chopin metronomic marking.

It remained for Riemann to make some radical changes. This learned and worthy doctor astonished the musical world a few years by his new marks of phrasing in the Beethoven symphonies. They topsy-turvied the old bowing. With Chopin, new dynamic and agogic accents are rather dangerous, at least to the peace of mind of worshippers of the Chopin fetish. Riemann breaks two bars into one. It is a finished period for him, and by detaching several of the six-teenths in the first group, the first and fourth, he makes the accent clearer, — at least to the eye. He indicates alla breve with 88 to the half. In later studies examples will be given of this phrasing, a phrasing that becomes a mannerism with the editor. He offers no startling finger changes. The value of his criticism throughout the volume seems to be in the phrasing, and this by no means conforms to accepted notions of how Chopin should be interpreted. I intend quoting more freely from Riemann than from the others, but not for the reason that I consider him as a cloud by day and a pillar of fire by night in the desirable land of the Chopin Études, rather because his piercing analysis lays bare the very roots of these shining examples of piano literature. Klindworth contents him-self with a straightforward version of the C major study, his fingering being the clearest and most admirable. The Mikuli edition makes one addition: it is a line which binds the last note of the first group to the first of the second. The device is useful, and occurs only on the upward flights of the arpeggio.

This study suggests that its composer wished to begin the exposition of his wonderful technical system with a skeletonized statement. It is the tree stripped of its bark, the flower of its leaves, yet, austere as is the result, there is compensating power, dignity and unswerving logic. This study is the key with which Chopin unlocked — not his heart, but the kingdom of technique. It should be played, for variety, unisono, with both hands, omitting, of course, the octave bass.

Von Bülow writes cannily enough, that the second study in A minor being chromatically related to Moscheles' étude, op. 70, No. 3, that piece should prepare the way for Chopin's more musical composition. In different degrees of tempo, strength and rhythmic accent it should be practised, omitting the thumb and first finger. Mikuli's metronome is 144 to the quarter, Von Bülow's, 114; Klindworth's, the same as Mikuli, and Riemann is 72 to the half, with an alla breve. The fingering in three of these authorities is almost identical. Riemann has ideas of his own, both in the phrasing and figuration. Look at these first two bars:

Von Bülow orders " the middle harmonies to be played throughout distinctly, and yet transiently " — in German, " flüchtig." In fact, the entire composition, with its murmuring, meandering, chromatic character, is a forerunner to the whispering, weaving, moonlit effects in some of his later studies. The technical purpose is clear, but not obtrusive. It is intended for the fourth and fifth finger of the right hand, but given in unison with both hands it becomes a veritable but laudable torture for the thumb of the left. With the repeat of the first at bar 36 Von Bülow gives a variation in fingering. Kullak's method of fingering is this: " Everywhere that two white keys occur in succession the fifth finger is to be used for C and F in the right hand, and for F and E in the left." He has also something to say about holding " the hand sideways, so that the back of the hand

148

and arm form an angle." This question of hand position, particularly in Chopin, is largely a matter of individual formation. No two hands are alike, no two pianists use the same muscular movements. Play along the easiest line of resistance.

We now have reached a study, the third, in which the more intimately known Chopin reveals himself. This one in E is among the finest flowering of the composer's choice garden. It is simpler, less morbid, sultry and languorous, therefore saner, than the much bepraised study in C sharp minor, No. 7, op. 25. Niecks writes that this study " may be counted among Chopin's loveliest compositions." It combines " classical chasteness of contour with the fragrance of romanticism." Chopin told his faithful Gutmann that "he had never in his life written another such melody," and once when hearing it raised his arms aloft and cried out: " Oh, ma patrie ! "

I cannot vouch for the sincerity of Chopin's utterance for as Runciman writes: " They were a very Byronic set, these young men ; and they took themselves with ludicrous seriousness."

Von Bülow calls it a study in expression — which is obvious — and thinks it should be studied in company with No. 6, in E flat minor. This reason is not patent. Emotions should not be hunted in couples and the very object of the collection, variety in mood as well as mechanism, is thus defeated. But Von Bülow was ever an ardent classifier. Perhaps he had his soul compartmentized. He also attempts to regulate the rubato — this is the first of the studies wherein the rubato's rights must be acknowledged. The bars are even mentioned 32, 33, 36 and 37, where tempo license may be indulged. But here is a case which innate taste and feeling must guide. You can no more teach a real Chopin rubato — not the mawkish imitation, — than you can make a donkey comprehend Kant. The metronome is the same in all editions, 100 to the eighth.

Kullak rightly calls this lovely study " ein wunderschönes, poetisches Tonstück," more in the nocturne than study style. He gives in the bravura-like cadenza, an alternate for small hands, but small hands should not touch this piece unless they can grapple the double sixths with ease. Klindworth fingers the study with great care. The figuration in three of the editions is the same, Mikuli separating the voices distinctly. Riemann exercises all his ingenuity to make the beginning clear to the eye.

What a joy is the next study, No. 4! How
well Chopin knew the value of contrast in
tonality and sentiment! A veritable classic is
this piece, which, despite its dark key color,
C sharp minor as a foil to the preceding one
in E, bubbles with life and spurts flame. It
reminds one of the story of the Polish peasants, who are happiest when they sing in the
minor mode. Kullak calls this "a bravura
study for velocity and lightness in both
hands. Accentuation fiery!" while Von
Bülow believes that "the irresistible interest
inspired by the spirited content of this truly
classical and model piece of music may become a stumbling block in attempting to
conquer the technical difficulties." Hardly.
The technics of this composition do not lie
beneath the surface. They are very much in
the way of clumsy fingers and heavy wrists.
Presto 88 to the half is the metronome indication in all five editions. Klindworth does

not comment, but I like his fingering and phrasing best of all. Riemann repeats his trick of breaking a group, detaching a note for emphasis; although he is careful to retain the legato bow. One wonders why this study does not figure more frequently on programmes of piano recitals. It is a fine, healthy technical test, it is brilliant, and the coda is very dramatic. Ten bars before the return of the theme there is a stiff digital hedge for the student. A veritable lance of tone is this study, if justly poised.

Riemann has his own ideas of the phrasing of the following one, the fifth and familiar "Black Key" étude. Examine the first bar:

Von Bülow would have grown jealous if he had seen this rather fantastic phrasing. It is a trifle too finical, though it must be confessed looks pretty. I like longer breathed phrasing. The student may profit by this analysis. The piece is indeed, as Kullak says, "full of Polish elegance." Von Bülow speaks rather disdainfully of it as a Damen-Salon Étude. It is certainly graceful, delicately witty, a trifle naughty, arch and roguish, and it is delightfully invented. Technically, it requires smooth, velvet-tipped fingers and a supple wrist. In the fourth bar, third group, third note of group, Klindworth and Riemann print E flat instead of D flat. Mikuli, Kullak and Von Bülow use the D flat. Now, which is right? The D flat is preferable. There are already two E flats in the bar. The change is an agreeable one. Joseffy has made a concert variation for this study. The metronome of the original is given at 116 to the quarter.

A dark, doleful nocturne is No. 6, in E flat minor. Niecks praises it in company with the preceding one in E. It is beautiful, if music so sad may be called beautiful, and the melody is full of stifled sorrow. The study figure is ingenious, but subordinated to the theme. In the E major section the piece broadens to dramatic vigor. Chopin was not yet the slave of his mood. There must be a psychical programme to this study, some record of a youthful disillusion, but the expression of it is kept well within chaste

lines. The Sarmatian composer had not yet
unlearned the value of reserve. The Klindworth reading of this troubled poem is the
best though Kullak used Chopin's autographic
copy. There is no metronomic sign in this
autograph. Tellefsen gives 69 to the quarter;
Klindworth, 60; Riemann, 69; Mikuli, the
same; Von Bülow and Kullak, 60. Kullak
also gives several variante from the text,
adding an A flat to the last group in bar 11.
Riemann and the others make the same addition. The note must have been accidentally
omitted from the Chopin autograph. Two
bars will illustrate what Riemann can accomplish when he makes up his mind to be
explicit, leaving little to the imagination:

sempre legatissimo

A luscious touch, and a sympathetic soul
is needed for this nocturne study.

We emerge into a clearer, more bracing
atmosphere in the C major study, No. 7. It
is a genuine toccata, with moments of tender

twilight, serving a distinct technical purpose
— the study of double notes and changing on
one key — and is as healthy as the toccata
by Robert Schumann. Here is a brave, an
undaunted Chopin, a gay cavalier, with the
sunshine shimmering about him. There are
times when this study seems like light drip-
ping through the trees of a mysterious forest;
with the delicato there are Puck-like rust-
lings, and all the while the pianist without
imagination is exercising wrist and fingers in
a technical exercise! Were ever Beauty and
Duty so mated in double harness? Pegasus
pulling a cloud charged with rain over an
arid country! For study, playing the entire
composition with a wrist stroke is advisable.
It will secure clear articulation, staccato and
finger-memory. Von Büow phrases the study
in groups of two, Kullak in sixes, Klindworth
and Mikuli the same, while Riemann in alternate twos, fours and sixes. One sees his
logic rather than hears it. Von Bülow plas-
tically reproduces the flitting, elusive character of the study far better than the others.

It is quite like him to suggest to the pant-
ing and ambitious pupil that the performance
in F sharp major, with the same fingering as
the next study in F, No. 8, would be bene-
ficial. It certainly would. By the same

token, the playing of the F minor Sonata, the Appassionata of Beethoven, in the key of F sharp minor, might produce good results. This was another crotchet of Wagner's friend and probably was born of the story that Beethoven transposed the Bach fugues in all keys. The same is said of Saint-Saëns.

In his notes to the F major study Theodor Kullak expatiates at length upon his favorite idea that Chopin must not be played according to his metronomic markings. The original autograph gives 96 to the half, the Tellefsen edition 88, Klindworth 80, Von Bülow 89, Mikuli 88, and Riemann the same. Kullak takes the slower tempo of Klindworth, believing that the old Herz and Czerny ideals of velocity are vanished, that the shallow dip of the keys in Chopin's day had much to do with the swiftness and lightness of his playing. The noble, more sonorous tone of a modern piano requires greater breadth of style and less speedy passage work. There can be no doubt as to the wisdom of a broader treatment of this charming display piece. How it makes the piano sound — what a rich, brilliant sweep it secures! It elbows the treble to its last euphonious point, glitters and crests itself, only to fall away as if the sea were melodic and could shatter and tumble into tuneful foam! The emotional content is not marked. The piece is for the fashionable salon or the concert hall. One catches at its close the overtones of bustling plaudits and the clapping of gloved palms. Ductility, an aristocratic ease, a delicate touch and fluent technique will carry off this study with good effect. Technically it is useful; one must speak of the usefulness of Chopin, even in these imprisoned, iridescent soap bubbles of his. On the fourth line and in the first bar of the Kullak version, there is a chord of the dominant seventh in dispersed position that does not occur in any other edition. Yet it must be Chopin or one of his disciples, for this autograph is in the Royal Library at Berlin. Kullak thinks it ought to be omitted, moreover he slights an E flat, that occurs in all the other editions situated in the fourth group of the twentieth bar from the end.

The F minor study, No. 9, is the first one of those tone studies of Chopin in which the mood is more petulant than tempestuous. The melody is morbid, almost irritating, and yet not without certain accents of grandeur. There is a persistency in repetition that foreshadows the Chopin of the later, sadder years. The figure in the left hand is the first in which a prominent part is given to that member. Not as noble and sonorous a figure as the one in the C minor study, it is a distinct forerunner of the bass of the D minor Prelude. In this F minor study the stretch is the technical object. It is rather awkward for close-knit fingers. The best fingering is Von Bülow's. It is 5, 3, 1, 4, 1, 3 for the first figure. All the other editions, except Riemann's, recommend the fifth finger on F, the fourth on C. Von Bülow believes that small hands beginning with his system will achieve quicker results than by the Chopin fingering. This is true. Riemann phrases the study with a multiplicity of legato bows and dynamic accents. Kullak prefers the Tellefsen metronome 80, rather than the traditional 96. Most of the others use 88 to the quarter, except Riemann, who espouses the more rapid gait of 96. Klindworth, with his 88, strikes a fair medium.

The verdict of Von Bülow on the following study in A flat, No. 10, has no uncertainty of tone in its proclamation:

He who can play this study in a really finished manner may congratulate himself on having climbed to the highest point of the pianist's Parnassus, as it is perhaps the most difficult piece of the entire set. The whole repertory of

piano music does not contain a study of perpetuum mobile so full of genius and fancy as this
particular one is universally acknowledged to be,
except perhaps Liszt's Feux Follets. The most
important point would appear to lie not so much
in the interchange of the groups of legato and staccato as in the exercise of rhythmic contrasts —
the alternation of two and three part metre (that
is, of four and six) in the same bar. To overcome
this fundamental difficulty in the art of musical reproduction is the most important thing here, and
with true zeal it may even be accomplished easily.

Kullak writes: "Harmonic anticipations;
a rich rhythmic life originating in the changing articulation of the twelve-eights in groups
of three and two each. . . . This étude is an
exceedingly piquant composition, possessing
for the hearer a wondrous, fantastic charm,
if played with the proper insight." The metronomic marking is practically the same in
all editions, 152 to the quarter notes. The
study is one of the most charming of the
composer. There is more depth in it than
in the G flat and F major studies, and its
effectiveness in the virtuoso sense is un-
questionable. A savor of the salon hovers
over its perfumed measures, but there is
grace, spontaneity and happiness. Chopin
must have been as happy **as his sensitive**

nature would allow when he conceived this vivacious caprice.

In all the editions, Riemann's excepted, there is no doubt left as to the alternations of metres. Here are the first few bars of Von Bülow's, which is normal phrasing:

Read Riemann's version of these bars:

Riemann is conducive to clear-sighted phrasing, and will set the student thinking, but the general effect of accentuation is certainly different. All the editors quoted agree with Von Bülow, Klindworth and Kullak.

But if this is a marked specimen of Riemann, examine his reading of the phrase wherein Chopin's triple rhythm is supplanted by duple. Thus Von Bülow — and who will dare cavil?

Riemann:

The difference is more imaginary than real, for the stems of the accented notes give us the binary metre. But the illustration serves to show how Dr. Riemann is disposed to refine upon the gold of Chopin.

Kullak dilates upon a peculiarity of Chopin: the dispersed position of his underlying harmonies. This in a footnote to the eleventh study of op. 10. Here one must let go the critical valve, else strangle in pedagogics. So much has been written, so much that is false, perverted sentimentalism and unmitigated cant about the nocturnes, that the wonder is the real Chopin lover has not rebelled. There are pearls and diamonds in the jewelled collection of nocturnes, many are dolorous, few dramatic, and others are sweetly insane and songful. I yield to none in my admiration for the first one of the two in G minor, for the psychical despair in the C sharp minor nocturne, for that noble drama called the C minor nocturne, for the B major, the Tuberose nocturne; and for the E, D flat and G major nocturnes, it remains unabated. But in the list there is no such picture painted, a Corot if ever there was one, as this E flat study.

Its novel design, delicate arabesques — as if the guitar had been dowered with a soul — and the richness and originality of its harmonic scheme, gives us pause to ask if Chopin's invention is not almost boundless. The melody itself is plaintive; a plaintive grace informs the entire piece. The harmonization is far more wonderful, but to us the chord of the tenth and more remote intervals, seem no longer daring; modern composition **has** devilled the musical alphabet into the very caverns of the grotesque, yet there are harmonies in the last page of this study that still excite wonder. The fifteenth bar from the end is one that Richard Wagner might have made. From that bar to the close, every group is a masterpiece.

Remember, this study is a nocturne, and even the accepted metronomic markings in most editions, 76 to the quarter, are not too slow; they might even be slower. Allegretto and not a shade speedier! The color scheme is celestial and the ending a sigh, not unmixed with happiness. Chopin, sensitive poet, had his moments of peace, of divine content — lebensruhe. The dizzy appoggiatura leaps in the last two bars set the seal of perfection upon this unique composition.

Touching upon the execution, one may say that it is not for small hands, nor yet for big fists. The former must not believe that any " arrangements " or simplified versions will ever produce the aerial effect, the swaying of the tendrils of tone, intended by Chopin. Very large hands are tempted by their reach to crush the life out of the study in not arpeggiating it. This I have heard, and the impression was indescribably brutal. As for

fingering, Mikuli, Von Bülow, Kullak, Riemann and Klindworth all differ, and from
them must most pianists differ. Your own
grasp, individual sense of fingering and tact
will dictate the management of technics. Von
Bülow gives a very sensible pattern to work
from, and Kullak is still more explicit. He
analyzes the melody and, planning the arpeggiating with scrupulous fidelity, he shows
why the arpeggiating " must be affected with
the utmost rapidity, bordering upon simulta-
neousness of harmony in the case of many
chords." Kullak has something to say about
the grace notes and this bids me call your attention to Von Bülow's change in the appoggiatura at the last return of the subject. A
bad misprint is in the Von Bülow edition : it
is in the seventeenth bar from the end, the
lowest note in the first bass group and should
read E natural, instead of the E flat that
stands.

Von Bülow does not use the arpeggio sign
after the first chord. He rightly believes it
makes unclear for the student the subtleties
of harmonic changes and fingering. He also
suggests — quite like the fertile Hans Guido
— that " players who have sufficient patience
and enthusiasm for the task would find it
worth their while to practise the arpeggi the

reverse way, from top to bottom; or in con trary motion, beginning with the top note in one hand and the bottom note in the other. A variety of devices like this would certainly help to give greater finish to the task."

Doubtless, but consider: man's years are but threescore and ten!

The phrasing of the various editions examined do not vary much. Riemann is excepted, who has his say in this fashion, at the beginning:

More remarkable still is the diversity of opinion regarding the first three bass chord groups in the fifteenth bar from the close: the bottom notes in the Von Bülow and Klindworth editions are B flat and two A naturals, and in the Riemann, Kullak and Mikuli editions the notes are two B flats and one A natural. The former sounds more varied, but we may suppose the latter to be correct because of Mikuli. Here is the particular bar, as given by Riemann:

Yet this exquisite flight into the blue, this nocturne which should be played before sundown, excited the astonishment of Mendelssohn, the perplexed wrath of Moscheles and the contempt of Rellstab, editor of the "Iris," who wrote in that journal in 1834 of the studies in op. 10: —

"Those who have distorted fingers may put them right by practising these studies; but those who have not, should not play them, at least not without having a surgeon at hand." What incredible surgery would have been needed to get within the skull of this narrow critic any savor of the beauty of these compositions! In the years to come the Chopin studies will be played for their music, without any thought of their technical problems.

Now the young eagle begins to face the

sun, begins to mount on wind-weaving pinions. We have reached the last study of op. 10, the magnificent one in C minor. Four pages suffice for a background upon which the composer has flung with overwhelming fury the darkest, the most demoniac expressions of his nature. Here is no veiled surmise, no smothered rage, but all sweeps along in tornadic passion. Karasowski's story may be true regarding the genesis of this work, but true or not, it is one of the greatest dramatic outbursts in piano literature. Great in outline, pride, force and velocity, it never relaxes its grim grip from the first shrill dissonance to the overwhelming chordal close. This end rings out like the crack of creation. It is elemental. Kullak calls it a " bravura study of the very highest order for the left hand. It was composed in 1831 in Stuttgart, shortly after Chopin had received tidings of the taking of Warsaw by the Russians, September 8, 1831." Karasowski wrote: " Grief, anxiety and despair over the fate of his relatives and his dearly-beloved father filled the measure of his sufferings. Under the influence of this mood he wrote the C minor Étude, called by many the Revolutionary Étude. Out of the mad and tempestuous storm of passages for the left hand the melody rises aloft, now passionate and anon proudly majestic, until thrills of awe stream over the listener, and the image is evoked of Zeus hurling thunderbolts at the world."

Niecks thinks it "superbly grand," and furthermore writes: "The composer seems fuming with rage; the left hand rushes impetuously along and the right hand strikes in with passionate ejaculations." Von Bülow said: "This C minor study must be considered a finished work of art in an even higher degree than the study in C sharp minor." All of which is pretty, but not enough to the point.

Von Bülow fingers the first passage for the left hand in a very rational manner; Klindworth differs by beginning with the third instead of the second finger, while Riemann — dear innovator — takes the group: second, first, third, and then, the fifth finger on D, if you please! Kullak is more normal, beginning with the third. Here is Riemann's phrasing and grouping for the first few bars. Notice the half note with peculiar changes of fingering at the end. It gives surety and variety. Von Bülow makes the changes ring on the second and fifth, instead of third and fifth, fingers. Thus Riemann:

In the above the accustomed phrasing is altered, for in all other editions the accent falls upon the first note of each group. In Riemann the accentuation seems perverse, but there is no question as to its pedagogic value. It may be ugly, but it is useful though I should not care to hear it in the concert room. Another striking peculiarity of the Riemann phrasing is his heavy accent on the top E flat in the principal passage for the left hand. He also fingers what Von Bülow calls the " chromatic meanderings," in an unusual manner, both on the first page

169

and the last. His idea of the enunciation of
the first theme is peculiar:

Mikuli places a legato bow over the first
three octaves — so does Kullak — Von Bülow
only over the last two, which gives a slightly
different effect, while Klindworth does the
same as Kullak. The heavy dynamic accents employed by Riemann are unmistakable. They signify the vital importance of
the phrase at its initial entrance. He does
not use it at the repetition, but throughout
both dynamic and agogic accents are un-
sparingly used, and the study seems to resound with the sullen booming of a park of
artillery. The working-out section, with
its anticipations of "Tristan and Isolde," is
phrased by all the editors as it is never played.
Here the technical figure takes precedence
over the law of the phrase, and so most virtuosi place the accent on the fifth finger, re-

gardless of the pattern. This is as it should be. In Klindworth there is a misprint at the beginning of the fifteenth bar from the end in the bass. It should read B natural, not B flat. The metronome is the same in all editions, 160 to the quarter, but speed should give way to breadth at all hazards. Von Bülow is the only editor, to my knowledge, who makes an enharmonic key change in this working-out section. It looks neater, sounds the same, but is it Chopin? He also gives a variant for public performance by transforming the last run in unisono into a veritable hurricane by interlocked octaves. The effect is brazen. Chopin needs no such clangorous padding in this étude, which gains by legitimate strokes the most startling contrasts.

The study is full of tremendous pathos; it compasses the sublime, and in its most torrential moments the composer never quite loses his mental equipoise. He, too, can evoke tragic spirits, and at will send them scurrying back to their dim profound. It has but one rival in the Chopin studies — No. 12, op. 25, in the same key.

II

OPUS 25, twelve studies by Frédéric Chopin, are dedicated to Madame la Comtesse d'Agoult. The set opens with the familiar study in A flat, so familiar that I shall not make further ado about it except to say that it is delicious, but played often and badly. All that modern editing can do since Miluki is to hunt out fresh accentuation. Von Bülow is the worst sinner in this respect, for he discovers quaint nooks and dells for his dynamics undreamed of by the composer. His edition should be respectfully studied and, when mastered, discarded for a more poetic interpretation. Above all, poetry, poetry and pedals. Without pedalling of the most varied sort this study will remain as dry as a dog-gnawed bone. Von Bülow says the " figure must be treated as a double triplet — twice three and not three times two — as indicated in the first two bars." Klindworth makes the group a sextolet. Von Bülow has set forth numerous directions in fingering and phrasing, giving the exact number of notes in the bass trill at the end. Kullak uses the most ingenious fingering. Look at the last group of the last bar, second line, third page. It is the last word in fingering.

Better to end with Robert Schumann's beautiful description of this study, as quoted by Kullak:

In treating of the present book of Études, Robert Schumann, after comparing Chopin to a strange star seen at midnight, wrote as follows: "Whither his path lies and leads, or how long, how brilliant its course is yet to be, who can say? As often, however, as it shows itself, there is ever seen the same deep dark glow, the same starry light and the same austerity, so that even a child could not fail to recognize it. But besides this, I have had the advantage of hearing most of these Études played by Chopin himself, and quite à la Chopin did he play them!"

Of the first one especially he writes: "Imagine that an æolian harp possessed all the musical scales, and that the hand of an artist were to cause them all to intermingle in all sorts of fantastic embellishments, yet in such a way as to leave everywhere audible a deep fundamental tone and a soft continuously-singing upper voice, and you will get the right idea of his playing. But it would be an error to think that Chopin permitted every one of the small notes to be distinctly heard. It was rather an undulation of the A flat major chord, here and there thrown aloft anew by the pedal. Throughout all the harmonies one always heard in great tones a wondrous melody, while once only, in the middle of the piece, besides that chief song, a tenor voice became prominent in the midst of chords. After the Étude a feeling came over one as of having seen in a dream a beatific picture which when half awake one would gladly recall."

After these words there can be no doubt as to the mode of delivery. No commentary is required to show that the melodic and other important tones indicated by means of large notes must emerge from within the sweetly whispering waves, and that the upper tones must be combined so as to form a real melody with the finest and most thoughtful shadings.

The twenty-fourth bar of this study in A major is so Lisztian that Liszt must have benefited by its harmonies.

"And then he played the second in the book, in F minor, one in which his individuality displays itself in a manner never to be forgotten. How charming, how dreamy it was! Soft as the song of a sleeping child." Schumann wrote this about the wonderful study in F minor, which whispers, not of baleful deeds in a dream, as does the last movement of the B flat minor sonata, but is — "the song of a sleeping child." No comparison could be prettier, for there is a sweet, delicate drone that sometimes issues from childish lips, having a charm for ears not attuned to grosser things.

This must have been the study that Chopin played for Henrietta Voigt at Leipsic, September 12, 1836. In her diary she wrote: "The over excitement of his fantastic manner is imparted to the keen eared. It made me hold my breath. Wonderful is the ease with which his velvet fingers glide, I might almost say fly, over the keys. He has enraptured me — in a way which hitherto had been unknown to me. What delighted me was the childlike, natural manner which he showed in his demeanor and in his playing." Von Bülow believes the interpretation of this magical music should be without sentimentality, almost without shading — clearly, delicately and dreamily executed. "An ideal pianissimo, an accentless quality, and completely without passion or rubato." There is little doubt this was the way Chopin played it. Liszt is an authority on the subject, and M. Mathias corroborates him. Regarding the rhythmical problem to be overcome, the combination of two opposing rhythms, Von Bülow indicates an excellent method, and Kullak devotes part of a page to examples of how the right, then the left, and finally both hands, are to be treated. Kullak furthermore writes: "Or, if one will, he may also betake himself in fancy to a still, green, dusky forest, and listen in profound solitude to the mysterious rustling and whispering of the foliage. What, indeed, despite the algebraic character of the tone-language, may not a lively fancy conjure out of, or, rather, into, this étude! But one thing is to be held fast: it is to be played in that Chopin-like whisper of which, among others, Mendelssohn also affirmed that for him nothing more enchanting existed."

But enough of subjective fancies. This study contains much beauty, and every bar rules over a little harmonic kingdom of its own. It is so lovely that not even the Brahms' distortion in double notes or the version in octaves can dull its magnetic crooning. At times so delicate is its design that it recalls the faint fantastic tracery made by frost on glass. In all instances save one it is written as four unbroken quarter triplets in the bar — right hand. Not so Riemann. He has views of his own, both as to fingering and phrasing:

Jean Kleczynski's interesting brochure, 'The Works of Frédéric Chopin and Their Proper Interpretation," is made up of three lectures delivered at Warsaw. While the subject is of necessity foreshortened, he says some practical things about the use of the pedals in Chopin's music. He speaks of this very study in F minor and the enchanting way Rubinstein and Essipowa ended it — the echo-like effects on the four C's, the pedal floating the tone. The pedals are half the battle in Chopin playing. *One can never play Chopin beautifully enough.* Realistic treatment dissipates his dream palaces, shatters his aërial architecture. He may be played broadly, fervently, dramatically but coarsely, never. I deprecate the rose-leaf sentimentalism in which he is swathed by nearly all pianists. "Chopin is a sigh, with something pleasing in it," wrote some one, and it is precisely this notion which has created such havoc among his interpreters. But if excess in feeling is objectionable, so too is the "healthy" reading accorded his works by pianists with more brawn than brain. The real Chopin player is born and can never be a product of the schools.

Schumann thinks the third study in F less novel in character, although "here the mas-

ter showed his admirable bravura powers.
"But," he continues, "they are all model
of bold, indwelling, creative force, truly poeti
creations, though not without small blots i
their details, but on the whole striking an
powerful. Yet, if I give my complete opin
ion, I must confess that his earlier collectio
seems more valuable to me. Not that
mean to imply any deterioration, for thes
recently published studies were nearly a
written at the same time as the earlier ones
and only a few were composed a little while
ago — the first in A flat and the last mag
nificent one in C minor, both of which displa
great mastership."

One may be permitted to disagree with
Schumann, for op. 25 contains at least tw
of Chopin's greater studies — A minor an
C minor. The most valuable point of th
passage quoted is the clenching of the fac
that the studies were composed in a bunch
That settles many important psychologica
details. Chopin had suffered much befor
going to Paris, had undergone the purifica
tion and renunciation of an unsuccessful lov
affair, and arrived in Paris with his style full
formed — in his case the style was mos
emphatically the man.

Kullak calls the study in F "a spirite

little caprice, whose kernel lies in the simultaneous application of four different little
rhythms to form a single figure in sound,
which figure is then repeated continuously
to the end. In these repetitions, however,
changes of accentuation, fresh modulations,
and piquant antitheses, serve to make the
composition extremely vivacious and effective." He pulls apart the brightly colored
petals of the thematic flower and reveals
the inner chemistry of this delicate growth.
Four different voices are distinguished in the
kernel.

"The third voice is the chief one, and after
it the first, because they determine the melodic and harmonic contents":

Kullak and Mikuli dot the C of the first
bar. Klindworth and Von Bülow do not.

As to phrasing and fingering I pin my faith
to Riemann. His version is the most satisfactory. Here are the first bars. The idea
is clearly expressed:

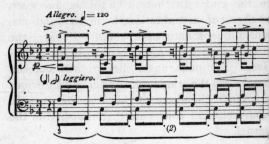

Best of all is the careful accentuation, and
at a place indicated in no other edition that
I have examined. With the arrival of the
thirty-second notes, Riemann punctuates the
theme this way:

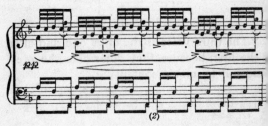

The melody, of course in profile, is in the
ghth notes. This gives meaning to the

decorative pattern of the passage. And what charm, buoyancy, and sweetness there is in this caprice! It has the tantalizing, elusive charm of a humming bird in full flight. The human element is almost eliminated. We are in the open, the sun blazes in the blue, and all is gay, atmospheric, and illuding. Even where the tone deepens, where the shadows grow cooler and darker in the B major section, there is little hint of preoccupation with sadness. Subtle are the harmonic shifts, admirable the ever changing devices of the figuration. Riemann accents the B, the E, A, B flat, C and F, at the close — perilous leaps for the left hand, but they bring into fine relief the exquisite harmonic web. An easy way of avoiding the tricky position in the left hand at this spot — thirteen bars from the close — is to take the upper C in bass with the right hand thumb and in the next bar the upper B in bass the same way. This minimizes the risk of the skip, and it is perfectly legitimate to do this — in public at least. The ending, to be "breathed" away, according to Kullak, is variously fingered. He also prescribes a most trying fingering for the first group, fourth finger on both hands. This is useful for study, but for performance the third finger is surer. Von

Bülow advises the player to keep the " uppe
part of the body as still as possible, as an
haste of movement would destroy the objec
in view, which is the acquisition of a loos
wrist." He also suggests certain phrasing i
bar seventeen, and forbids a sharp, cuttin
manner in playing the sforzati at the las
return of the subject. Kullak is copious i
his directions, and thinks the touch shoul
be light and the hand gliding, and in the
major part " fiery, wilful accentuation of th
inferior beats." Capricious, fantastic, an
graceful, this study is Chopin in rare spirit
Schumann has the phrase — the study shoul
be executed with " amiable bravura." Ther
is a misprint in the Kullak edition: at th
beginning of the thirty-second notes an
instead of an F upsets the tonality, beside
being absurd.

Of the fourth study in A minor there
little to add to Theodor Kullak, who writes

" In the broadest sense of the word, every pie
of music is an étude. In a narrower sense, hov
ever, we demand of an étude that it shall have
special end in view, promote facility in somethin
and lead to the conquest of some particular dif
culty, whether of technics, of rhythm, expressic
or delivery." (Robert Schumann, Collected Wri
ings, i., 201.) The present study is less interes

ing from a technical than a rhythmical point of view. While the chief beats of the measure (1st, 3d, 5th and 7th eighths) are represented only by single tones (in the bass part), which are to a certain extent "free and unconcerned, and void of all encumbrance," the inferior parts of the measure (2d, 4th, 6th and 8th eighths) are burdened with chords, the most of which, moreover, are provided with accents in opposition to the regular beats of the measure. Further, there is associated with these chords, or there may be said to grow out of them, a cantilene in the upper voice, which appears in syncopated form opposite to the strong beats of the bass. This cantilene begins on a weak beat, and produces numerous suspensions, which, in view of the time of their entrance, appear as so many retardations and delayals of melodic tones.

All these things combine to give the composition a wholly peculiar coloring, to render its flow somewhat restless and to stamp the étude as a little characteristic piece, a capriccio, which might well be named " Inquietude."

As regards technics, two things are to be studied : the staccato of the chords and the execution of the cantilena. The chords must be formed more by pressure than by striking. The fingers must support themselves very lightly upon the chord keys and then rise again with the back of the hand in the most elastic manner. The upward movement

of the hand must be very slight. Everything must
be done with the greatest precision, and not merely
in a superficial manner. Where the cantilena appears, every melodic tone must stand apart from
the tones of the accompaniment as if in "relief."
Hence the fingers for the melodic tones must press
down the keys allotted to them with special force,
in doing which the back of the hand may be permitted to turn lightly to the right (sideward stroke),
especially when there is a rest in the accompaniment. Compare with this étude the introduction
to the Capriccio in B minor, with orchestra, by
Felix Mendelssohn, first page. Aside from a few
rallentando places, the étude is to be played
strictly in time.

I prefer the Klindworth editing of this
rather sombre, nervous composition, which
may be merely an étude, but it also indicates a
slightly pathologic condition. With its breath-
catching syncopations and narrow emotional
range, the A minor study has nevertheless
moments of power and interest. Riemann's
phrasing, while careful, is not more enlighten-
ing than Klindworth's. Von Bülow says:
"The bass must be strongly marked throughout — even when piano — and brought out
in imitation of the upper part." Singularly
enough, his is the only edition in which the
left hand arpeggios at the close, though in

the final bar "both hands may do so." This is editorial quibbling. Stephen Heller remarked that this study reminded him of the first bar of the Kyrie — rather the Requiem Aeternam of Mozart's Requiem.

It is safe to say that the fifth study in E minor is less often heard in the concert room than any one of its companions. I cannot recall having heard it since Annette Essipowa gave that famous recital during which she played the entire twenty-seven studies. Yet it is a sonorous piano piece, rich in embroideries and general decorative effect in the middle section. Perhaps the rather perverse, capricious and not altogether amiable character of the beginning has caused pianists to be wary of introducing it at a recital. It is hugely effective and also difficult, especially if played with the same fingering throughout, as Von Bülow suggests. Niecks quotes Stephen Heller's partiality for this very study. In the "Gazette Musicale," February 24, 1839, Heller wrote of Chopin's op. 25:

What more do we require to pass one or several evenings in as perfect a happiness as possible? As for me, I seek in this collection of poesy — this is the only name appropriate to the works of Chopin — some favorite pieces which I might fix in my memory, rather than others. Who could retain everything? For this reason I have in my notebook quite particularly marked the numbers four, five and seven of the present poems. Of these twelve much loved studies — every one of which has a charm of its own — the three numbers are those I prefer to all the rest.

The middle part of this E minor study recalls Thalberg. Von Bülow cautions the student against "the accenting of the first note with the thumb — right hand — as it does not form part of the melody, but only comes in as an unimportant passing note." This refers to the melody in E. He also writes that the addition of the third in the left hand, Klindworth edition, needs no special justification. I discovered one marked difference in the Klindworth edition. The leap in the left hand — first variant of the theme, tenth bar from beginning — is preceded by an appoggiatura, E natural. The jump is to F sharp, instead of G, as in the Mikuli, Kullak and Riemann editions. Von Bülow uses the F sharp, but without the ninth below. Riemann phrases the piece so as to get the top melody, B, E and G, and his stems are below instead of above, as in Mikuli and Von Bülow. Kullak dots the eighth note. Riemann uses a sixteenth, thus:

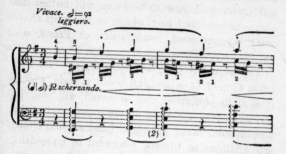

Kullak writes that the figure 184 is not found on the older metronomes. This is not too fast for the capriccio, with its pretty and ingenious rhythmical transformations. As regards the execution of the 130th bar, Von Bülow says: "The acciaccature — prefixes — are to be struck simultaneously with the other parts, as also the shake in bar 134 and following bars; this must begin with the upper auxiliary note." These details are important. Kullak concludes his notes thus:

Despite all the little transformations of the motive member which forms the kernel, its recognizability remains essentially unimpaired. Meanwhile out of these little metamorphoses there is developed a rich rhythmic life, which the performer must bring out with great precision. If in addition, he possesses a fine feeling for what is graceful, coquettish, or agreeably capricious, he will understand how to heighten still further the charm of the chief part, which, as far as its character is concerned, reminds one of Étude, op. 25, No. 3.

The secondary part, in major, begins. Its kernel is formed of a beautiful broad melody, which, if soulfully conceived and delivered, will sing its way deep into the heart of the listener. For the accompaniment in the right hand we find chord arpeggiations in triplets, afterward in sixteenths, calmly ascending and descending, and surrounding the melody as with a veil. They are to be played almost without accentuation.

It was Louis Ehlert who wrote of the celebrated study in G sharp minor op. 25, No. 6: "Chopin not only versifies an exercise in thirds; he transforms it into such a work of art that in studying it one could sooner fancy himself on Parnassus than at a lesson. He deprives every passage of all mechanical appearance by promoting it to become the embodiment of a beautiful thought, which in turn finds graceful expression in its motion."

And indeed in the piano literature no more remarkable merging of matter and manner exists. The means justifies the end, and the means employed by the composer are beautiful, there is no other word to describe the style and architectonics of this noble study. It is seldom played in public because of its difficulty. With the Schumann Toccata, the G sharp minor study stands at the portals of the delectable land of Double Notes. Both compositions have a common ancestry in the Czerny Toccata, and both are the parents of such a sensational offspring as Balakirew's "Islamey." In reading through the double note studies for the instrument it is in the nature of a miracle to come upon Chopin's transfiguration of such a barren subject. This study is first music, then a technical problem.

Where two or three pianists are gathered together in the name of Chopin, the conversation is bound to formulate itself thus: "How do you finger the double chromatic thirds in the G sharp minor study?" That question answered, your digital politics are known. You are classified, ranged. If you are heterodox you are eagerly questioned; if you follow Von Bülow and stand by the Czerny fingering, you are regarded as a curiosity. As the interpretation of the study is not taxing, let us examine the various fingerings. First, a fingering given by Leopold Godowsky. It is for double chromatic thirds:

You will now be presented with a battalion of authorities, so that you may see at a glance the various efforts to climb those slippery chromatic heights. Here is Mikuli:

Kullak's is exactly the same as above. It is the so-called Chopin fingering, as contrasted with the so-called Czerny fingering — though in reality Clementi's, as Mr. John Kautz contends. "In the latter the third and fifth fingers fall upon C sharp and E and F sharp and A in the right hand, and upon C and E flat and G and B flat in the left." Klindworth also employs the Chopin fingering. Von Bülow makes this statement: "As the peculiar fingering adopted by Chopin for chromatic scales in thirds appears to us to render their performance in legatissimo utterly unattainable on our modern instruments, we have exchanged it, where necessary, for the older method of Hummel. Two of the greatest executive artists of modern times, Alexander Dreyschock and Carl Tausig, were, theoretically and practically, of the same opinion. It is to be conjectured that Chopin was influenced in his method of fingering by the piano of his favorite makers, Pleyel and Wolff, of Paris — who, before they adopted the double échappement, certainly produced instruments with the most pliant touch possible — and therefore regarded the use of the thumb in the ascending scale on two white keys in succession — the semitones E F and B C — as practicable. On the grand piano of the present day we regard it as irreconcilable with conditions of crescendo legato." This Chopin fingering in reality derives directly from Hummel. See his "Piano School."

So he gives this fingering:

He also suggests the following phrasing for the left hand. This is excellent:

Riemann not only adopts new fingering for the double note scale, but also begins the study with the trill on first and third, second and fourth, instead of the usual first and fourth, second and fifth fingers, adopted by the rest. This is his notion of the run in chromatic thirds:

For the rest the study must be played like the wind, or, as Kullak says: "Apart from a few places and some accents, the Étude is to be played almost throughout in that Chopin whisper. The right hand must play its thirds, especially the diatonic and chromatic scales, with such equality that no angularity of motion shall be noticeable where the fingers pass under or over each other. The left hand, too, must receive careful attention and special study. The chord passages and all similar ones must be executed discreetly and legatissimo. Notes with double stems must be distinguished from notes with single stems by means of stronger shadings, for they are mutually interconnected."

Von Bülow calls the seventh study, the one in C sharp minor, a nocturne — a duo for 'cello and flute. He ingeniously smooths out the unequal rhythmic differences of the two hands, and justly says the piece does not work out any special technical matter. This study is the most lauded of all. Yet I cannot help agreeing with Niecks, who writes of it — he oddly enough places it in the key of E: " A duet between a He and a She, of whom the former shows himself more talkative and emphatic than the latter, is, indeed, very sweet, but, perhaps, also somewhat tiresomely monotonous, as such tête-à-têtes naturally are to third parties."

For Chopin's contemporaries this was one of his greatest efforts. Heller wrote: " It engenders the sweetest sadness, the most enviable torments, and if in playing it one feels oneself insensibly drawn toward mournful and melancholy ideas, it is a disposition of the soul which I prefer to all others. Alas! how I love these sombre and mysterious dreams, and Chopin is the god who creates them." In this étude Kleczynski thinks there are traces of weariness of life, and quotes Orlowski, Chopin's friend, " He is only afflicted with homesickness." Willeby calls this study the most beautiful of them all. For me it is both morbid and elegiac. There is nostalgia in it, the nostalgia of a sick, lacerated soul. It contains in solution all the most objectionable and most endearing qualities of the master. Perhaps we have heard its sweet, highly perfumed measures too often. Its interpretation is a matter of taste. Kullak has written the most ambitious programme for it. Here is a quotation from Albert R. Parsons' translation in Schirmer's edition of Kullak.

Throughout the entire piece an elegiac mood prevails. The composer paints with psychologic truthfulness a fragment out of the life of a deeply clouded soul. He lets a broken heart, filled with grief, proclaim its sorrow in a language of pain which is incapable of being misunderstood. The heart has lost — not something, but everything. The tones, however, do not always bear the im-

press of a quiet, melancholy resignation. More
passionate impulses awaken, and the still plaint
becomes a complaint against cruel fate. It seeks
the conflict, and tries through force of will to
burst the fetters of pain, or at least to alleviate it
through absorption in a happy past. But in vain !
The heart has not lost something — it has lost
everything. The musical poem divides into three,
or if one views the little episode in B major
as a special part, into four parts (strophes), of
which the last is an elaborated repetition of the
first with a brief closing part appended. The
whole piece is a song, or, better still, an aria,
in which two principal voices are to be brought
out ; the upper one is in imitation of a human
voice, while the lower one must bear the character
throughout of an obligato violoncello. It is well
known that Chopin was very fond of the violoncello and that in his piano compositions he imitated
the style of passages peculiar to that instrument.
The two voices correspond closely, supplementing
and imitating each other reciprocally. Between
the two a third element exists : an accompaniment
of eighths in uniform succession without any significance beyond that of filling out the harmony.
This third element is to be kept wholly subordi-
nate. The little, one-voiced introduction in recitative style which precedes the aria reminds one
vividly of the beginning of the Ballade in G minor,
op 23.

The D flat study, No. 8, is called by Von Bülow " the most useful exercise in the whole range of étude literature. It might truly be called 'l'indispensable du pianiste,' if the term, through misuse, had not fallen into disrepute. As a remedy for stiff fingers and preparatory to performing in public, playing it six times through is recommended, even to the most expert pianist." Only six times! The separate study of the left hand is recommended. Kullak finds this study " surprisingly euphonious, but devoid of depth of content." It is an admirable study for the cultivation of double sixths. It contains a remarkable passage of consecutive fifths that set the theorists by the ears. Riemann manages to get some new editorial comment upon it.

The nimble study, No. 9, which bears the title of " The Butterfly," is in G flat. Von Bülow transposes it enharmonically to F sharp, avoiding numerous double flats. The change is not laudable. He holds anything but an elevated opinion of the piece, classing it with a composition of the Charles Mayer order. This is unjust; the study if not deep is graceful and certainly very effective. It has lately become the stamping ground for the display of piano athletics.

Nearly all modern virtuosi pull to pieces the wings of this gay little butterfly. They smash it, they bang it, and, adding insult to cruelty, they finish it with three chords, mounting an octave each time, thus giving a conventional character to the close — the very thing the composer avoids. Much distorted phrasing is also indulged in. The Tellefsen's edition and Klindworth's give these differences:

Mikuli, Von Bülow and Kullak place the legato bow over the first three notes of the group. Riemann, of course, is different:

The metronomic markings are about the same in all editions.

Asiatic wildness, according to Von Bülow,
pervades the B minor study, op. 25, No. 10,
although Willeby claims it to be only a
study in octaves "for the left hand"! Von
Bülow furthermore compares it, because of
its monophonic character, to the Chorus
of Dervishes in Beethoven's "Ruins of
Athens." Niecks says it is "a real pande-
monium; for a while holier sounds intervene,
but finally hell prevails." The study is for
Kullak "somewhat far fetched and forced
in invention, and leaves one cold, although
it plunges on wildly to the end." Von
Bülow has made the most complete edition.
Klindworth strengthens the first and the seventh eighth notes of the fifth bar before the
last by filling in the harmonics of the left hand.
This étude is an important one, technically;
because many pianists make little of it that
does not abate its musical significance, and I
am almost inclined to group it with the last
two studies of this opus. The opening is portentous and soon becomes a driving whirlwind
of tone. Chopin has never penned a love-
lier melody than the one in B — the middle
section of this étude — it is only to be compared to the one in the same key in the B
minor Scherzo, while the return to the first
subject is managed as consummately as in

the E flat minor Scherzo, from op. 35. I confess to being stirred by this B minor study, with its tempo at a forced draught and with its precipitous close. There is a lushness about the octave melody; the tune may be a little overripe, but it is sweet, sensuous music, and about it hovers the hush of a rich evening in early autumn.

And now the " Winter Wind " — the study in A minor, op. 25, No. 11. Here even Von Bülow becomes enthusiastic:

" It must be mentioned as a particular merit of this, the longest and, in every respect, the grandest of Chopin's studies, that, while producing the greatest fulness of sound imaginable, it keeps itself so entirely and utterly unorchestral, and represents piano music in the most accurate sense of the word. To Chopin is due the honor and credit of having set fast the boundary between piano and orchestral music, which through other composers of the romantic school, especially Robert Schumann, has been defaced and blotted out, to the prejudice and damage of both species."

Kullak is equally as warm in his praise of it:

One of the grandest and most ingenious of Chopin's études, and a companion piece to op.

10, No. 12, which perhaps it even surpasses. It is a bravura study of the highest order; and is captivating through the boldness and originality of its passages, whose rising and falling waves, full of agitation, overflow the entire keyboard; captivating through its harmonic and modulatory shadings; and captivating, finally, through a wonderfully invented little theme which is drawn like a "red thread" through all the flashing and glittering waves of tone, and which, as it were, prevents them from scattering to all quarters of the heavens. This little theme, strictly speaking only a phrase of two measures, is, in a certain sense, the motto which serves as a superscription for the étude, appearing first one voiced, and immediately afterward four voiced. The slow time (Lento) shows the great importance which is to be attached to it. They who have followed thus far and agree with what has been said cannot be in doubt concerning the proper artistic delivery. To execute the passages quite in the rapid time prescribed one must possess a finished technique. Great facility, lightness of touch, equality, strength and endurance in the forte passages, together with the clearest distinctness in the piano and pianissimo — all of this must have been already achieved, for the interpreter must devote his whole attention to the poetic contents of the composition, especially to the delivery of the march-like rhythms, which possess a life of their own, appearing now calm and circumspect, and anon bold and challenging. The march-like element naturally requires strict playing in time.

This study is magnificent, and moreover it is music.

In bar fifteen Von Bülow makes B natural the second note of the last group, although all other editions, except Klindworth, use a B flat. Von Bülow has common sense on his side. The B flat is a misprint. The same authority recommends slow staccato practice, with the lid of the piano closed. Then the hurly-burly of tone will not intoxicate the player and submerge his critical faculty.

Each editor has his notion of the phrasing of the initial sixteenths. Thus Mikuli's— which is normal:

Klindworth fingers this passage more ingeniously, but phrases it about the same,

omitting the sextolet mark. Kullak retains
it. Von Bülow makes his phrase run in this
fashion:

As regards grouping, Riemann follows Von
Bülow, but places his accents differently.

The canvas is Chopin's largest — for the
idea and its treatment are on a vastly
grander scale than any contained in the two
concertos. The latter are after all miniatures, precious ones if you will, joined and
built with cunning artifice; in neither work
is there the resistless overflow of this étude,
which has been compared to the screaming
of the winter blasts. Ah, how Chopin puts
to flight those modern men who scheme out
a big decorative pattern and then have nothing wherewith to fill it! He never relaxes
his theme, and its fluctuating surprises are
many. The end is notable for the fact that

scales appear. Chopin very seldom uses scale figures in his studies. From Hummel to Thalberg and Herz the keyboard had glittered with spangled scales. Chopin must have been sick of them, as sick of them as of the left-hand melody with arpeggiated accompaniment in the right, à la Thalberg. Scales had been used too much, hence Chopin's sparing employment of them. In the first C sharp minor study, op. 10, there is a run for the left hand in the coda. In the seventh study, same key, op. 25, there are more. The second study of op. 10, in A minor, is a chromatic scale study; but there are no other specimens of the form until the mighty run at the conclusion of this A minor study.

It takes prodigious power and endurance to play this work, prodigious power, passion and no little poetry. It is open air music, storm music, and at times moves in processional splendor. Small souled men, no matter how agile their fingers, should avoid it.

The prime technical difficulty is the management of the thumb. Kullak has made a variant at the end for concert performance. It is effective. The average metronomic marking is sixty-nine to the half.

Kullak thinks the twelfth and last study

of op. 25 in C minor "a grand, magnificent composition for practice in broken chord passages for both hands, which requires no comment." I differ from this worthy teacher. Rather is Niecks more to my taste: "No. 12, C minor, in which the emotions rise not less high than the waves of arpeggios which symbolize them."

Von Bülow is didactic:

The requisite strength for this grandiose bravura study can only be attained by the utmost clearness, and thus only by a gradually increasing speed. It is therefore most desirable to practise it piano also by way of variety, for otherwise the strength of tone might easily degenerate into hardness, and in the poetic striving after a realistic portrayal of a storm on the piano the instrument, as well as the piece, would come to grief.

The pedal is needful to give the requisite effect, and must change with every new harmony; but it should only be used in the latter stages of study, when the difficulties are nearly mastered.

We have our preferences. Mine in op. 25 is the C minor study, which, like the prelude in D minor, is "full of the sound of great guns." Willeby thinks otherwise. On page 81 in his life of Chopin he has the courage to write: "Had Professor Niecks applied the term monotonous to No. 12 we should have been more ready to indorse his opinion, as, although great power is manifested, the very 'sameness' of the form of the arpeggio figure causes a certain amount of monotony to be felt." The C minor study is, in a degree, a return to the first study in C. While the idea in the former is infinitely nobler, more dramatic and tangible, there is in the latter naked, primeval simplicity, the larger eloquence, the elemental puissance. Monotonous? A thousand times no! Monotonous as is the thunder and spray of the sea when it tumbles and roars on some sullen, savage shore. Beethov-ian, in its ruggedness, the Chopin of this C minor study is as far removed from the musical dandyisms of the Parisian drawing rooms as is Beethoven himself. It is orchestral in intention and a true epic of the piano.

Riemann places half notes at the beginning of each measure, as a reminder of the necessary clinging of the thumbs. I like Von Bülow's version the best of all. His directions are most minute. He gives the Liszt method of working up the climax in octave triplets. How Liszt must have thundered through this tumultuous work! Before it all criticism should be silenced that fails to allow Chopin a place among the greatest creative musicians. We are here in the presence of Chopin the musician, not Chopin the composer for piano.

III

In 1840, Trois Nouvelles Études, by Frédéric Chopin, appeared in the " Méthode des Méthodes pour le piano," by F. J. Fétis and I. Moscheles. It was odd company for the Polish composer. " Internal evidence seems to show," writes Niecks, " that these weakest of the master's studies — which, however, are by no means uninteresting and certainly very characteristic — may be regarded more than op. 25 as the outcome of a gleaning."

The last decade has added much to the artistic stature of these three supplementary studies. They have something of the concision of the Preludes. The first is a masterpiece. In F minor the theme in triplet quarters, broad, sonorous and passionate, is unequally pitted against four-eight notes in the bass. The technical difficulty to be overcome is purely rhythmic, and Kullak takes pains to show how it may be overcome. It is the musical, the emotional content of the study that fascinates. The worthy editor calls it a companion piece to the F minor study in op. 25. The comparison is not an apt one. Far deeper is this new study, and although the doors never swing quite open, we divine the tragic issues concealed.

Beautiful in a different way is the A flat study which follows. Again the problem is a rhythmical one, and again the composer demonstrates his exhaustless invention and his power of evoking a single mood, viewing all its lovely contours and letting it melt away like dream magic. Full of gentle sprightliness and lingering sweetness is this study. Chopin has the hypnotic quality more than any composer of the century, Richard Wagner excepted. After you have enjoyed playing this study read Kullak and his "triplicity in biplicity." It may do you good, and it will not harm the music.

In all the editions save one that I have seen the third study in D flat begins on A flat, like the famous Valse in D flat. The exception is Klindworth, who starts with B flat, the note above. The study is full of sunny, good humor, spiritualized humor, and leaves the most cheering impression after its performance. Its technical object is a simultaneous legato and staccato. The result is an idealized Valse in allegretto tempo, the very incarnation of joy, tempered by aristocratic reserve. Chopin never romps, but he jests wittily, and always in supremely good taste. This study fitly closes his extraordinary labors in this form, and it is as if he had signed it " F. Chopin, et ego in Arcady."

Among the various editions let me recommend Klindworth for daily usage, while frequent reference to Von Bülow, Riemann and Kullak cannot fail to prove valuable, curious and interesting.

Of the making of Chopin editions there is seemingly no end. In 1894 I saw in manuscript some remarkable versions of the Chopin Studies by Leopold Godowsky. The study in G sharp minor was the first one published and played in public by this young pianist. Unlike the Brahms derangements, they are musical but immensely difficult. Topsy-turvied as are the figures, a Chopin, even if lop-sided, hovers about, sometimes with eyebrows uplifted, sometimes with angry, knitted forehead and not seldom amused to the point of smiling. You see his narrow shoulders, shrugged in the Polish fashion as he examines the study in double-thirds transposed to the left hand! Curiously enough this transcription, difficult as it is, does not tax the fingers as much as a bedevilment of the

A minor, op. 25, No. 4, which is extremely difficult, demanding color discrimination and individuality of finger.

More breath-catching, and a piece at which one must cry out: " Hats off, gentlemen! A tornado!" is the caprice called "Badinage." But if it is meant to badinage, it is no sport for the pianist of everyday technical attainments. This is formed of two studies. In the right hand is the G flat study, op. 25, No. 9, and in the left the black key study, op. 10, No. 5. The two go laughing through the world like old friends; brother and sister they are tonally, trailing behind them a cloud of iridescent glory. Godowsky has cleverly combined the two, following their melodic curves as nearly as is possible. In some places he has thickened the harmonies and shifted the " black key" figures to the right hand. It is the work of a remarkable pianist. This is the way it looks on paper at the beginning:

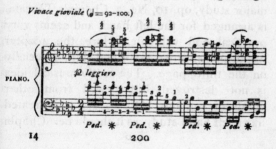

Vivace gioviale (♩ = 92–100.)

PIANO.

leggiero

Ped. ✳   Ped. ✳   Ped. ✳   Ped. ✳

The same study G flat, op. 10, No. 5, is also treated separately, the melody being transferred to the treble. The Butterfly octaves, in another study, are made to hop nimbly along in the left hand, and the C major study, op. 10, No. 7, Chopin's Toccata, is arranged for the left hand, and seems very practical and valuable. Here the adapter has displayed great taste and skill, especially on the third page. The pretty musical idea is not destroyed, but viewed from other points of vantage. Op. 10, No. 2, is treated like a left hand study, as it should be. Chopin did not always give enough work to the left hand, and the first study of this opus in C is planned on brilliant lines for both hands. Ingenious is the manipulation of the seldom played op. 25, No. 5, in E minor. As a study in rhythms and double notes it is very welcome. The F minor study, op. 25, No. 2, as considered by the ambidextrous Godowsky, is put in the bass, where it whirrs along to the melodic encouragement of a theme of the paraphraser's own, in the right. This study has suffered the most of all, for Brahms, in his heavy, Teutonic way, set it grinding double sixths, while Isidor Philipp, in his "Studies for the Left Hand," has harnessed it to sullen octaves. This Frenchman, by the way, has also arranged for left hand alone the G sharp minor, the D flat double sixths, the A minor — "Winter Wind" — studies, the B flat minor prelude, and, terrible to relate, the last movement of the Chopin B flat minor Sonata.

Are the Godowsky transcriptions available? Certainly. In ten years — so rapid is the technical standard advancing — they will be used in the curriculum of students. Whether he has treated Chopin with reverence I leave my betters to determine. What has reverence to do with the case, anyhow? Plato is parsed in the schoolroom, and Beethoven taught in conservatories! Therefore why worry over the question of Godowsky's attitude! Besides, he is writing for the next generation — presumably a generation of Rosenthals.

And now, having passed over the salt and stubbly domain of pedagogics, what is the dominant impression gleaned from the twenty-seven Chopin studies? Is it not one of admiration, tinged with wonder at such a prodigal display of thematic and technical invention? Their variety is great, the æsthetic side is nowhere neglected for the purely mechanical, and in the most poetic of them stuff may be found for delicate fingers. Astounding, canorous, enchanting, alembicated and dramatic, the Chopin studies are exemplary essays in emotion and manner. In them is mirrored all of Chopin, the planetary as well as the secular Chopin. When most of his piano music has gone the way of all things fashioned by mortal hands, these studies will endure, will stand for the nineteenth century as Beethoven crystallized the eighteenth, Bach the seventeenth centuries in piano music. Chopin is a classic.

VII

MOODS IN MINIATURE: — THE PRELUDES.

I

THE Preludes bear the opus number 28 and are dedicated to J. C. Kessler, a composer of well-known piano studies. It is only the German edition that bears his name, the French and English being inscribed by Chopin "à son ami Pleyel." As Pleyel advanced the pianist 2,000 francs for the Preludes he had a right to say: "These are my Preludes." Niecks is authority for Chopin's remark: " I sold the Preludes to Pleyel because he liked them." This was in 1838, when Chopin's health demanded a change of climate. He wished to go to Majorca with Madame Sand and her children, and had applied for money to the piano maker and publisher, Camille Pleyel. He received but five hundred francs in advance, the balance being paid on delivery of the manuscript.

The Preludes were published in 1839, yet there is internal evidence which proves that most of them had been composed before the trip to the Balearic Islands. This will upset the very pretty legend of music making at the monastery of Valdemosa. Have we not all read with sweet credulity the eloquent pages in George Sand in which the storm is described that overtook the novelist and her son Maurice? After terrible trials, dangers and delays, they reached their home and found Chopin at the piano. Uttering a cry, he arose and stared at the pair. "Ah! I knew well that you were dead." It was the sixth prelude, the one in B minor, that he played, and dreaming, as Sand writes, that "he saw himself drowned in a lake; heavy, ice cold drops of water fell at regular intervals upon his breast; and when I called his attention to those drops of water which were actually falling upon the roof, he denied having heard them. He was even vexed at what I translated by the term, imitative harmony. He protested with all his might, and he was right, against the puerility of these imitations for the ear. His genius was full of mysterious harmonies of nature."

Yet this prelude was composed previous to the Majorcan episode. "The Preludes," says Niecks, "consist — to a great extent, at least — of pickings from the composer's portfolios, of pieces, sketches and memoranda written at various times and kept to be utilized when occasion might offer."

Gutmann, Chopin's pupil, who nursed him to the last, declared the Preludes to have been composed before he went away with Madame Sand, and to Niecks personally he maintained that he had copied all of them. Niecks does not credit him altogether, for there are letters in which several of the Preludes are mentioned as being sent to Paris, so he reaches the conclusion that "Chopin's labors at Majorca on the Preludes were confined to selecting, filing and polishing." This seems to be a sensible solution.

Robert Schumann wrote of these Preludes: "I must signalize them as most remarkable. I will confess I expected something quite different, carried out in the grand style of his studies. It is almost the contrary here; these are sketches, the beginning of studies, or, if you will, ruins, eagles' feathers, all strangely intermingled. But in every piece we find in his own hand, 'Frédéric Chopin wrote it.' One recognizes him in his pauses, in his impetuous respiration. He is the boldest, the proudest poet soul of his time. To be sure the book also contains some morbid, feverish, repellant traits; but let everyone look in it for something that will enchant him. Philistines, however, must keep away."

It was in these Preludes that Ignaz Moscheles first comprehended Chopin and his methods of execution. The German pianist had found his music harsh and dilettantish in modulation, but Chopin's originality of performance — "he glides lightly over the keys in a fairy-like way with his delicate fingers" — quite reconciled the elder man to this strange music.

To Liszt the Preludes seem modestly named, but "are not the less types of perfection in a mode created by himself, and stamped like all his other works with the high impress of his poetic genius. Written in the commencement of his career, they are characterized by a youthful vigor not to be found in some of his subsequent works, even when more elaborate, finished and richer in combinations; a vigor which is entirely lost in his latest productions, marked by an over-excited sensibility, a morbid irritability, and giving painful intimations of his own state of suffering and exhaustion."

Liszt, as usual, erred on the sentimental side. Chopin, being essentially a man of moods, like many great men, and not necessarily feminine in this respect, cannot always be pinned down to any particular period. Several of the Preludes are very morbid — I purposely use this word — as is some of his early music, while he seems quite gay just before his death.

"The Preludes follow out no technical idea, are free creations on a small basis, and exhibit the musician in all his versatility," says Louis Ehlert. "No work of Chopin's portrays his inner organization so faithfully and completely. Much is embryonic. It is as though he turned the leaves of his fancy without completely reading any page. Still, one finds in them the thundering power of the Scherzi, the half satirical, half coquettish elegance of the Mazurkas, and the southern, luxuriously fragrant breath of the Nocturnes. Often it is as though they were small falling stars dissolved into tones as they fall."

Jean Kleczynski, who is credited with understanding Chopin, himself a Pole and a pianist, thinks that "people have gone too far in seeking in the Preludes for traces of that misanthropy, of that weariness of life to which he was prey during his stay in the Island of Majorca. . . . Very few of the Preludes present this character of ennui, and that which is the most marked, the second one, must have been written, according to Count Tarnowski, a long time before he went to Majorca. . . . What is there to say concerning the other Preludes, full of good humor and gaiety — No. 18, in E flat; No. 21, in B flat; No. 23, in F, or the last, in D minor? Is it not strong and energetic, concluding, as it does, with three cannon shots?"

Willeby in his " Frédéric François Chopin " considers at length the Preludes. He agrees in the main with Niecks, that certain of these compositions were written at Valdemosa — Nos. 4, 6, 9, 13, 20 and 21 — and that " Chopin, having sketches of others with him, completed the whole there, and published them under one opus number. . . . The atmosphere of those I have named is morbid and azotic; to them there clings a faint flavor of disease, a something which is overripe in its lusciousness and febrile in its passion. This in itself inclines me to believe they were written at the time named."

This is all very well, but Chopin was faint and febrile in his music before he went to Majorca, and the plain facts adduced by Gutmann and Niecks cannot be passed over. Henry James, an old admirer of Madame Sand, admits her utter unreliability, and so we may look upon her evidence as romantic but by no means infallible. The case now stands: Chopin may have written a few of the Preludes at Majorca, filed them, finished them, but the majority of them were in his portfolio in 1837 and 1838. Op. 45, a separate Prelude in C sharp minor, was published in December, 1841. It was composed at Nohant in August of that year. It is dedicated to Mme. la Princesse Elizabeth Czernicheff, whose name, as Chopin confesses in a letter, he knows not how to spell.

II

Theodore Kullak is curt and pedagogic in his preface to the Preludes. He writes:

Chopin's genius nowhere reveals itself more charmingly than within narrowly bounded musical forms. The Preludes are, in their aphoristic brevity, masterpieces of the first rank. Some of them appear like briefly sketched mood pictures related to the nocturne style, and offer no technical hindrance even to the less advanced player. I mean Nos. 4, 6, 7, 9, 15 and 20. More difficult are Nos. 17, 25 and 11, without, however, demanding eminent virtuosity. The other Preludes belong to a species of character-étude. Despite their brevity of outline they are on a par with the great collections op. 10 and op. 25. In so far as it is practicable — special cases of individual endowments not being taken into consideration — I would propose the following order of succession : Begin with Nos. 1, 14, 10, 22, 23, 3 and 18. Very great bravura is demanded by Nos. 12, 8, 16 and 24. The difficulty of the other Preludes, Nos. 2, 5, 13, 19 and 21, lies in the delicate piano and legato technique, which, on account of the extended positions, leaps and double notes, presupposes a high degree of development.

This is eminently a common sense grouping. The first prelude, which, like the first étude, begins in C, has all the characteristics of an impromptu. We know the wonderful Bach Preludes, which grew out of a free improvisation to the collection of dance forms called a suite, and the preludes which precede his fugues. In the latter Bach sometimes exhibits all the objectivity of the study or toccata, and often wears his heart in full view. Chopin's Preludes — the only preludes to be compared to Bach's — are largely personal, subjective, and intimate. This first one is not Bach-ian, yet it could have been written by no one but a devout Bach student. The pulsating, passionate, agitated, feverish, hasty qualities of the piece are modern; so is the changeful modulation. It is a beau-

tiful composition, rising to no dramatic
heights, but questioning and full of life.
Klindworth writes in triplet groups, Kullak
in quintolets. Breitkopf & Härtel do not.
Dr. Hugo Riemann, who has edited a few of
the Preludes, phrases the first bars thus:

Desperate and exasperating to the nerves
is the second prelude in A minor. It is
an asymmetric tune. Chopin seldom wrote
ugly music, but is this not ugly, forlorn, despairing, almost grotesque, and discordant?
It indicates the deepest depression in its
sluggish, snake-like progression. Willeby
finds a resemblance to the theme of the first
nocturne. And such a theme! The tonality
is vague, beginning in E minor. Chopin's
method of thematic parallelism is here very
clear. A small figure is repeated in descending keys until hopeless gloom and depraved
melancholy are reached in the closing chords.

Chopin now is morbid, here are all his most antipathetic qualities. There is aversion to life — in this music he is a true lycanthrope. A self-induced hypnosis, a mental, an emotional atrophy are all present.

Kullak divides the accompaniment, difficult for small hands, between the two. Riemann detaches the eighth notes of the bass figures, as is his wont, for greater clearness. Like Klindworth, he accents heavily the final chords. He marks his metronome 50 to the half note. All the editions are lento with alla breve.

That the Preludes are a sheaf of moods, loosely held together by the rather vague title, is demonstrated by the third, in the key of G. The rippling, rain-like figure for the left hand is in the nature of a study. The melody is delicate in sentiment, Gallic in its esprit. A true salon piece, this prelude has no hint of artificiality. It is a precise antithesis to the mood of the previous one. Graceful and gay, the G major prelude is a fair reflex of Chopin's sensitive and naturally buoyant nature. It requires a light hand and nimble fingers. The melodic idea requires no special comment. Kullak phrases it differently from Riemann and Klindworth. The latter is the preferable. Klindworth gives 72 to the half note as his metronomic marking, Riemann only 60 — which is too slow — while Klindworth contents himself by marking a simple Vivace. Regarding the fingering one may say that all tastes are pleased in these three editions. Klindworth's is the easiest. Riemann breaks up the phrase in the bass figure, but I cannot see the gain on the musical side.

Niecks truthfully calls the fourth prelude in E minor " a little poem, the exquisitely sweet, languid pensiveness of which defies description. The composer seems to be absorbed in the narrow sphere of his ego, from which the wide, noisy world is for the time shut out." Willeby finds this prelude to be " one of the most beautiful of these spontaneous sketches ; for they are no more than sketches. The melody seems literally to wail, and reaches its greatest pitch of intensity at the stretto." For Karasowski it is a " real gem, and alone would immortalize the name of Chopin as a poet." It must have been this number that impelled Rubinstein to assert that the Preludes were the pearls of his works. In the Klindworth edition, fifth bar from the last, the editor has filled in the harmonies to the first six notes of the left hand, added thirds, which is not reprehensible, although uncalled for. Kullak makes some new dynamic markings and several enharmonic changes. He also gives as metronome 69 to the quarter. This tiny prelude contains wonderful music. The grave reiteration of the theme may have suggested to Peter Cornelius his song " Ein Ton." Chopin expands a melodic unit, and one singularly pathetic. The whole is like some canvas by Rembrandt, Rembrandt who first dramatized the shadow in which a single motif is powerfully handled; some sombre effect of echoing light in the profound of a Dutch interior. For background Chopin has substituted his soul; no one in art, except Bach or Rembrandt, could paint as Chopin did in this composition. Its despair has the antique flavor, and there is a breadth, nobility and proud submission quite free from the tortured, whimpering complaint of the second prelude. The picture is small, but the subject looms large in meanings.

The fifth prelude in D is Chopin at his happiest. Its arabesque pattern conveys a most charming content; and there is a dewy freshness, a joy in life, that puts to flight much of the morbid tittle-tattle about Chopin's sickly soul. The few bars of this prelude, so seldom heard in public, reveal musicianship of the highest order. The harmonic scheme is intricate; Klindworth phrases the first four bars so as to bring out the alternate B and B flat. It is Chopin spinning his finest, his most iridescent web.

The next prelude, the sixth, in B minor, is doleful, pessimistic. As George Sand says: " It precipitates the soul into frightful depression." It is the most frequently played — and oh! how meaninglessly — prelude of the set; this and the one in D flat. Classical is its repression of feeling, its pure contour. The echo effect is skilfully managed, monotony being artfully avoided. Klindworth rightfully slurs the duple group of eighths; Kullak tries for the same effect by different means. The duality of the voices should be clearly expressed. The tempo, marked in both editions, lento assai, is fast. To be precise, Klindworth gives 66 to the quarter.

The plaintive little mazurka of two lines, the seventh prelude, is a mere silhouette of the national dance. Yet in its measures is compressed all Mazovia. Klindworth makes a variant in the fourth bar from the last, a G sharp instead of an F sharp. It is a more piquant climax, perhaps not admissible to the Chopin purist.

In the F sharp minor prelude No. 7, Chopin gives us a taste of his grand manner. For
Niecks the piece is jerky and agitated, and
doubtless suggests a mental condition bordering on anxiety; but if frenzy there is, it is
kept well in check by the exemplary taste of
the composer. The sadness is rather elegiac,
remote, and less poignant than in the E minor
prelude. Harmonic heights are reached on
the second page — surely Wagner knew these
bars when he wrote " Tristan and Isolde " —
while the ingenuity of the figure and avoid-
ance of a rhythmical monotone are evidences
of Chopin's feeling for the decorative. It is
a masterly prelude. Klindworth accents the
first of the bass triplets, and makes an unnecessary enharmonic change at the sixth
and seventh lines.

There is a measure of grave content in the
ninth prelude in E. It is rather gnomic, and
contains hints of both Brahms and Beethoven. It has an ethical quality, but that
may be because of its churchly rhythm and
color.

The C sharp minor prelude, No. 10, must
be the " eagle wings " of Schumann's critique.
There is a flash of steel gray, deepening
into black, and then the vision vanishes as
though some huge bird aloft had plunged

down through blazing sunlight, leaving a color-echo in the void as it passed to its quarry. Or, to be less figurative, this prelude is a study in arpeggio, with double notes interspersed, and is too short to make more than a vivid impression.

No. 11 in B is all too brief. It is vivacious, dolce indeed, and most cleverly constructed. Klindworth gives a more binding character to the first double notes. Another gleam of the Chopin sunshine.

Storm clouds gather in the G sharp minor, the twelfth prelude, so unwittingly imitated by Grieg in his Menuetto of the same key, and in its driving presto we feel the passionate clench of Chopin's hand. It is convulsed with woe, but the intellectual grip, the self-command are never lost in these two pages of perfect writing. The figure is suggestive, and there is a well defined technical problem, as well as a psychical character. Disputed territory is here: the editors do not agree about the twelfth and eleventh bars from the last. According to Breitkopf & Härtel the bass octaves are E both times. Mikuli gives G sharp the first time instead of E; Klindworth, G sharp the second time; Riemann, E, and also Kullak. The G sharp seems more various.

CHOPIN

In the thirteenth prelude, F sharp major, there is lovely atmosphere, pure and peaceful. The composer has found mental rest. Exquisitely poised are his pinions for flight, and in the piu lento he wheels significantly and majestically about in the blue. The return to earth is the signal for some strange modulatory tactics. It is an impressive close. Then, almost without pause, the blood begins to boil in this fragile man's veins. His pulse beat increases, and with stifled rage he rushes into the battle. It is the fourteenth prelude in the sinister key of E flat minor, and its heavy, sullen-arched triplets recalls for Niecks the last movement of the B flat minor Sonata; but there is less interrogation in the prelude, less sophistication, and the heat of conflict over it all. There is not a break in the clouds until the beginning of the fifteenth, the familiar prelude in D flat.

This must be George Sand's: " Some of them create such vivid impressions that the shades of dead monks seem to rise and pass before the hearer in solemn and gloomy funereal pomp." The work needs no programme. Its serene beginning, lugubrious interlude, with the dominant pedal never ceasing, a basso ostinato, gives color to

Kleczynski's contention that the prelude in B minor is a mere sketch of the idea fully elaborated in No. 15. "The foundation of the picture is the drops of rain falling at regular intervals" — the echo principle again — "which by their continual patter bring the mind to a state of sadness; a melody full of tears is heard through the rush of the rain; then passing to the key of C sharp minor, it rises from the depths of the bass to a prodigious crescendo, indicative of the terror which nature in its deathly aspect excites in the heart of man. Here again the form does not allow the ideas to become too sombre; notwithstanding the melancholy which seizes you, a feeling of tranquil grandeur revives you." To Niecks, the C sharp minor portion affects one as in an oppressive dream: "The re-entrance of the opening D flat, which dispels the dreadful nightmare, comes upon one with the smiling freshness of dear, familiar nature."

The prelude has a nocturnal character. It has become slightly banal from frequent repetition, likewise the C sharp minor study in opus 25. But of its beauty, balance and exceeding chastity there can be no doubt. The architecture is at once Greek and Gothic.

The sixteenth prelude in the relative key of B flat minor is the boldest of the set. Its scale figures, seldom employed by Chopin, boil and glitter, the thematic thread of the idea never being quite submerged. Fascinating, full of perilous acclivities and sudden treacherous descents, this most brilliant of preludes is Chopin in riotous spirits. He plays with the keyboard: it is an avalanche, anon a cascade, then a swift stream, which finally, after mounting to the skies, descends to an abyss. Full of imaginative lift, caprice and stormy dynamics, this prelude is the darling of the virtuoso. Its pregnant introduction is like a madly jutting rock from which the eagle spirit of the composer precipitates itself.

In the twenty-third bar there is curious editorial discrepancy. Klindworth uses an A natural in the first of the four groups of sixteenths, Kullak a B natural; Riemann follows Kullak. Nor is this all. Kullak in the second group, right hand, has an E flat, Klindworth a D natural. Which is correct? Klindworth's texture is more closely chromatic and it sounds better, the chromatic parallelism being more carefully preserved. Yet I fancy that Kullak has tradition on his side.

THE PRELUDES

The seventeenth prelude Niecks finds Mendelssohn-ian. I do not. It is suave, sweet, well developed, yet Chopin to the core, and its harmonic life surprisingly rich and novel. The mood is one of tranquillity. The soul loses itself in early autumnal revery while there is yet splendor on earth and in the skies. Full of tonal contrasts, this highly finished composition is grateful to the touch. The eleven booming A flats on the last page are historical. Klindworth uses a B flat instead of a G at the beginning of the melody. It is logical, but is it Chopin?

The fiery recitatives of No. 18 in F minor are a glimpse of Chopin, muscular and not hectic. In these editions you will find three different groupings of the cadenzas. It is Riemann's opportunity for pedagogic editing, and he does not miss it. In the first long breathed group of twenty-two sixteenth notes he phrases as shown on the following page.

It may be noticed that Riemann even changes the arrangement of the bars. This prelude is dramatic almost to an operatic degree. Sonorous, rather grandiloquent, it is a study in declamation, the declamation of the slow movement in the F minor concerto. Schumann may have had the first phrase in his mind when he wrote his Auf-

schwung. This page of Chopin's, the torso
of a larger idea, is nobly rhetorical.

What piano music is the nineteenth prelude in E flat! Its widely dispersed harmonies, its murmuring grace and June-like
beauty, are they not Chopin, the Chopin
we best love? He is ever the necromancer,
ever invoking phantoms, but with its whirring
melody and furtive caprice this particular
shape is an alluring one. And difficult it
is to interpret with all its plangent lyric
freedom.

No. 20 in C minor contains in its thirteen bars the sorrows of a nation. It is without doubt a sketch for a funeral march, and of it George Sand must have been thinking when she wrote that one prelude of Chopin contained more music than all the trumpetings of Meyerbeer.

Of exceeding loveliness is the B flat major prelude, No. 21. It is superior in content and execution to most of the nocturnes. In feeling it belongs to that form. The melody is enchanting. The accompaniment figure shows inventive genius. Klindworth employs a short appoggiatura, Kullak the long, in the second bar. Judge of what is true editorial sciolism when I tell you that Riemann — who evidently believes in a rigid melodic structure — has inserted an E flat at the end of bar four, thus maiming the tender, elusive quality of Chopin's theme. This is cruelly pedantic. The prelude arrests one in ecstasy; the fixed period of contemplation of the saint or the hypnotized sets in, and the awakening is almost painful. Chopin, adopting the relative minor key as a pendant to the picture in B flat, thrills the nerves by a bold dissonance in the next prelude, No. 22. Again, concise paragraphs filled with the smoke of revolt and conflict.

CHOPIN

The impetuosity of this largely moulded piece in G minor, its daring harmonics,—read the seventeenth and eighteenth bars, —and dramatic note make it an admirable companion to the Prelude in F minor. Technically it serves as an octave study for the left hand.

In the concluding bar, but one, Chopin has in the F major Prelude attempted a most audacious feat in harmony. An E flat in the bass of the third group of sixteenths leaves the whole composition floating enigmatically in thin air. It deliciously colors the close, leaving a sense of suspense, of anticipation which is not tonally realized, for the succeeding number is in a widely divorced key. But it must have pressed hard the philistines. And this prelude, the twenty-third, is fashioned out of the most volatile stuff. Aerial, imponderable, and like a sun-shot spider web oscillating in the breeze of summer, its hues change at every puff. It is in extended harmonics and must be delivered with spirituality. The horny hand of the toilsome pianist would shatter the delicate, swinging fantasy of the poet. Kullak points out a variant in the fourteenth bar, G instead of B natural being used by Riemann. Klindworth prefers the latter.

We have reached the last prelude of op.

THE PRELUDES

28. In D minor, it is sonorously tragic, troubled by fevers and visions, and capricious, irregular and massive in design. It may be placed among Chopin's greater works: the two Études in C minor, the A minor, and the F sharp minor Prelude. The bass requires an unusual span, and the suggestion by Kullak, that the thumb of the right hand may eke out the weakness of the left is only for the timid and the small of fist. But I do not counsel following his two variants in the fifth and twenty-third bars. Chopin's text is more telling. Like the vast reverberation of monstrous waves on the implacable coast of a remote world is this prelude. Despite its fatalistic ring, its note of despair is not dispiriting. Its issues are larger, more impersonal, more elemental than the other preludes. It is a veritable Appassionata, but its theatre is cosmic and no longer behind the closed doors of the cabinet of Chopin's soul. The Seelenschrei of Stanislaw Przybyszewski is here, explosions of wrath and revolt; not Chopin suffers, but his countrymen. Kleczynski speaks of the three tones at the close. They are the final clangor of oppressed, almost overthrown, reason. After the subject reappears in C minor there is a shift to D flat, and for a

CHOPIN

moment a point of repose is gained, but this elusive rest is brief. The theme reappears in the tonic and in octaves, and the tension becomes too great; the accumulated passion discharges and dissolves in a fierce gust of double chromatic thirds and octaves. Powerful, repellant, this prelude is almost infernal in its pride and scorn. But in it I discern no vestige of uncontrolled hysteria. It is well-nigh as strong, rank and human as Beethoven. The various editorial phraseology is not of much moment. Riemann uses thirty-second notes for the cadenzas, Kullak eighths and Klindworth sixteenths.

Niecks writes of the Prelude in C sharp minor, op. 45, that it " deserves its name better than almost any one of the twenty-four; still I would rather call it improvisata. It seems unpremeditated, a heedless outpouring, when sitting at the piano in a lonely, dreary hour, perhaps in the twilight. The quaver figure rises aspiringly, and the sustained parts swell out proudly. The piquant cadenza forestalls in the progression of diminished chords favorite effects of some of our more modern composers. The modulation from C sharp minor to D major and back again — after the cadenza — is very striking and equally beautiful."

236

THE PRELUDES

Elsewhere I have called attention to the Brahmsian coloring of this prelude. Its mood is fugitive and hard to hold after capture. Recondite it is and not music for the multitude.

Niecks does not think Chopin created a new type in the Preludes. "They are too unlike each other in form and character." Yet notwithstanding the fleeting, evanescent moods of the Preludes, there is designedly a certain unity of feeling and contrasted tonalities, all being grouped in approved Bach-ian manner. This may be demonstrated by playing them through at a sitting, which Arthur Friedheim, the Russian virtuoso, did in a concert with excellent effect. As if wishing to exhibit his genius in perspective, Chopin carved these cameos with exceeding fineness, exceeding care. In a few of them the idea overbalances the form, but the greater number are exquisite examples of a just proportion of manner and matter, a true blending of voice and vision. Even in the more microscopic ones the tracery, echoing like the spirals in strange seashells, is marvellously measured. Much in miniature are these sculptured Preludes of the Polish poet.

VIII

IMPROMPTUS AND VALSES

To write of the four Impromptus in their own key of unrestrained feeling and pondered intention would not be as easy as recapturing the first "careless rapture" of the lark. With all the freedom of an improvisation the Chopin impromptu has a well defined form. There is structural impulse, although the patterns are free and original. The mood-color is not much varied in three, the first, third and fourth, but in the second there is a ballade-like quality that hints of the tragic. The A flat Impromptu, op. 29, is, if one is pinned down to the title, the happiest named of the set. Its seething, prankish, nimble, bubbling quality is indicated from the start; the D natural in the treble against the C and E flat — the dominant — in the bass is a most original effect, and the flowing triplets of the first part of this piece give a ductile, gracious, high-bred character to it. The chromatic involutions are many and interesting. When the F minor part is reached the ear experiences the relief of a strongly contrasted rhythm. The simple duple measure, so naturally ornamented, is nobly, broadly melodious. After the return of the first dimpling theme there is a short coda, a chiaroscura, and then with a few chords the composition goes to rest. A bird flew that way! Rubato should be employed, for, as Kleczynski says, " Here everything totters from foundation to summit, and everything is, nevertheless, so beautiful and so clear." But only an artist with velvety fingers should play this sounding arabesque.

There is more limpidezza, more pure grace of line in the first Impromptu than in the second in F sharp, op. 36. Here symmetry is abandoned, as Kullak remarks, but the compensation of intenser emotional issues is offered. There is something sphinx-like in the pose of this work. Its nocturnal beginning with the carillon-like bass — a bass that ever recalls to me the faint, buried tones of Hauptmann's " Sunken Bell," the sweetly grave close of the section, the faint hoof-beats of an approaching cavalcade, with the swelling thunders of its passage, surely suggests a narrative, a programme. After the D major episode there are two bars of anonymous modulation — these bars creak on their hinges — and the first subject reappears in F, then climbs to F sharp, thence merges into a glittering melodic organ-point, exciting, brilliant, the whole subsiding into an echo of earlier harmonies. The final octaves are marked fortissimo which always seems brutal. Yet its logic lies in the scheme of the composer. Perhaps he wished to arouse us harshly from his dreamland, as was his habit while improvising for friends — a glissando would send them home shivering after an evening of delicious reverie.

Niecks finds this Impromptu lacking the pith of the first. To me it is of more moment than the other three. It is irregular and wavering in outline, the moods are wandering and capricious, yet who dares deny its power, its beauty? In its use of accessory figures it does not reveal so much ingenuity, but just because the "figure in the carpet" is not so varied in pattern, its passion is all the deeper. It is another Ballade, sadder, more meditative of the tender grace of vanished days.

The third Impromptu in G flat, op. 51, is not often played. It may be too difficult for the vandal with an average technique, but it is neither so fresh in feeling nor so spontaneous in utterance as its companions.

There is a touch of the faded, blasé, and it is hardly healthy in sentiment. Here are some ophidian curves in triplets, as in the first Impromptu, but with interludes of double notes, in coloring tropical and rich to morbidity. The E flat minor trio is a fine bit of melodic writing. The absence of simplicity is counterbalanced by greater freedom of modulation and complexity of pattern. The impromptu flavor is not missing, and there is allied to delicacy of design a strangeness of sentiment — that strangeness which Edgar Poe declared should be a constituent element of all great art.

The Fantaisie-Impromptu in C sharp minor, op. 66, was published by Fontana in 1855, and is one of the few posthumous works of Chopin worthy of consideration. It was composed about 1834. A true Impromptu, but the title of Fantaisie given by Fontana is superfluous. The piece presents difficulties, chiefly rhythmical. Its involuted first phrases suggest the Bellini-an fioriture so dear to Chopin, but the D flat part is without nobility. Here is the same kind of saccharine melody that makes mawkish the trio in the "Marche Funèbre." There seems no danger that this Fantaisie-Impromptu will suffer from neglect, for it is the joy of the

piano student, who turns its presto into a
slow, blurred mess of badly related rhythms,
and its slower movement into a long drawn
sentimental agony; but in the hands of a
master the C sharp minor Impromptu is
charming, though not of great depth.

The first Impromptu, dedicated to Mlle.
la Comtesse de Lobau, was published December, 1837; the second, May, 1840; the
third, dedicated to Madame la Comtesse
Esterhazy, February, 1843. Not one of these
four Impromptus is as naïve as Schubert's;
they are more sophisticated and do not smell
of nature and her simplicities.

Of the Chopin Valses it has been said that
they are dances of the soul and not of the
body. Their animated rhythms, insouciant
airs and brilliant, coquettish atmosphere, the
true atmosphere of the ballroom, seem to
smile at Ehlert's poetic exaggeration. The
valses are the most objective of the Chopin
works, and in few of them is there more than
a hint of the sullen, Sargasson seas of the
nocturnes and scherzi. Nietzsche's la Gaya
Scienza — the Gay Science — is beautifully
set forth in the fifteen Chopin valses. They
are less intimate, in the psychic sense, but
exquisite exemplars of social intimacy and
aristocratic abandon. As Schumann declared,

the dancers of these valses should be at least countesses. There is a high-bred reserve despite their intoxication, and never a hint of the brawling peasants of Beethoven, Grieg, Brahms, Tschaikowsky, and the rest. But little of Vienna is in Chopin. Around the measures of this most popular of dances he has thrown mystery, allurement, and in them secret whisperings and the unconscious sigh. It is going too far not to dance to some of this music, for it is putting Chopin away from the world he at times loved. Certain of the valses may be danced: the first, second, fifth, sixth, and a few others. The dancing would be of necessity more picturesque and less conventional than required by the average valse, and there must be fluctuations of tempo, sudden surprises and abrupt languors. The mazurkas and polonaises are danced to-day in Poland, why not the valses? Chopin's genius reveals itself in these dance forms, and their presentation should be not solely a psychic one. Kullak, stern old pedagogue, divides these dances into two groups, the first dedicated to " Terpsichore," the second a frame for moods. Chopin admitted that he was unable to play valses in the Viennese fashion, yet he has contrived to rival Strauss in his own genre. Some of these valses are trivial, artificial, most of them are bred of candlelight and the swish of silken attire, and a few are poetically morbid and stray across the border into the rhythms of the mazurka. All of them have been edited to death, reduced to the commonplace by vulgar methods of performance, but are altogether sprightly, delightful specimens of the composer's careless, vagrant and happy moods.

Kullak utters words of warning to the "unquiet" sex regarding the habitual neglect of the bass. It should mean something in valse tempo, but it usually does not. Nor need it be brutally banged; the fundamental tone must be cared for, the subsidiary harmonies lightly indicated. The rubato in the valses need not obtrude itself as in the mazurkas.

Opus 18, in E flat, was published in June, 1834, and dedicated to Mlle. Laura Harsford. It is a true ballroom picture, spirited and infectious in rhythms. Schumann wrote rhapsodically of it. The D flat section has a tang of the later Chopin. There is bustle, even chatter, in this valse, which in form and content is inferior to op. 34, No. 1, A flat. The three valses of this set were published December, 1838. There are many editorial differences in the A flat Valse, owing to the

careless way it was copied and pirated. Klindworth and Kullak are the safest for dynamic
markings. This valse may be danced as far
as its dithyrhambic coda. Notice in this coda
as in many other places the debt Schumann
owes Chopin for a certain passage in the Pré-
ambule of his " Carneval."

The next Valse in A minor has a tinge
of Sarmatian melancholy, indeed, it is one
of Chopin's most desponding moods. The
episode in C rings of the mazurka, and the
A major section is of exceeding loveliness;
Its coda is characteristic. This valse is a favorite, and who need wonder? The F major
Valse, the last of this series, is a whirling,
wild dance of atoms. It has the perpetuum
mobile quality, and older masters would have
prolonged its giddy arabesques into pages of
senseless spinning. It is quite long enough
as it is. The second theme is better, but
the appoggiatures are flippant. It buzzes to
the finish. Of it is related that Chopin's cat
sprang upon his keyboard and in its feline
flight gave him the idea of the first measures.
I suppose as there is a dog valse, there had
to be one for the cat.

But as Rossini would have said, "Ça sent de
Scarlatti !"

The A minor Valse was, of the three, Chopin's favorite. When Stephen Heller told him this too was his beloved valse, Chopin was greatly pleased, inviting the Hungarian composer, Niecks relates, to luncheon at the Café Riche.

Not improvised in the ballroom as the preceding, yet a marvellous epitome is the A flat Valse, op. 42, published July, 1840. It is the best rounded specimen of Chopin's experimenting with the form. The prolonged trill on E flat, summoning us to the ballroom, the suggestive intermingling of rhythms, duple and triple, the coquetry, hesitation, passionate avowal and the superb coda, with its echoes of evening — have not these episodes a charm beyond compare? Only Schumann in certain pages of his "Carneval" seizes the secret of young life and love, but his is not so finished, so glowing a tableau.

Regarding certain phrasing of this valse Moriz Rosenthal wrote to the London "Musical Standard":

In Music there is Liberty and Fraternity, but seldom Equality, and in music Social Democracy has no voice. Notes have a right to the Aftertone (Nachton), and this right depends upon their rôle in the key. The Vorhalt (accented passing note) will always have an accent. On this point Riemann

246

must without question be considered right. Likewise the feeling player will mark those notes that introduce the transition to another key. We will consider now our example and set down my accents:

In the first bar we have the tonic chord of its major key as bass, and are thus not forced to any accent. In the second bar we have the dominant harmony in the bass, and in the treble, C, which falls upon the down beat as Vorhalt to the next tone (B flat), so it must be accented. Also in the fourth bar the B flat is Vorhalt to the B flat, and likewise requires an accent. In bars 6, 7 and 8 the notes, A flat, B flat and C, are without doubt the characteristic ones of the passage, and the E flat has in each case only a secondary significance.

That a genius like Chopin did not indicate everything accurately is quite explainable. He flew where we merely limp after. Moreover, these accents must be felt rather than executed, with softest touch, and as tenderly as possible.

The D flat Valse—"le valse du petit chien" —is of George Sand's own prompting. One evening at her home in the Square d'Orléans, she was amused by her little pet dog, chasing its tail. She begged Chopin, her little pet pianist, to set the tail to music. He did so, and behold the world is richer for this piece. I do not dispute the story. It seems well grounded, but then it is so ineffably silly! The three valses of this op. 64 were published September, 1847, and are respectively dedicated to the Comtesse Delphine Potocka, the Baronne Nathaniel de Rothschild and the Baronne Bronicka.

I shall not presume to speak of the execution of the D flat Valse; like the rich, it is always with us. It is usually taken at a meaningless, rapid gait. I have heard it played by a genuine Chopin pupil, M. Georges Mathias, and he did not take it prestissimo. He ran up the D flat scale, ending with a sforzato at the top, and gave a variety of nuance to the composition. The cantabile is nearly always delivered with sloppiness of sentiment. This valse has been served up in a highly indigestible condition for concert purposes by Tausig, Joseffy—whose arrangement was the first to be heard here—Theodore Ritter, Rosenthal and Isidor Philipp.

The C sharp minor Valse is the most poetic of all. The first theme has never been excelled by Chopin for a species of veiled melancholy. It is a fascinating, lyrical sorrow, and what Kullak calls the psychologic motivation of the first theme in the curving figure of the second does not relax the spell. A space of clearer skies, warmer, more consoling winds are in the D flat interlude, but the spirit of unrest, ennui returns. The elegiac imprint is unmistakable in this soul dance. The A flat Valse which follows is charming. It is for superior souls who dance with intellectual joy, with the joy that comes of making exquisite patterns and curves. Out of the salon and from its brilliantly lighted spaces the dancers do not wander, do not dance into the darkness and churchyard, as Ehlert imagines of certain other valses.

The two valses in op. 69, three valses, op. 70, and the two remaining valses in E minor and E major, need not detain us. They are posthumous. The first of op. 69 in F minor was composed in 1836; the B minor in 1829; G flat, op. 70, in 1835; F minor in 1843, and D flat major, 1830. The E major and E minor were composed in 1829. Fontana gave these compositions to the world. The F minor Valse, op. 69, No. 1, has a charm of its own. Kullak prints the Fontana and Klindworth variants. This valse is suavely melancholy, but not so melancholy as the B minor of the same opus. It recalls in color the B minor mazurka. Very gay and sprightly is the G flat Valse, op. 70, No. 1. The next in F minor has no special physiognomy, while the third in D flat contains, as Niecks points out, germs of the op. 42 and the op. 34 Valses. It recalls to me the D flat study in the supplementary series. The E minor Valse, without opus, is beloved. It is very graceful and not without sentiment. The major part is the early Chopin. The E major Valse is published in the Mikuli edition. It is commonplace, hinting of its composer only in places. Thus ends the collection of valses, not Chopin's most signal success in art, but a success that has dignified and given beauty to this conventional dance form.

IX

NIGHT AND ITS MELANCHOLY MYS-
TERIES:—THE NOCTURNES

HERE is the chronology of the nocturnes:
Op. 9, three nocturnes, January, 1833; op.
15, three nocturnes, January, 1834; op. 27,
two nocturnes, May, 1836; op. 32, two nocturnes, December, 1837; op. 37, two nocturnes, May, 1840; op. 48, two nocturnes,
November, 1841; op. 55, two nocturnes,
August, 1844; op. 62, two nocturnes, September, 1846. In addition there is a nocturne written in 1828 and published by
Fontana, with the opus number 72, No. 2, and
the lately discovered one in C sharp minor,
written when Chopin was young and published in 1895. This completes the nocturne
list, but following Niecks' system of formal
grouping I include the Berceuse and Barcarolle as full fledged specimens of nocturnes.

John Field has been described as the forerunner of Chopin. The limpid style of this
pupil and friend of Clementi, his beautiful
touch and finished execution, were certainly
admired and imitated by the Pole. Field's

nocturnes are now neglected — so curious are Time's caprices — and without warrant, for not only is Field the creator of the form, but in both his concertos and nocturnes he has written charming, sweet and sane music. He rather patronized Chopin, for whose melancholy pose he had no patience. " He has a talent of the hospital," growled Field in the intervals between his wine drinking, pipe smoking and the washing of his linen — the latter economical habit he contracted from Clementi. There is some truth in his stricture. Chopin, seldom exuberantly cheerful, is morbidly sad and complaining in many of the nocturnes. The most admired of his compositions, with the exception of the valses, they are in several instances his weakest. Yet he ennobled the form originated by Field, giving it dramatic breadth, passion and even grandeur. Set against Field's naïve and idyllic specimens, Chopin's efforts are often too bejewelled for true simplicity, too lugubrious, too tropical — Asiatic is a better word — and they have the exotic savor of the heated conservatory, and not the fresh scent of the flowers reared in the open by the less poetic Irishman. And, then, Chopin is so desperately sentimental in some of these compositions. They are not altogether to the taste of this generation; they seem to be suffering from anæmia. However, there are a few noble nocturnes; and methods of performance may have much to answer for the sentimentalizing of some others. More vigor, a quickening of the time-pulse, and a less languishing touch will rescue them from lush sentiment. Chopin loved the night and its soft mysteries as much as did Robert Louis Stevenson, and his nocturnes are true night pieces, some with agitated, remorseful countenance, others seen in profile only, while many are whisperings at dusk. Most of them are called feminine, a term psychologically false. The poetic side of men of genius is feminine, and in Chopin the feminine note was over emphasized — at times it was almost hysterical — particularly in these nocturnes.

The Scotch have a proverb: "She wove her shroud, and wore it in her lifetime." In the nocturnes the shroud is not far away. Chopin wove his to the day of his death, and he wore it sometimes but not always, as many think.

One of the most elegiac of his nocturnes is the first in B flat minor. It is one of three, op. 9, dedicated to Mme. Camille Pleyel. Of far more significance than its two companions, it is, for some reason, neglected. While I am far from agreeing with those who hold that in the early Chopin all his genius was completely revealed, yet this nocturne is as striking as the last, for it is at once sensuous and dramatic, melancholy and lovely. Emphatically a mood, it is best heard on a gray day of the soul, when the times are out of joint; its silken tones will bring a triste content as they pour out upon one's hearing. The second section in octaves is of exceeding charm. As a melody it has all the lurking voluptuousness and mystic crooning of its composer. There is flux and reflux throughout, passion peeping out in the coda.

The E flat nocturne is graceful, shallow of content, but if it is played with purity of touch and freedom from sentimentality it is not nearly so banal as it usually seems. It is Field-like, therefore play it as did Rubinstein, in a Field-like fashion.

Hadow calls attention to the " remote and recondite modulations" in the twelfth bar, the chromatic double notes. For him they only are one real modulation, "the rest of the passage is an iridescent play of color, an effect of superficies, not an effect of substance." It was the E flat nocturne

that unloosed Rellstab's critical wrath in the
"Iris." Of it he wrote: "Where Field smiles,
Chopin makes a grinning grimace; where
Field sighs, Chopin groans; where Field
shrugs his shoulders, Chopin twists his whole
body; where Field puts some seasoning
into the food, Chopin empties a handful of
cayenne pepper. In short, if one holds
Field's charming romances before a distort-
ing, concave mirror, so that every delicate
impression becomes a coarse one, one gets
Chopin's work. We implore Mr. Chopin to
return to nature."

Rellstab might have added that while
Field was often commonplace, Chopin never
was. Rather is to be preferred the sound
judgment of J. W. Davison, the English
critic and husband of the pianist, Arabella
Goddard. Of the early works he wrote:

Commonplace is instinctively avoided in all the
works of Chopin — a stale cadence or a trite progression — a hum-drum subject or a worn-out passage — a vulgar twist of the melody or a hackneyed
sequence — a meagre harmony or an unskilful
counterpoint — may in vain be looked for throughout the entire range of his compositions, the prevailing characteristics of which are a feeling as
uncommon as beautiful; a treatment as original as
felicitous; a melody and a harmony as new, fresh.

vigorous and striking as they are utterly unexpected and out of the original track. In taking up one of the works of Chopin you are entering, as it were, a fairyland untrodden by human footsteps — a path hitherto unfrequented but by the great composer himself.

Gracious, even coquettish, is the first part of the B major Nocturne of this opus. Well knit, the passionate intermezzo has the true dramatic Chopin ring. It should be taken alla breve. The ending is quite effective.

I do not care much for the F major Nocturne, op. 15, No. 1. The opus is dedicated to Ferdinand Hiller. Ehlert speaks of " the ornament in triplets with which he brushes the theme as with the gentle wings of a butterfly," and then discusses the artistic value of the ornament which may be so profitably studied in the Chopin music. " From its nature, the ornament can only beautify the beautiful." Music like Chopin's, " with its predominating elegance, could not forego ornament. But he surely did not purchase it of a jeweller; he designed it himself, with a delicate hand. He was the first to surround a note with diamond facets and to weave the rushing floods of his emotions with the silver beams of the moonlight

In his nocturnes there is a glimmering as of distant stars. From these dreamy, heavenly gems he has borrowed many a line. The Chopin nocturne is a dramatized ornament. And why may not Art speak for once in such symbols? In the much admired F sharp major Nocturne the principal theme makes its appearance so richly decorated that one cannot avoid imagining that his fancy confined itself to the Arabesque form for the expression of its poetical sentiments. Even the middle part borders upon what I should call the tragic style of ornament. The ground thought is hidden behind a dense veil, but a veil, too, can be an ornament."

In another place Ehlert thinks that the F sharp major Nocturne seems inseparable from champagne and truffles. It is certainly more elegant and dramatic than the one in F major, which precedes it. That, with the exception of the middle part in F minor, is weak, although rather pretty and confiding. The F sharp Nocturne is popular. The "doppio movemento" is extremely striking and the entire piece is saturated with young life, love and feelings of good will to men. Read Kleczynski. The third nocturne of the three is in G minor, and contains some fine, picturesque writing. Kullak does not find in it aught of the fantastic. The languid, earth-weary voice of the opening and the churchly refrain of the chorale, is not this fantastic contrast! This nocturne contains in solution all that Chopin developed later in a nocturne of the same key. But I think the first stronger — its lines are simpler, more primitive, its coloring less complicated, yet quite as rich and gloomy. Of it Chopin said: "After Hamlet," but changed his mind. "Let them guess for themselves," was his sensible conclusion. Kullak's programme has a conventional ring. It is the lament for the beloved one, the lost Lenore, with the consolation of religion thrown in. The "bell-tones" of the plain chant bring to my mind little that consoles, although the piece ends in the major mode. It is like Poe's "Ulalume." A complete and tiny tone poem, Rubinstein made much of it. In the fourth bar and for three bars there is a held note F, and I heard the Russian virtuoso, by some miraculous means, keep this tone prolonged. The tempo is abnormally slow, and the tone is not in a position where the sustaining pedal can sensibly help it. Yet under Rubinstein's fingers it swelled and diminished, and went singing into D, as if the instrument were an organ. I suspected the inaudible changing of fingers on the note or a sustaining pedal. It was wonderfully done.

The next nocturne, op. 27, No. 1, brings us before a masterpiece. With the possible exception of the C minor Nocturne, this one in the sombre key of C sharp minor is the great essay in the form. Kleczynski finds it " a description of a calm night at Venice, where, after a scene of murder, the sea closes over a corpse and continues to serve as a mirror to the moonlight." This is melodramatic. Willeby analyzes it at length with the scholarly fervor of an English organist. He finds the accompaniment to be " mostly on a double pedal," and remarks that " higher art than this one could not have if simplicity of means be a factor of high art." The wide-meshed figure of the left hand supports a morbid, persistent melody that grates on the nerves. From the piu mosso the agitation increases, and here let me call to your notice the Beethoven-ish quality of these bars, which continue until the change of signature. There is a surprising climax followed by sunshine and favor in the D flat part, then after mounting dissonances a bold succession of octaves returns to the feverish plaint of the opening. Kullak speaks of a resemblance to Meyerbeer's song, Le Moine. The composition reaches exalted states. Its psychological tension is so great at times as to border on a pathological condition. There is unhealthy power in this nocturne, which is seldom interpreted with sinister subtlety. Henry T. Finck rightfully thinks it "embodies a greater variety of emotion and more genuine dramatic spirit on four pages than many operas on four hundred."

The companion picture in D flat, op. 27, No. 2, has, as Karasowski writes, "a profusion of delicate fioriture." It really contains but one subject, and is a song of the sweet summer of two souls, for there is obvious meaning in the duality of voices. Often heard in the concert room, this nocturne gives us a surfeit of sixths and thirds of elaborate ornamentation and monotone of mood. Yet it is a lovely, imploring melody, and harmonically most interesting. A curious marking, and usually overlooked by pianists, is the crescendo and con forza of the cadenza. This is obviously erroneous. The theme, which occurs three times, should first be piano, then pianissimo, and lastly forte. This opus is dedicated to the Comtesse d'Appony.

THE NOCTURNES

The best part of the next nocturne, — B major, op. 32, No. 1, dedicated to Madame de Billing — is the coda. It is in the minor and is like the drum-beat of tragedy. The entire ending, a stormy recitative, is in stern contrast to the dreamy beginning. Kullak in the first bar of the last line uses a G; Fontana, F sharp, and Klindworth the same as Kullak. The nocturne that follows in A flat is a reversion to the Field type, the opening recalling that master's B flat Nocturne. The F minor section of Chopin's broadens out to dramatic reaches, but as an entirety this opus is a little tiresome. Nor do I admire inordinately the Nocturne in G minor, op. 37, No. 1. It has a complaining tone, and the choral is not noteworthy. This particular part, so Chopin's pupil Gutmann declared, is taken too slowly, the composer having forgotten to mark the increased tempo. But the Nocturne in G, op. 37, No. 2, is charming. Painted with Chopin's most ethereal brush, without the cloying splendors of the one in D flat, the double sixths, fourths and thirds are magically euphonious. The second subject, I agree with Karasowski, is the most beautiful melody Chopin ever wrote. It is in true barcarolle vein; and most subtle are the shifting harmonic hues. Pianists usually

take the first part too fast, the second too
slowly, transforming this poetic composition
into an étude. As Schumann wrote of this
opus:

"The two nocturnes differ from his earlier
ones chiefly through greater simplicity of
decoration and more quiet grace. We know
Chopin's fondness in general for spangles,
gold trinkets and pearls. He has already
changed and grown older; decoration he still
loves, but it is of a more judicious kind, behind which the nobility of the poetry shim-
mers through with all the more loveliness:
indeed, taste, the finest, must be granted him."

Both numbers of this opus are without
dedication. They are the offspring of the
trip to Majorca.

Niecks, writing of the G major Nocturne,
adjures us "not to tarry too long in the
treacherous atmosphere of this Capua — it
bewitches and unmans." Kleczynski calls
the one in G minor "homesickness," while
the celebrated Nocturne in C minor "is the
tale of a still greater grief told in an agitated
recitando; celestial harps" — ah! I hear the
squeak of the old romantic machinery —
"come to bring one ray of hope, which is
powerless in its endeavor to calm the
wounded soul, which . . . sends forth to

heaven a cry of deepest anguish." It doubtless has its despairing movement, this same
Nocturne in C minor, op. 48, No. 1, but
Karasowski is nearer right when he calls it
"broad and most imposing with its powerful
intermediate movement, a thorough departure from the nocturne style." Willeby finds
it "sickly and labored," and even Niecks
does not think it should occupy a foremost
place among its companions. The ineluc-
table fact remains that this is the noblest
nocturne of them all. Biggest in conception
it seems a miniature music drama. It requires the grand manner to read it adequately,
and the doppio movemento is exciting to
a dramatic degree. I fully agree with Kullak
that too strict adherence to the marking of
this section produces the effect of an "inartistic precipitation" which robs the movement
of clarity. Kleczynski calls the work The
Contrition of a Sinner and devotes several
pages to its elucidation. De Lenz chats
most entertainingly with Tausig about it. Indeed, an imposing march of splendor is the
second subject in C. A fitting pendant is
this work to the C sharp minor Nocturne.
Both have the heroic quality, both are free
from mawkishness and are of the greater
Chopin, the Chopin of the mode masculine.

Niecks makes a valuable suggestion: "In playing these nocturnes — op. 48 — there occurred to me a remark of Schumann's, when he reviewed some nocturnes by Count Wièlhorski. He said that the quick middle movements which Chopin frequently introduced into his nocturnes are often weaker than his first conceptions; meaning the first portions of his nocturnes. Now, although the middle part in the present instances are, on the contrary, slower movements, yet the judgment holds good; at least with respect to the first nocturne, the middle part of which has nothing to recommend it but a full, sonorous instrumentation, if I may use this word in speaking of one instrument. The middle part of the second — D flat, molto piu lento — however, is much finer; in it we meet again, as we did in some other nocturnes, with soothing, simple chord progressions. When Gutmann studied the C sharp minor Nocturne with Chopin, the master told him that the middle section — the molto piu lento in D flat major — should be played as a recitative. 'A tyrant commands' — the first two chords — he said, 'and the other asks for mercy.'"

Of course Niecks means the F sharp minor, not the C sharp minor Nocturne, op. 48,

No. 2, dedicated, with the C minor, to Mlle L. Duperré.

Opus 55, two nocturnes in F minor and E flat major, need not detain us long. The first is familiar. Kleczynski devotes a page or more to its execution. He seeks to vary the return of the chief subject with nuances as would an artistic singer the couplets of a classic song. There are "cries of despair" in it, but at last a "feeling of hope." Kullak writes of the last measures: "Thank God — the goal is reached!" It is the relief of a major key after prolonged wanderings in the minor. It is a nice nocturne, neat in its sorrow, yet not epoch-making. The one following has "the impression of an improvisation." It has also the merit of being seldom heard. These two nocturnes are dedicated to Mlle. J. W. Stirling.

Opus 62 brings us to a pair in B major and E major inscribed to Madame de Konneritz. The first, the Tuberose Nocturne, is faint with a sick, rich odor. The climbing trellis of notes, that so unexpectedly leads to the tonic, is charming and the chief tune has charm, a fruity charm. It is highly ornate, its harmonies dense, the entire surface overrun with wild ornamentation and a profusion of trills. The piece — the third of its sort in

the key of B — is not easy.   Mertke gives
the following explication of the famous chain
trills:

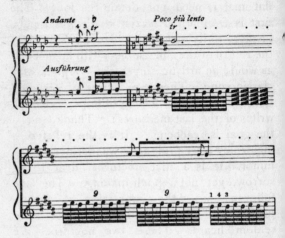

Although this nocturne is luxuriant in
style, it deserves warmer praise than is
accorded it.   Irregular as its outline is, its
troubled lyrism is appealing, is melting, and
the A flat portion, with its hesitating, timid
accents, has great power of attraction.   The
E major Nocturne has a bardic ring.   Its
song is almost declamatory and not at all
sentimental — unless so distorted — as Niecks
would have us imagine.   The intermediate
portion is wavering and passionate, like the

middle of the F sharp major Nocturne. It
shows no decrease in creative vigor or lyrical
fancy. The Klindworth version differs from
the original, as an examination of the following examples will show, the upper being
Chopin's:

The posthumous nocturne in E minor,
composed in 1827, is weak and uninteresting.
Moreover, it contains some very un-Chopin-
like modulations. The recently discovered
nocturne in C sharp minor is hardly a trea-
sure trove. It is vague and reminiscent.

CHOPIN

The following note was issued by its London publishers, Ascherberg & Co.:

The first question, suggested by the announcement of a new posthumous composition of Chopin's, will be "What proof is there of its authenticity?" To musicians and amateurs who cannot recognize the beautiful Nocturne in C sharp minor as indeed the work of Chopin, it may in the first place be pointed out that the original manuscript (of which a facsimile is given on the title-page) is in Chopin's well-known handwriting, and, secondly, that the composition, which is strikingly characteristic, was at once accepted as the work of Chopin by the distinguished composer and pianist Balakireff, who played it for the first time in public at the Chopin Commemoration Concert, held in the autumn of 1894 at Zelazowa Wola, and afterward at Warsaw. This nocturne was addressed by Chopin to his sister Louise, at Warsaw, in a letter from Paris, and was written soon after the production of the two lovely piano concertos, when Chopin was still a very young man. It contains a quotation from his most admired Concerto in F minor, and a brief reference to the charming song known as the Maiden's Wish, two of his sister's favorite melodies. The manuscript of the nocturne was supposed to have been destroyed in the sacking of the Zamojski Palace, at Warsaw, toward the end of the insurrection of 1863, but it was discovered quite recently among papers of various kinds in the possession of a Polish gentleman, a great collector, whose son offered Mr. Polinski the privilege of selecting from such papers. His choice was three manuscripts of Chopin's, one of them being this nocturne. A letter from Mr. Polinski on the subject of this nocturne is in the possession of Miss Janotha.

Is this the nocturne of which Tausig spoke to his pupil Joseffy as belonging to the master's "best period," or did he refer to the one in E minor?

The Berceuse, op. 57, published June, 1845, and dedicated to Mlle. Elise Gavard, is the very sophistication of the art of musical ornamentation. It is built on a tonic and dominant bass — the triad of the tonic and the chord of the dominant seventh. A rocking theme is set over this basso ostinato and the most enchanting effects are produced. The rhythm never alters in the bass, and against this background, the monotone of a dark, gray sky, the composer arranges an astonishing variety of fireworks, some florid, some subdued, but all delicate in tracery and design. Modulations from pigeon egg blue to Nile green, most misty and subtle modulations, dissolve before one's eyes, and for a moment the sky is peppered with tiny stars in doubles, each independently tinted. Within a small segment of the chromatic bow Chopin has imprisoned new, strangely dissonant colors. It is a miracle; and after the drawn-out chord of the dominant seventh and the rain of silvery fire ceases one realizes that the whole piece is a delicious illusion, but an ululation in the key of D flat, the apotheosis of pyrotechnical colorature.

Niecks quotes Alexandre Dumas fils, who calls the Berceuse "muted music," but introduces a Turkish bath comparison, which crushes the sentiment. Mertke shows the original and Klindworth's reading of a certain part of the Berceuse, adding a footnote to the examples:

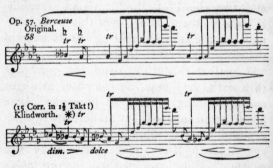

* Das tr (flat) der Originale (Scholtz tr natural-flat) zeigt, dass Ch. den Triller mit Ganzton und nach Mikuli den Trilleranfang mit Hauptton wollte.

The Barcarolle, op. 60, published September, 1846, is another highly elaborated work. Niecks must be quoted here: "One day Tausig, the great piano virtuoso, promised W. de Lenz to play him Chopin's Barcarolle, adding, ' That is a performance which must not be undertaken before more than two persons. I shall play you my own self. I love the piece, but take it rarely.' Lenz got the music, but it did not please him — it seemed to him a long movement in the nocturne style, a Babel of figuration on a lightly laid foundation. But he found that he had made a mistake, and, after hearing it played by Tausig, confessed that the virtuoso had infused into the ' nine pages of enervating music, of one and the same long-breathed rhythm, so much interest, so much motion, so much action,' that he regretted the long piece was not longer."

Tausig's conception of the barcarolle was this: "There are two persons concerned in the affair; it is a love scene in a discrète gondola; let us say this mise-en-scène is the symbol of a lover's meeting generally."

"This is expressed in thirds and sixths; the dualism of two notes — persons — is maintained throughout; all is two-voiced, two-souled. In this modulation in C sharp major — superscribed dolce sfogato — there are kiss and embrace! This is evident! When, after three bars of introduction, the theme, "lightly rocking in the bass solo, enters in the fourth, this theme is nevertheless made use of throughout the whole fabric only as an accompaniment, and *on* this the cantilena in two parts is laid; we have thus a continuous, tender dialogue."

The Barcarolle is a nocturne painted on a large canvas, with larger brushes. It has Italian color in spots — Schumann said that, melodically, Chopin sometimes "leans over Germany into Italy" — and is a masterly one in sentiment, pulsating with amorousness. To me it sounds like a lament for the splendors, now vanished, of Venice the Queen. In bars 8, 9, and 10, counting backward, Louis Ehlert finds obscurities in the middle voices. It is dedicated to the Baronne de Stockhausen.

The nocturnes — including the Berceuse and Barcarolle — should seldom be played in public and not the public of a large hall. Something of Chopin's delicate, tender warmth and spiritual voice is lost in larger spaces. In a small auditorium, and from the fingers of a sympathetic pianist, the nocturnes should be heard, that their intimate,

night side may be revealed. Many are like
the music en sourdine of Paul Verlaine' in
his "Chanson D'Automne" or "Le Piano
que Baise une Main Frêle." They are essentially for the twilight, for solitary enclosures,
where their still, mysterious tones — "silent
thunder in the leaves" as Yeats sings —
become eloquent and disclose the poetry and
pain of their creator.

X

THE BALLADES:—FAËRY DRAMAS

W. H. HADOW has said some pertinent things about Chopin in "Studies in Modern Music." Yet we cannot accept unconditionally his statement that "in structure Chopin is a child playing with a few simple types, and almost helpless as soon as he advances beyond them; in phraseology he is a master whose felicitous perfection of style is one of the abiding treasures of the art."

Chopin then, according to Hadow, is no "builder of the lofty rhyme," but the poet of the single line, the maker of the phrase exquisite. This is hardly comprehensive. With the more complex, classical types of the musical organism Chopin had little sympathy, but he contrived nevertheless to write two movements of a piano sonata that are excellent — the first half of the B flat minor Sonata. The idealized dance forms he preferred; the Polonaise, Mazurka and Valse were already there for him to handle, but the Ballade was not. Here he is not imitator, but creator. Not loosely-jointed, but compact structures glowing with genius and presenting definite unity of form and expression, are the ballades — commonly written in six-eight and six-four time. "None of Chopin's compositions surpasses in masterliness of form and beauty and poetry of contents his ballades. In them he attains the acme of his power as an artist," remarks Niecks.

I am ever reminded of Andrew Lang's lines, "the thunder and surge of the Odyssey," when listening to the G minor Ballade, op. 23. It is the Odyssey of Chopin's soul. That 'cello-like largo with its noiseless suspension stays us for a moment in the courtyard of Chopin's House Beautiful. Then, told in his most dreamy tones, the legend begins. As in some fabulous tales of the Genii this Ballade discloses surprising and delicious things. There is the tall lily in the fountain that nods to the sun. It drips in cadenced monotone and its song is repeated on the lips of the slender-hipped girl with the eyes of midnight — and so might I weave for you a story of what I see in the Ballade and you would be aghast or puzzled. With such a composition any programme could be sworn to, even the silly story of the Englishman who haunted Chopin, beseeching him to teach him this Ballade. That Chopin had a programme, a definite one, there can be no doubt; but he has, wise artist, left us no clue beyond Mickiewicz's, the Polish bard Lithuanian poems. In Leipzig, Karasowski relates, that when Schumann met Chopin, the pianist confessed having "been incited to the creation of the ballades by the poetry" of his fellow countryman. The true narrative tone is in this symmetrically constructed Ballade, the most spirited, most daring work of Chopin, according to Schumann. Louis Ehlert says of the four Ballades: "Each one differs entirely from the others, and they have but one thing in common — their romantic working out and the nobility of their motives. Chopin relates in them, not like one who communicates something really experienced; it is as though he told what never took place, but what has sprung up in his inmost soul, the anticipation of something longed for. They may contain a strong element of national woe, much outwardly expressed and inwardly burning rage over the sufferings of his native land; yet they do not carry with a positive reality like that which in a Beethoven Sonata will often call words to our lips."

THE BALLADES

Which means that Chopin was not such a realist as Beethoven? Ehlert is one of the few sympathetic German Chopin commentators, yet he did not always indicate the salient outlines of his art. Only the Slav may hope to understand Chopin thoroughly. But these Ballades are more truly touched by the universal than any other of his works. They belong as much to the world as to Poland.

The G minor Ballade after "Konrad Wallenrod," is a logical, well knit and largely planned composition. The closest parallelism may be detected in its composition of themes. Its second theme in E flat is lovely in line, color and sentiment. The return of the first theme in A minor and the quick answer in E of the second are evidences of Chopin's feeling for organic unity. Development, as in strict cyclic forms, there is not a little. After the cadenza, built on a figure of wavering tonality, a valse-like theme emerges and enjoys a capricious, butterfly existence. It is fascinating. Passage work of an etherealized character leads to the second subject, now augmented and treated with a broad brush. The first questioning theme is heard again, and with a perpendicular roar the presto comes upon us.

For two pages the dynamic energy displayed
by the composer is almost appalling. A
whirlwind I have called it elsewhere. It
is a storm of the emotions, muscular in
its virility. I remember de Pachmann — a
close interpreter of certain sides of Chopin
— playing this coda piano, pianissimo and
prestissimo. The effect was strangely irritating to the nerves, and reminded me of
a tornado seen from the wrong end of an
opera glass. According to his own lights
the Russian virtuoso was right: his strength
was not equal to the task, and so, imitating
Chopin, he topsy-turvied the shading. It
recalled Moscheles' description of Chopin's
playing: "His piano is so softly breathed
forth that he does not require any strong
forte to produce the wished for contrast."

This G minor Ballade was published in
June, 1836, and is dedicated to Baron Stockhausen. The last bar of the introduction
has caused some controversy. Gutmann,
Mikuli and other pupils declare for the E
flat; Klindworth and Kullak use it. Xaver
Scharwenka has seen fit to edit Klindworth,
and gives a D natural in the Augener edition. That he is wrong internal testimony
abundantly proves. Even Willeby, who personally prefers the D natural, thinks Chopin

intended the E flat, and quotes a similar effect twenty-eight bars later. He might have added that the entire composition contains examples — look at the first bar of the valse episode in the bass. As Niecks thinks, "This dissonant E flat may be said to be the emotional keynote of the whole poem. It is a questioning thought that, like a sudden pain, shoots through mind and body."

There is other and more confirmatory evidence. Ferdinand Von Inten, a New York pianist, saw the original Chopin manuscript at Stuttgart. It was the property of Professor Lebert (Levy), since deceased, and in it, without any question, stands the much discussed E flat. This testimony is final. The D natural robs the bar of all meaning. It is insipid, colorless.

Kullak gives 60 to the half note at the moderato. On the third page, third bar, he uses F natural in the treble. So does Klindworth, although F sharp may be found in some editions. On the last page, second bar, first line, Kullak writes the passage beginning with E flat in eighth notes, Klindworth in sixteenths. The close is very striking, full of the splendors of glancing scales and shrill octave progressions. "It would inspire a poet to write words to it,' said Robert Schumann.

"Perhaps the most touching of all that Chopin has written is the tale of the F major Ballade. I have witnessed children lay aside their games to listen thereto. It appears like some fairy tale that has become music. The four-voiced part has such a clearness withal, it seems as if warm spring breezes were waving the lithe leaves of the palm tree. How soft and sweet a breath steals over the senses and the heart!"

And how difficult it seems to be to write of Chopin except in terms of impassioned prose! Louis Ehlert, a romantic in feeling and a classicist in theory, is the writer of the foregoing. The second Ballade, although dedicated to Robert Schumann, did not excite his warmest praise. "A less artistic work than the first," he wrote, "but equally fantastic and intellectual. Its impassioned episodes seem to have been afterward inserted. I recollect very well that when Chopin played this Ballade for me it finished in F major; it now closes in A minor." Willeby gives its key as F minor. It is really in the keys of F major — A minor. Chopin's psychology was seldom at fault. A major ending would have

crushed this extraordinary tone-poem, writ
ten, Chopin admits, under the direct inspira
tion of Adam Mickiewicz's "Le Lac de
Willis." Willeby accepts Schumann's dictum of the inferiority of this Ballade to its
predecessor. Niecks does not. Niecks is
quite justified in asking how "two such
wholly dissimilar things can be compared
and weighed in this fashion."

In truth they cannot. "The second Ballade possesses beauties in no way inferior to
those of the first," he continues. "What
can be finer than the simple strains of the
opening section! They sound as if they had
been drawn from the people's store-house of
song. The entrance of the presto surprises,
and seems out of keeping with what precedes; but what we hear after the return of
tempo primo — the development of those
simple strains, or rather the cogitations on
them — justifies the presence of the presto.
The second appearance of the latter leads to
an urging, restless coda in A minor, which
closes in the same key and pianissimo with
a few bars of the simple, serene, now veiled
first strain."

Rubinstein bore great love for this second
Ballade. This is what it meant for him:
"Is it possible that the interpreter does not

feel the necessity of representing to his audience — a field flower caught by a gust of wind, a caressing of the flower by the wind; the resistance of the flower, the stormy struggle of the wind; the entreaty of the flower, which at last lies there broken; and paraphrased — the field flower a rustic maiden, the wind a knight."

I can find "no lack of affinity" between the andantino and presto. The surprise is a dramatic one, withal rudely vigorous. Chopin's robust treatment of the first theme results in a strong piece of craftmanship. The episodical nature of this Ballade is the fruit of the esoteric moods of its composer. It follows a hidden story, and has the quality — as the second Impromptu in F sharp — of great, unpremeditated art. It shocks one by its abrupt but by no means fantastic transitions. The key color is changeful, and the fluctuating themes are well contrasted. It was written at Majorca while the composer was only too noticeably disturbed in body and soul.

Presto con fuoco Chopin marks the second section. Kullak gives 84 to the quarter, and for the opening 66 to the quarter. He also wisely marks crescendos in the bass at the first thematic development. He prefers the E — as does Klindworth — nine bars before the return of the presto. At the eighth bar, after this return, Kullak adheres to the E instead of F at the beginning of the bar, treble clef. Klindworth indicates both. Nor does Kullak follow Mikuli in using a D in the coda. He prefers a D sharp, instead of a natural. I wish the second Ballade were played oftener in public. It is quite neglected for the third in A flat, which, as Ehlert says, has the voice of the people.

This Ballade, the "Undine" of Mickiewicz, published November, 1841, and dedicated to Mlle. P. de Noailles, is too well known to analyze. It is the schoolgirls' delight, who familiarly toy with its demon, seeing only favor and prettiness in its elegant measures. In it " the refined, gifted Pole, who is accustomed to move in the most distinguished circles of the French capital, is pre-eminently to be recognized." Thus Schumann. Forsooth, it is aristocratic, gay, graceful, piquant, and also something more. Even in its playful moments there is delicate irony, a spiritual sporting with graver and more passionate emotions. Those broken octaves which usher in each time the second theme, with its fascinating,

infectious, rhythmical lilt, what an ironi
cally joyous fillip they give the imagination!

"A coquettish grace — if we accept by
this expression that half unconscious toying
with the power that charms and fires, that
follows up confession with reluctance —
seems the very essence of Chopin's being."

"It becomes a difficult task to transcribe
the easy transitions, full of an irresistible
charm, with which he portrays Love's game.
Who will not recall the memorable passage
in the A flat Ballade, where the right hand
alone takes up the dotted eighths after the
sustained chord of the sixth of A flat?
Could a lover's confusion be more deliciously
enhanced by silence and hesitation?" Ehlert
above evidently sees a ballroom picture of
brilliancy, with the regulation tender avowal.
The episodes of this Ballade are so attenuated of any grosser elements that none but
psychical meanings should be read into
them.

The disputed passage is on the fifth page
of the Kullak edition, after the trills. A
measure is missing in Kullak, who, like
Klindworth, gives it in a footnote. To my
mind this repetition adds emphasis, although
it is a formal blur. And what an irresistible moment it is, this delightful terri-

tory, before the darker mood of the C sharp minor part is reached! Niecks becomes enthusiastic over the insinuation and persuasion of this composition: "the composer showing himself in a fundamentally caressing mood." The ease with which the entire work is floated proves that Chopin in mental health was not daunted by larger forms. There is moonlight in this music, and some sunlight, too. The prevailing moods are coquetry and sweet contentment.

Contrapuntal skill is shown in the working out section. Chopin always wears his learning lightly; it does not oppress us. The inverted dominant pedal in the C sharp minor episode reveals, with the massive coda, a great master. Kullak suggests some variants. He uses the transient shake in the third bar, instead of the appoggiatura which Klindworth prefers. Klindworth attacks the trill on the second page with the upper tone — A flat. Kullak and Mertke, in the Steingräber edition, play the passage in this manner:

Here is Klindworth:

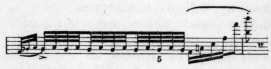

Of the fourth and glorious Ballade in F minor dedicated to Baronne C. de Rothschild I could write a volume. It is Chopin in his most reflective, yet lyric mood. Lyrism is the keynote of the work, a passionate lyrism, with a note of self-absorption, suppressed feeling — truly Slavic, this shyness! — and a concentration that is remarkable even for Chopin. The narrative tone is missing after the first page, a rather moody and melancholic pondering usurping its place. It is the mood of a man who examines with morbid, curious insistence the malady that is devouring his soul. This Ballade is the companion of the Fantaisie-Polonaise, but as a Ballade "fully worthy of its sisters," to quote Niecks. It was published December, 1843. The theme in F minor has the elusive charm of a slow, mournful valse, that returns twice, bejewelled, yet never overladen. Here is the very apotheosis of the ornament; the figuration sets off the idea in dazzling relief. There are episodes, transitional passage work, distinguished by novelty and the finest art. At no place is there display for display's sake. The cadenza in A is a pause for breath, rather a sigh, before the rigorously logical imitations which presage the re-entrance of the theme. How wonderfully the introduction comes in for its share of thoughtful treatment. What a harmonist! And consider the D flat scale runs in the left hand; how suave, how satisfying is this page. I select for especial admiration this modulatory passage:

And what could be more evocative of dramatic suspense than the sixteen bars before the mad, terrifying coda! How the solemn splendors of the half notes weave an atmosphere of mystic tragedy! This soul-suspension recalls Maeterlinck. Here is the episode:

A story of de Lenz that lends itself to quotation is about this piece:

Tausig impressed me deeply in his interpretation of Chopin's Ballade in F minor. It has three requirements: The comprehension of the programme as a whole, — for Chopin writes according to a programme, to the situations in life best known to, and understood by himself; and in an adequate manner; the conquest of the stupendous difficulties in complicated figures, winding harmonies and formidable passages.

Tausig fulfilled these requirements, presenting an embodiment of the signification and the feeling of the work. The Ballade — andante con moto, six-eighths — begins in the major key of the domi-

nant; the seventh measure comes to a stand
before a fermata on C major. The easy han-
dling of these seven measures Tausig interpreted
thus: 'The piece has not yet begun;' in his
firmer, nobly expressive exposition of the principal
theme, free from sentimentality — to which one
might easily yield — the grand style found due
scope. An essential requirement in an instru-
mental virtuoso is that he should understand how
to breathe, and how to allow his hearers to take
breath — giving them opportunity to arrive at a
better understanding. By this I mean a well
chosen incision — the cesura, and a lingering —
" letting in air," Tausig cleverly called it — which
in no way impairs rhythm and time, but rather
brings them into stronger relief; a *lingering* which
our signs of notation cannot adequately express,
because it is made up of atomic time values. Rub
the bloom from a peach or from a butterfly —
what remains will belong to the kitchen, to natural
history ! It is not otherwise with Chopin; the
bloom consisted in Tausig's treatment of the
Ballade.

He came to the first passage — the motive
among blossoms and leaves — a figurated recur-
rence to the principal theme is in the inner parts
— its polyphonic variant. A little thread con-
nects this with the chorale-like introduction of
the second theme. The theme is strongly and
abruptly modulated, perhaps a little too much so.

Tausig tied the little thread to a doppio movimento in two-four time, but thereby resulted sextolets, which threw the chorale into still bolder relief. Then followed a passage a tempo, in which the principal theme played hide and seek. How clear it all became as Tausig played it! Of technical difficulties he knew literally nothing; the intricate and evasive parts were as easy as the easiest — I might say easier!

I admired the short trills in the left hand, which were trilled out quite independently, as if by a second player; the gliding ease of the cadence marked dolcissimo. It swung itself into the higher register, where it came to a stop before A major, just as the introduction stopped before C major. Then, after the theme has once more presented itself in a modified form — variant — it comes under the pestle of an extremely figurate coda, which demands the study of an artist, the strength of a robust man — the most vigorous pianistic health, in a word! Tausig overcame this threatening group of terrific difficulties, whose appearance in the piece is well explained by the programme, without the slightest effect. The coda, in modulated harp tones, came to a stop before a fermata which corresponded to those before mentioned, in order to cast anchor in the haven of the dominant, finishing with a witches' dance of triplets, doubled in thirds. This piece winds up with extreme bravura.

THE BALLADES

The "lingering" mentioned by de Lenz
is tempo rubato, so fatally misunderstood by
most Chopin players. De Lenz in a note
quotes Meyerbeer as saying — Meyerbeer,
who quarrelled with Chopin about the
rhythm of a mazurka — " Can one reduce
women to notation? They would breed
mischief, were they emancipated from the
measure."

There is passion, refined and swelling, in
the curves of this most eloquent composition. It is Chopin at the supreme summit
of his art, an art alembicated, personal and
intoxicating. I know of nothing in music
like the F minor Ballade. Bach in the Chromatic Fantasia — be not deceived by its
classical contours, it is music hot from the
soul — Beethoven in the first movement of
the C sharp minor Sonata, the arioso of the
Sonata op. 110, and possibly Schumann in
the opening of his C major Fantaisie, are as
intimate, as personal as the F minor Ballade,
which is as subtly distinctive as the hands
and smile of Lisa Gioconda. Its inaccessible position preserves it from rude and
irreverent treatment. Its witchery is irresistible.

XI

CLASSICAL CURRENTS

GUY DE MAUPASSANT put before us a widely diverse number of novels in a famous essay attached to the definitive edition of his masterpiece, " Pierre et Jean," and puzzlingly demanded the real form of the novel. If " Don Quixote " is one, how can " Madame Bovary " be another? If " Les Misérables " is included in the list, what are we to say to Huysmans' " La Bas "?

Just such a question I should like to propound, substituting sonata for novel. If Scarlatti wrote sonatas, what is the Appassionata? If the A flat Weber is one, can the F minor Brahms be called a sonata? Is the Haydn form orthodox and the Schumann heterodox? These be enigmas to make weary the formalists. Come, let us confess, and in the open air: there is a great amount of hypocrisy and cant in this matter. We can, as can any conservatory student, give the recipe for turning out a smug specimen of the form, but when we study the

great examples, it is just the subtle eluding
of hard and fast rules that distinguishes the
efforts of the masters from the machine
work of apprentices and academic monsters.
Because it is no servile copy of the Mozart
Sonata, the F sharp minor of Brahms is a
piece of original art.   Beethoven at first
trod in the well blazed path of Haydn, but
study his second period, and it sounds the
big Beethoven note.   There is no final court
of appeal in the matter of musical form, and
there is none in the matter of literary style.
The history of the sonata is the history of
musical evolution.   Every great composer,
Schubert included, added to the form, filed
here, chipped away there, introduced law-
lessness where reigned prim order — witness
the Schumann F sharp minor Sonata — and
then came Chopin.

The Chopin sonata has caused almost as
much warfare as the Wagner music drama.
It is all the more ludicrous, for Chopin
never wrote but one piano sonata that has a
classical complexion: in C minor, op. 4, and
it was composed as early as 1828.   Not
published until July, 1851, it demonstrates
without a possibility of doubt that the composer had no sympathy with the form.   He
tried so hard and failed so dismally that it is

293

a relief when the second and third sonatas are reached, for in them there are only traces of formal beauty and organic unity. But then there is much Chopin, while little of his precious essence is to be tasted in the first sonata.

Chopin wrote of the C minor Sonata: "As a pupil I dedicated it to Elsner," and — oh, the irony of criticism! — it was praised by the critics because not so revolutionary as the Variations, op. 2. This, too, despite the larghetto in five-four time. The first movement is wheezing and all but lifeless. One asks in astonishment what Chopin is doing in this gallery. And it is technically difficult. The menuetto is excellent, its trio being a faint approach to Beethoven in color. The unaccustomed rhythm of the slow movement is irritating. Our young Chopin does not move about as freely as Benjamin Godard in the scherzo of his violin and piano sonata in the same bizarre rhythm. Niecks sees naught but barren waste in the finale. I disagree with him. There is the breath of a stirring spirit, an imitative attempt that is more diverting than the other movements. Above all there is movement, and the close is vigorous, though banal. The sonata is the dullest music penned by

Chopin, but as a whole it hangs together as a sonata better than its two successors. So much for an attempt at strict devotion to scholastic form.

From this schoolroom we are transported in op. 35 to the theatre of larger life and passion. The B flat minor Sonata was published May, 1840. Two movements are masterpieces; the funeral march that forms the third movement is one of the Pole's most popular compositions, while the finale has no parallel in piano music. Schumann says that Chopin here "bound together four of his maddest children," and he is not astray. He thinks the march does not belong to the work. It certainly was written before its companion movements. As much as Hadow admires the first two movements, he groans at the last pair, though they are admirable when considered separately.

These four movements have no common life. Chopin says he intended the strange finale as a gossiping commentary on the march. "The left hand unisono with the right hand are gossiping after the march." Perhaps the last two movements do hold together, but what have they in common with the first two? Tonality proves nothing. Notwithstanding the grandeur and beauty of the grave, the power and passion of the scherzo, this Sonata in B flat minor is not more a sonata than it is a sequence of ballades and scherzi. And again we are at the de Maupassant crux. The work never could be spared; it is Chopin mounted for action and in the thick of the fight. The doppio movimento is pulse-stirring — a strong, curt and characteristic theme for treatment. Here is power, and in the expanding prologue flashes more than a hint of the tragic. The D flat Melody is soothing, charged with magnetism, and urged to a splendid fever of climax. The working out section is too short and dissonantal, but there is development, perhaps more technical than logical — I mean by this more pianistic than intellectually musical — and we mount with the composer until the B flat version of the second subject is reached, for the first subject, strange to say, does not return. From that on to the firm chords of the close there is no misstep, no faltering or obscurity. Noble pages have been read, and the scherzo is approached with eagerness. Again there is no disappointment. On numerous occasions I have testified my regard for this movement in warm and uncritical terms. It is simply unapproachable, and has no equal for lucidity, brevity and polish among the works of Chopin, except the Scherzo in C sharp minor; but there is less irony, more muscularity, and more native sweetness in this E flat minor Scherzo. I like the way Kullak marks the first B flat octave. It is a pregnant beginning. The second bar I have never heard from any pianist save Rubinstein given with the proper crescendo. No one else seems to get it explosive enough within the walls of one bar. It is a true Rossin-ian crescendo. And in what a wild country we are landed when the F sharp minor is crashed out! Stormy chromatic double notes, chords of the sixth, rush on with incredible fury, and the scherzo ends on the very apex of passion. A Trio in G flat is the song of songs, its swaying rhythms and phrase-echoings investing a melody at once sensuous and chaste. The second part and the return to the scherzo are proofs of the composer's sense of balance and knowledge of the mysteries of anticipation. The closest parallelisms are noticeable, the technique so admirable that the scherzo floats in mid-air — Flaubert's ideal of a miraculous style.

And then follows that deadly Marche Funèbre! Ernest Newman, in his remark-

able "Study of Wagner," speaks of the fun
damental difference between the two orders
of imagination, as exemplified by Beethoven
and Chopin on the one side, Wagner on the
other. This regarding the funeral marches
of the three. Newman finds Wagner's the
more concrete imagination; the "inward
picture" of Beethoven, and Chopin "much
vaguer and more diffused." Yet Chopin is
seldom so realistic; here are the bell-like
basses, the morbid coloring. Schumann
found "it contained much that is repulsive,"
and Liszt raves rhapsodically over it; for
Karasowski it was the "pain and grief of an
entire nation," while Ehlert thinks "it owes
its renown to the wonderful effect of two
triads, which in their combination possess
a highly tragical element. The middle
movement is not at all characteristic. Why
could it not at least have worn second
mourning? After so much black crêpe
drapery one should not at least at once display white lingerie!" This is cruel.

The D flat Trio is a logical relief after
the booming and glooming of the opening.
That it is "a rapturous gaze into the beatific
regions of a beyond," as Niecks writes, I
am not prepared to say. We do know, however, that the march, when isolated, has a

much more profound effect than in its normal sequence. The presto is too wonderful for words. Rubinstein, or was it originally Tausig who named it "Night winds sweeping over the churchyard graves"? Its agitated, whirring, unharmonized triplets are strangely disquieting, and can never be mistaken for mere étude passage work. The movement is too sombre, its curves too full of half-suppressed meanings, its rush and sub-human growling too expressive of something that defies definition. Schumann compares it to a "sphinx with a mocking smile." To Henri Barbadette "C'est Lazare grattant de ses ongles la pierre de son tombeau," or, like Mendelssohn, one may abhor it, yet it cannot be ignored. It has Asiatic coloring, and to me seems like the wavering outlines of light-tipped hills seen sharply en silhouette, behind which rises and falls a faint, infernal glow. This art paints as many differing pictures as there are imaginations for its sonorous background; not alone the universal solvent, as Henry James thinks, it bridges the vast, silent gulfs between human souls with its humming eloquence. This sonata is not dedicated.

The third Sonata in B minor, op. 58, has more of that undefinable "organic unity," yet, withal, it is not so powerful, so pathos-breeding or so compact of thematic interest as its forerunner. The first page, to the chromatic chords of the sixth, promises much. There is a clear statement, a sound theme for developing purposes, the crisp march of chord progressions, and then — the edifice goes up in smoke. After wreathings and curlings of passage work, and on the rim of despair, we witness the exquisite budding of the melody in D. It is an aubade, a nocturne of the morn — if the contradictory phrase be allowed. There is morning freshness in its hue and scent, and, when it bursts, a parterre of roses. The close of the section is inimitable. All the more sorrow at what follows: wild disorder and the luxuriance called tropical. When B major is compassed we sigh, for it augurs us a return of delight. The ending is not that of a sonata, but a love lyric. For Chopin is not the cool breadth and marmoreal majesty of blank verse. He sonnets to perfection, but the epical air does not fill his nostrils.

Vivacious, charming, light as a harebell in the soft breeze is the Scherzo in E flat. It has a clear ring of the scherzo and harks back to Weber in its impersonal, amiable hurry. The largo is tranquilly beautiful, rich in its reverie, lovely in its tune. The trio is reserved and hypnotic. The last movement, with its brilliancy and force, is a favorite, but it lacks weight, and the entire sonata is, as Niecks writes, "affiliated, but not cognate." It was published June, 1845, and is dedicated to Comtesse E. de Perthuis.

So these sonatas of Chopin are not sonatas at all, but, throwing titles to the dogs, would we forego the sensations that two of them evoke? There is still another, the Sonata in G minor, op. 65, for piano and 'cello. It is dedicated to Chopin's friend, August Franchomme, the violoncellist. Now, while I by no means share Finck's exalted impression of this work, yet I fancy the critics have dealt too harshly with it. Robbed of its title of sonata — though sedulously aping this form — it contains much pretty music. And it is grateful for the 'cello. There is not an abundant literature for this kingly instrument, in conjunction with the piano, so why flaunt Chopin's contribution? I will admit that he walks stiffly, encased in his borrowed garb, but there is the andante, short as it is, an effective scherzo and a carefully made allegro and finale. Tonal monotony is the worst charge to be brought against this work.

The trio, also in **G** minor, op. 8, is more alluring. It was published March, 1833, and dedicated to Prince Anton Radziwill. Chopin later, in speaking of it to a pupil, admitted that he saw things he would like to change. He regretted not making it for viola, instead of violin, 'cello and piano.

It was worked over a long time, the first movement being ready in 1833. When it appeared it won philistine praise, for its form more nearly approximates the sonata than any of his efforts in the cyclical order, excepting op. 4. In it the piano receives better treatment than the other instruments; there are many virtuoso passages, but again key changes are not frequent or disparate enough to avoid a monotone. Chopin's imagination refuses to become excited when working in the open spaces of the sonata form. Like creatures that remain drab of hue in unsympathetic or dangerous environment, his music is transformed to a bewildering bouquet of color when he breathes native air. Compare the wildly modulating Chopin of the ballades to the tame-pacing Chopin of the sonatas, trio and concertos!

The trio opens with fire, the scherzo is
fanciful, and the adagio charming, while the
finale is cheerful to loveliness. It might
figure occasionally on the programmes of
our chamber music concerts, despite its
youthful puerility.

There remain the two concertos, which I
do not intend discussing fully. Not Chopin
at his very best, the E minor and F minor
concertos are frequently heard because of the
chances afforded the solo player. I have
written elsewhere at length of the Klindworth, Tausig and Burmeister versions of
the two concertos. As time passes I see no
reason for amending my views on this
troublous subject. Edgar S. Kelly holds a
potent brief for the original orchestration,
contending that it suits the character of the
piano part. Rosenthal puts this belief into
practice by playing the older version of the
E minor with the first long tutti curtailed.
But he is not consistent, for he uses the
Tausig octaves at the close of the rondo.
While I admire the Tausig orchestration,
these particlar octaves are hideously caca-
phonic. The original triplet unisons are so
much more graceful and musical.

The chronology of the concertos has given
rise to controversy. The trouble arose from

the F minor Concerto, it being numbered op. 21, although composed before the one in E minor. The former was published April, 1836; the latter September, 1833. The slow movement of the F minor Concerto was composed by Chopin during his passion for Constantia Gladowska. She was "the ideal" he mentions in his letters, the adagio of this concerto. This larghetto in A flat is a trifle too ornamental for my taste, mellifluous and serene as it is. The recitative is finely outlined. I think I like best the romanze of the E minor Concerto. It is less flowery. The C sharp minor part is imperious in its beauty, while the murmuring mystery of the close mounts to the imagination. The rondo is frolicksome, tricky, genial and genuine piano music. It is true the first movement is too long, too much in one set of keys, and the working-out section too much in the nature of a technical study. The first movement of the F minor far transcends it in breadth, passion and musical feeling, but it is short and there is no coda. Richard Burmeister has supplied the latter deficiency in a capitally made cadenza, which Paderewski plays. It is a complete summing up of the movement. The mazurka-like finale is very graceful and full of pure, sweet melody. This concerto is altogether more human than the E minor.

Both derive from Hummel and Field. The passage work is superior in design to that of the earlier masters, the general character episodical, — but episodes of rare worth and originality. As Ehlert says, "Noblesse oblige — and thus Chopin felt himself compelled to satisfy all demands exacted of a pianist, and wrote the unavoidable piano concerto. It was not consistent with his nature to express himself in broad terms. His lungs were too weak for the pace in seven league boots, so often required in a score. The trio and 'cello sonata were also tasks for whose accomplishment Nature did not design him. He must touch the keys by himself without being called upon to heed the players sitting next him. He is at his best when without formal restraint, he can create out of his inmost soul."

"He must touch the keys by himself!" There you have summed up in a phrase the reason Chopin never succeeded in impressing his individuality upon the sonata form and his playing upon the masses. His was the lonely soul. George Sand knew this when she wrote, "He made an instrument speak the language of the infinite. Often

in ten lines that a child might play he has
introduced poems of unequalled elevation,
dramas unrivalled in force and energy. He
did not need the great material methods to
find expression for his genius. Neither
saxophone nor ophicleide was necessary for
him to fill the soul with awe. Without
church organ or human voice he inspired
faith and enthusiasm."

It might be remarked here that Beethoven,
too, aroused a wondering and worshipping
world without the aid of saxophone or
ophicleide. But it is needless cruelty to
pick at Madame Sand's criticisms. She
had no technical education, and so little
appreciation of Chopin's peculiar genius for
the piano that she could write, "The day
will come when his music will be arranged
for orchestra without change of the piano
score;" which is disaster-breeding non-
sense. We have sounded Chopin's weakness when writing for any instrument but
his own, when writing in any form but his
own.

The E minor Concerto is dedicated to
Frederick Kalkbrenner, the F minor to the
Comtesse Deiphine Potocka. The latter
dedication demonstrates that he could forget his only "ideal" in the presence of the

charming Potocka! Ah! these vibratile and versatile Poles!

Robert Schumann, it is related, shook his head wearily when his early work was mentioned. "Dreary stuff," said the composer, whose critical sense did not fail him even in so personal a question. What Chopin thought of his youthful music may be discovered in his scanty correspondence. To suppose that the young Chopin sprang into the arena a fully equipped warrior is one of those nonsensical notions which gains currency among persons unfamiliar with the law of musical evolution. Chopin's musical ancestry is easily traced; as Poe had his Holley Chivers, Chopin had his Field. The germs of his second period are all there; from op. 1 to opus 22 virtuosity for virtuosity's sake is very evident. Liszt has said that in every young artist there is the virtuoso fever, and Chopin being a pianist did not escape the fever of the footlights. He was composing, too, at a time when piano music was well nigh strangled by excess of ornament, when acrobats were kings, when the Bach Fugue and Beethoven Sonata lurked neglected and dusty in the memories of the few. Little wonder, then, we find this individual, youthful Pole, not

timidly treading in the path of popular composition, but bravely carrying his banner,
spangled, glittering and fanciful, and out-
stripping at their own game all the virtuosi
of Europe. His originality in this bejewelled work caused Hummel to admire and
Kalkbrenner to wonder. The supple fingers
of the young man from Warsaw made quick
work of existing technical difficulties. He
needs must invent some of his own, and
when Schumann saw the pages of op. 2 he
uttered his historical cry. To-day we wonder somewhat at his enthusiasm. It is the
old story — a generation seeks to know, a
generation comprehends and enjoys, and a
generation discards.

Opus 1, a Rondo in C minor, dedicated to
Madame de Linde, saw the light in 1825,
but it was preceded by two polonaises, a set
of variations, and two mazurkas in G and B
flat major. Schumann declared that Chopin's
first published work was his tenth, and that
between op. 1 and 2 there lay two years and
twenty works. Be this as it may, one cannot help liking the C minor Rondo. In the
A flat section we detect traces of his F
minor Concerto. There is lightness, joy in
creation, which contrast with the heavy,
dour quality of the C minor Sonata, op. 4

Loosely constructed, in a formal sense, and too exuberant for his strict confines, this op. 1 is remarkable, much more remarkable, than Schumann's Abegg variations.

The Rondo à la Mazur, in F, is a further advance. It is dedicated to Comtesse Moriolles, and was published in 1827 (?). Schumann reviewed it in 1836. It is sprightly, Polish in feeling and rhythmic life, and a glance at any of its pages gives us the familiar Chopin impression — florid passage work, chords in extensions and chromatic progressions. The Concert Rondo, op. 14, in F, called Krakowiak, is built on a national dance in two-four time, which originated in Cracovia. It is, to quote Niecks, a modified polonaise, danced by the peasants with lusty abandon. Its accentual life is usually manifested on an unaccented part of the bar, especially at the end of a section or phrase. Chopin's very Slavic version is spirited, but the virtuoso predominates. There is lushness in ornamentation, and a bold, merry spirit informs every page. The orchestral accompaniment is thin. Dedicated to the Princesse Czartoryska, it was published June, 1834. The Rondo, op. 16, with an Introduction, is in great favor at the conservatories, and is neat rather than poetical, although the introduction has dramatic touches. It is to this brilliant piece, with its Weber-ish affinities, that Richard Burmeister has supplied an orchestral accompaniment.

The remaining Rondo, posthumously published as op. 73, and composed in 1828, was originally intended, so Chopin writes in 1828, for one piano. It is full of fire, but the ornamentation runs mad, and no traces of the poetical Chopin are present. He is preoccupied with the brilliant surfaces of the life about him. His youthful expansiveness finds a fair field in these variations, rondos and fantasias.

Schumann's enthusiasm over the variations on "La ci darem la mano" seems to us a little overdone. Chopin had not much gift for variation in the sense that we now understand variation. Beethoven, Schumann and Brahms — one must include Mendelssohn's Serious Variations — are masters of a form that is by no means structurally simple or a reversion to mere spielerei, as Finck fancies. Chopin plays with his themes prettily, but it is all surface display, all heat lightning. He never smites, as does Brahms with his Thor hammer, the subject full in the middle, cleaving it to its core. Chopin is slightly effeminate in his variations, and they are true specimens of spielerei, despite the cleverness of design in the arabesques, their brilliancy and euphony. Op. 2 has its dazzling moments, but its musical worth is inferior. It is written to split the ears of the groundlings, or rather to astonish and confuse them, for the Chopin dynamics in the early music are never very rude. The indisputable superiority to Herz and the rest of the shallow-pated variationists caused Schumann's passionate admiration. It has, however, given us an interesting page of music criticism. Rellstab, grumpy old fellow, was near right when he wrote of these variations that "the composer runs down the theme with roulades, and throttles and hangs it with chains of shakes." The skip makes its appearance in the fourth variation, and there is no gainsaying the brilliancy and piquant spirit of the Alla Polacca. Op. 2 is orchestrally accompanied, an accompaniment that may be gladly dispensed with, and dedicated by Chopin to the friend of his youth, Titus Woyciechowski.

Je Vends des Scapulaires is a tune in Herold and Halévy's "Ludovic." Chopin varied it in his op. 12. This rondo in B flat is the weakest of Chopin's muse. It is

Chopin and water, and Gallic eau sucrée at
that. The piece is written tastefully, is not
difficult, but woefully artificial. Published
in 1833, it was dedicated to Miss Emma
Horsford. In May, 1851, appeared the Variations in E, without an opus number. They
are not worth the trouble. Evidently composed before Chopin's op. 1 and before 1830,
they are musically light waisted, although
written by one who already knew the keyboard. The last, a valse, is the brightest of
the set. The theme is German.

The Fantaisie, op 13, in A, on Polish
airs, preceded by an introduction in F sharp
minor, is dedicated to the pianist J. P.
Pixis. It was published in April, 1834. It
is Chopin brilliant. Its orchestral background does not count for much, but the
energy, the color and Polish character of the
piece endeared it to the composer. He
played it often, and as Kleczynski asks,
"Are these brilliant passages, these cascades
of pearly notes, these bold leaps the sadness
and the despair of which we hear? Is it not
rather youth exuberant with intensity and
life? Is it not happiness, gayety, love for
the world and men? The melancholy notes
are there to bring out, to enforce the principal ideas. For instance, in the Fantaisie,

op. 13, the theme of Kurpinski moves and saddens us; but the composer does not give time for this impression to become durable; he suspends it by means of a long trill, and then suddenly by a few chords and with a brilliant prelude leads us to a popular dance, which makes us mingle with the peasant couples of Mazovia. Does the finale indicate by its minor key the gayety of a man devoid of hope — as the Germans say?" Kleczynski then tells us that a Polish proverb, "A fig for misery," is the keynote of a nation that dances furiously to music in the minor key. "Elevated beauty, not sepulchral gayety," is the character of Polish, of Chopin's music. This is a valuable hint. There are variations in the Fantaisie which end with a merry and vivacious Kujawiak.

The F minor Fantaisie will be considered later. Neither by its magnificent content, construction nor opus number (49) does it fall into this chapter.

The Allegro de Concert in A, op. 46, was published in November, 1841, and dedicated to Mlle. Friederike Müller, a pupil of Chopin. It has all the characteristics of a concerto, and is indeed a truncated one — much more so than Schumann's F minor Sonata, called Concert Sans Orchestre.

There are tutti in the Chopin work, the solo part not really beginning until the eighty-seventh bar. But it must not be supposed that these long introductory passages are ineffective for the player. The Allegro is one of Chopin's most difficult works. It abounds in risky skips, ambuscades of dangerous double notes, and the principal themes are bold and expressive. The color note is strikingly adapted for public performance, and perhaps Schumann was correct in believing that Chopin had originally sketched this for piano and orchestra. Niecks asks if this is not the fragment of a concerto for two pianos, which Chopin, in a letter written at Vienna, December 21, 1830, said he would play in public with his friend Nidecki, if he succeeded in writing it to his satisfaction. And is there any significance in the fact that Chopin, when sending this manuscript to Fontana, probably in the summer of 1841, calls it a concerto?

While it adds little to Chopin's reputation, it has the potentialities of a powerful and more manly composition than either of the two concertos. Jean Louis Nicodé has given it an orchestral garb, besides arranging it for two pianos. He has added a develop-

ing section of seventy bars. This version
was first played in New York a decade ago
by Marie Geselschap, a Dutch pianist, under
the direction of the late Anton Seidl. The
original, it must be acknowledged, is preferable.

The Bolero, op. 19, has a Polonaise flavor.
There is but little Spanish in its ingre-
dients. It is merely a memorandum of
Chopin's early essays in dance forms. It
was published in 1834, four years before
Chopin's visit to Spain. Niecks thinks it
an early work. That it can be made effective was proven by Emil Sauer. It is for
fleet-fingered pianists, and the principal
theme has the rhythmical ring of the Polonaise, although the most Iberian in character.
It is dedicated to Comtesse E. de Flahault.
In the key of A minor, its coda ends in A
major. Willeby says it is in C major!

The Tarantella is in A flat, and is numbered op. 43. It was published in 1841 (?),
and bears no dedication. Composed at
Nohant, it is as little Italian as the Bolero is
Spanish. Chopin's visit to Italy was of too
short a duration to affect him, at least in
the style of dance. It is without the necessary ophidian tang, and far inferior to
Heller and Liszt's efforts in the constricted

form. One finds little of the frenzy ascribed to it by Schumann in his review. It breathes of the North, not the South, and ranks far below the A flat Impromptu in geniality and grace.

The C minor Funeral March, composed, according to Fontana, in 1829, sounds like Mendelssohn. The trio has the processional quality of a Parisian funeral cortège. It is modest and in no wise remarkable. The three Écossaises, published as op. 73, No. 3, are little dances, schottisches, nothing more. No. 2 in G is highly popular in girls' boarding schools.

The Grand Duo Concertant for 'cello and piano is jointly composed by Chopin and Franchomme on themes from "Robert le Diable." It begins in E and ends in A major, and is without opus number. Schumann thinks "Chopin sketched the whole of it, and that Franchomme said 'Yes' to everything." It is for the salon of 1833, when it was published. It is empty, tiresome and only slightly superior to compositions of the same sort by De Beriot and Osborne. Full of rapid elegancies and shallow passage work, this duo is certainly a pièce d'occasion — the occasion probably being the need of ready money.

The seventeen Polish songs were composed between 1824 and 1844. In the psychology of the Lied Chopin was not happy. Karasowski writes that many of the songs were lost and some of them are still sung in Poland, their origin being hazy. The Third of May is cited as one of these. Chopin had a habit of playing songs for his friends, but neglected putting some of them on paper. The collected songs are under the opus head 74. The words are by his friends, Stephen Witwicki, Adam Mickiewicz, Bogdan Zaleski and Sigismond Krasinski. The first in the key of A, the familiar Maiden's Wish, has been brilliantly paraphrased by Liszt. This pretty mazurka is charmingly sung and played by Marcella Sembrich in the singing lesson of "The Barber of Seville." There are several mazurkas in the list. Most of these songs are mediocre. Poland's Dirge is an exception, and so is Horsemen Before the Battle. "Was ein junges Mädchen liebt" has a short introduction, in which the reminiscence hunter may find a true bit of "Meistersinger" color. Simple in structure and sentiment, the Chopin lieder seem almost rudimentary compared to essays in this form by Schubert, Schumann, Franz, Brahms and Tschaikowsky.

CHOPIN

A word of recommendation may not be amiss here regarding the technical study of Chopin. Kleczynski, in his two books, gives many valuable hints, and Isidor Philipp has published a set of Exercises Quotidiens, made up of specimens in double notes, octaves and passages taken from the works. Here skeletonized are the special technical problems. In these Daily Studies, and his edition of the Études, are numerous examples dealt with practically. For a study of Chopin's ornaments, Mertke has discussed at length the various editorial procedure in the matter of attacking the trill in single and double notes, also the easiest method of executing the flying scud and vapors of the fioriture. This may be found in No. 179 of the Edition Steingräber. Philipp's collection is published in Paris by J. Hamelle, and is prefixed by some interesting remarks of Georges Mathias. Chopin's portrait in 1833, after Vigneron, is included.

One composition more is to be considered. In 1837 Chopin contributed the sixth variation of the march from "I Puritani." These variations were published under the title: "Hexameron: Morceau de Concert. Grandes Variations de bravoure sur la marche des Puritans de Bellini, composées

pour le concert de Madame la Princesse
Belgiojoso au bénéfice des pauvres, par MM.
Liszt, Thalberg, Pixis, H. Herz, Czerny
et Chopin." Liszt wrote an orchestral accompaniment, never published. His pupil,
Moriz Rosenthal, is the only modern virtuoso who plays the Hexameron in his
concerts, and play it he does with overwhelming splendor. Chopin's contribution
in E major is in his sentimental, salon
mood. Musically, it is the most impressive of this extraordinary mastodonic survival
of the "pianistic" past.

The newly published Fugue — or fugato —
in A minor, in two voices, is from a manuscript in the possession of Natalie Janotha,
who probably got it from the late Princess
Czartoryska, a pupil of the composer. The
composition is ineffective, and in spots ugly
— particularly in the stretta — and is no
doubt an exercise during the working years
with Elsner. The fact that in the coda the
very suspicious octave pedal-point and trills
may be omitted — so the editorial note runs
— leads one to suspect that out of a fragment Janotha has evolved, Cuvier-like, an
entire composition. Chopin as fugue-maker
does not appear in a brilliant light. Is the
Polish composer to become a musical Hugh

Conway? Why all these disjecta membra
of a sketch-book?

In these youthful works may be found the
beginnings of the greater Chopin, but not
his vast subjugation of the purely technical
to the poetic and spiritual. That came
later. To the devout Chopinist the first
compositions are so many proofs of the
joyful, victorious spirit of the man whose
spleen and pessimism have been wrongfully
compared to Leopardi's and Baudelaire's.
Chopin was gay, fairly healthy and bubbling
over with a pretty malice. His first period
shows this; it also shows how thorough and
painful the processes by which he evolved
his final style.

XII

THE POLONAISES:—HEROIC HYMNS
OF BATTLE.

How is one to reconcile "the want of manliness, moral and intellectual," which Hadow asserts is "the one great limitation of Chopin's province," with the power, splendor and courage of the Polonaises? Here are the cannon buried in flowers of Robert Schumann, here overwhelming evidences of versatility, virility and passion. Chopin blinded his critics and admirers alike; a delicate, puny fellow, he could play the piano on occasion like a devil incarnate. He, too, had his demon as well as Liszt, and only, as Ehlert puts it, "theoretical fear" of this spirit driving him over the cliffs of reason made him curb its antics. After all the couleur de rose portraits and lollipop miniatures made of him by pensive, poetic persons it is not possible to conceive Chopin as being irascible and almost brutal. Yet he was at times even this. "Beethoven was scarce more vehement and irritable," writes Ehlert. And we remember

the stories of friends and pupils who have
seen this slender, refined Pole wrestling
with his wrath as one under the obsession of
a fiend. It is no desire to exaggerate this
side of his nature that impels this plain
writing. Chopin left compositions that bear
witness to his masculine side. Diminutive
in person, bad-temper became him ill; besides, his whole education and tastes were
opposed to scenes of violence. So this
energy, spleen and raging at fortune found
escape in some of his music, became psychical
in its manifestations.

But, you may say, this is feminine hysteria, the impotent cries of an unmanly, weak
nature. Read the E flat minor, the C
minor, the A major, the F sharp minor and
the two A flat major Polonaises! Ballades,
Scherzi, Studies, Preludes and the great F
minor Fantaisie are purposely omitted from
this awing scheme. Chopin was weak in
physique, but he had the soul of a lion.
Allied to the most exquisite poetic sensibilities — one is reminded here of Balzac's "Ce
beau génie est moins un musicien qu'une âme
qui se rend sensible " — there was another
nature, fiery, implacable. He loved Poland,
he hated her oppressors. There is no doubt
he idealized his country and her wrongs

322

until the theme grew out of all proportion. Politically the Poles and Celts rub shoulders. Niecks points out that if Chopin was "a flattering idealist as a national poet, as a personal poet he was an uncompromising realist." So in the polonaises we find two distinct groups: in one the objective, martial side predominates, in the other is Chopin the moody, mournful and morose. But in all the Polish element pervades. Barring the mazurkas, these dances are the most Polish of his works. Appreciation of Chopin's wide diversity of temperament would have spared the world the false, silly, distorted portraits of him. He had the warrior in him, even if his mailed fist was seldom used. There are moments when he discards gloves and soft phrases and deals blows that reverberate with formidable clangor.

By all means read Liszt's gorgeous description of the Polonaise. Originating during the last half of the sixteenth century, it was at first a measured procession of nobles and their womankind to the sound of music. In the court of Henry of Anjou, in 1574, after his election to the Polish throne, the Polonaise was born, and throve in the hardy, warlike atmosphere. It became a dance political, and had words set to it.

Thus came the Kosciuszko, the Oginski, the Moniuszko, the Kurpinski, and a long list written by composers with names ending in "ski." It is really a march, a processional dance, grave, moderate, flowing, and by no means stereotyped. Liszt tells of the capricious life infused into its courtly measures by the Polish aristocracy. It is at once the symbol of war and love, a vivid pageant of martial splendor, a weaving, cadenced, voluptuous dance, the pursuit of shy, coquettish woman by the fierce warrior.

The Polonaise is in three-four time, with the accent on the second beat of the bar. In simple binary form — ternary if a trio is added — this dance has feminine endings to all the principal cadences. The rhythmical cast of the bass is seldom changed. Despite its essentially masculine mould, it is given a feminine title; formerly it was called Polonais. Liszt wrote of it:

"In this form the noblest traditional feelings of ancient Poland are represented. The Polonaise is the true and purest type of Polish national character, as in the course of centuries it was developed, partly through the political position of the kingdom toward east and west, partly through an undefinable, peculiar, inborn disposition of the entire race. In the development of the Polonaise everything co-operated which specifically distinguished the nation from others. In the Poles of departed times manly resolution was united with glowing devotion to the object of their love. Their knightly heroism was sanctioned by high-soaring dignity, and even the laws of gallantry and the national costume exerted an influence over the turns of this dance. The Polonaises are the keystone in the development of this form. They belong to the most beautiful of Chopin inspirations. With their energetic rhythm they electrify, to the point of excited demonstration, even the sleepiest indifferentism. Chopin was born too late, and left his native hearth too early, to be initiated into the original character of the Polonaise as danced through his own observation. But what others imparted to him in regard to it was supplemented by his fancy and his nationality."

Chopin wrote fifteen Polonaises, the authenticity of one in G flat major being doubted by Niecks. This list includes the Polonaise for violoncello and piano, op. 3, and the Polonaise, op. 22, for piano and orchestra. This latter Polonaise is preceded by an andante spianato in G in six-eight time, and unaccompanied. It is a charming, liquid-toned, nocturne-like composition, Chopin in his most suave, his most placid mood: a barcarolle, scarcely a ripple of emotion, disturbs the mirrored calm of this lake. After sixteen bars of a crudely harmonized tutti comes the Polonaise in the widely remote key of E flat; it is brilliant, every note telling, the figuration rich and novel, the movement spirited and flowing. Perhaps it is too long and lacks relief. The theme on each re-entrance is varied ornamentally. The second theme, in C minor, has a Polish and poetic ring, while the coda is effective. This opus is vivacious, but not characterized by great depth. Crystalline, gracious, and refined, the piece is stamped "Paris," the elegant Paris of 1830. Composed in that year and published in July, 1836, it is dedicated to the Baronne D'Est. Chopin introduced it at a Conservatoire concert for the benefit of Habeneck, April 26, 1835. This, according to Niecks, was the only time he played the Polonaise with orchestral accompaniment. It was practically a novelty to New York when Rafael Joseffy played it here, superlatively well, in 1879.

The orchestral part seems wholly superfluous, for the scoring is not particularly effective, and there is a rumor that Chopin cannot be held responsible for it. Xaver Scharwenka made a new instrumentation that is discreet and extremely well sounding. With excellent tact he has managed the added accompaniment to the introduction, giving some thematic work of the slightest texture to the strings, and in the pretty coda to the wood-wind. A delicately managed allusion is made by the horns to the second theme of the nocturne in G. There are even five faint taps of the triangle, and the idyllic atmosphere is never disturbed. Scharwenka first played this arrangement at a Seidl memorial concert, in Chickering Hall, New York, April, 1898. Yet I cannot truthfully say the Polonaise sounds so characteristic as when played solo.

The C sharp minor Polonaise, op. 26, has had the misfortune of being sentimentalized to death. What can be more "appassionata" than the opening with its "grand rhythmical swing"? It is usually played by timid persons in a sugar-sweet fashion, although *fff* stares them in the face. The first three lines are hugely heroic, but the indignation soon melts away, leaving an apathetic humor; after the theme returns and is re-

peated we get a genuine love motif tender
enough in all faith wherewith to woo a
princess. On this the Polonaise closes, an
odd ending for such a fiery opening.

In no such mood does No. 2 begin. In E
flat minor it is variously known as the
Siberian, the Revolt Polonaise. It breathes
defiance and rancor from the start. What
suppressed and threatening rumblings are
there! Volcanic mutterings these:

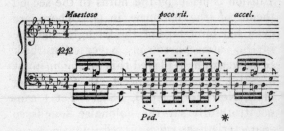

It is a sinister page, and all the more
so because of the injunction to open with
pianissimo. One wishes that the shrill,
high G flat had been written in full chords
as the theme suffers from a want of massive-
ness. Then follows a subsidiary, but the
principal subject returns relentlessly. The
episode in B major gives pause for breath-
ing. It has a hint of Meyerbeer. But again
with smothered explosions the Polonaise

proper appears, and all ends in gloom and the impotent clanking of chains. It is an awe-provoking work, this terrible Polonaise in E flat minor, op. 26; it was published July, 1836, and is dedicated to M. J. Dessauer.

Not so the celebrated A major Polonaise, op. 40, Le Militaire. To Rubinstein this seemed a picture of Poland's greatness, as its companion in C minor is of Poland's downfall. Although Karasowski and Kleczynski give to the A flat major Polonaise the honor of suggesting a well-known story, it is really the A major that provoked it — so the Polish portrait painter Kwiatowski informed Niecks. The story runs, that after composing it, Chopin in the dreary watches of the night was surprised — terrified is a better word — by the opening of his door and the entrance of a long train of Polish nobles and ladies, richly robed, who moved slowly by him. Troubled by the ghosts of the past he had raised, the composer, hollow eyed, fled the apartment. All this must have been at Majorca, for op. 40 was composed or finished there. Ailing, weak and unhappy as he was, Chopin had grit enough to file and polish this brilliant and striking composition into its present shape. It is the best known and, though the most muscular of his compositions, it is the most played. It is dedicated to J. Fontana, and was published November, 1840. This Polonaise has the festive glitter of Weber.

The C minor Polonaise of the same set is a noble, troubled composition, large in accents and deeply felt. Can anything be more impressive than this opening?

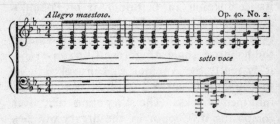

It is indeed Poland's downfall. The Trio in A flat, with its kaleidoscopic modulations, produces an impression of vague unrest and suppressed sorrow. There is loftiness of spirit and daring in it.

What can one say new of the tremendous F sharp minor Polonaise? Willeby calls it noisy! And Stanislaw Przybyszewski — whom Vance Thompson christened a prestidigious noctambulist — has literally stormed over it. It is barbaric, it is perhaps pathologic, and of it Liszt has said most eloquent things. It is for him a dream poem, the "lurid hour that precedes a hurricane" with a "convulsive shudder at the close." The opening is very impressive, the nerve-pulp being harassed by the gradually swelling prelude. There is defiant power in the first theme, and the constant reference to it betrays the composer's exasperated mental condition. This tendency to return upon himself, a tormenting introspection, certainly signifies a grave state. But consider the musical weight of the work, the recklessly bold outpourings of a mind almost distraught! There is no greater test for the poet-pianist than the F sharp minor Polonaise. It is profoundly ironical — what else means the introduction of that lovely mazurka, "a flower between two abysses"? This strange dance is ushered in by two of the most enigmatic pages of Chopin. The A major intermezzo, with its booming cannons and reverberating overtones, is not easily defensible on the score of form, yet it unmistakably fits in the picture. The mazurka is full of interrogation and emotional nuanciren. The return of the tempest is not long delayed. It bursts, wanes, and with the coda comes sad yearning, then the savage drama passes tremblingly into the

331

night after fluid and wavering affirmations,
a roar in F sharp and finally a silence
that marks the cessation of an agitating
nightmare. No "sabre dance" this, but a
confession from the dark depths of a self-
tortured soul. Op. 44 was published November, 1841, and is dedicated to Princesse de
Beauvau. There are few editorial differences. In the eighteenth bar from the beginning, Kullak, in the second beat, fills
out an octave. Not so in Klindworth nor in
the original. At the twentieth bar Klindworth differs from the original as follows.
The Chopin text is the upper one:

The A flat Polonaise, op. 53, was published December, 1843, and is said by Karasowski to have been composed in 1840, after
Chopin's return from Majorca. It is dedicated to A. Leo. This is the one Karasowski calls the story of Chopin's vision of
the antique dead in an isolated tower of
Madame Sand's chateau at Nohant. We

have seen this legend disproved by one who
knows. This Polonaise is not as feverish
and as exalted as the previous one. It is,
as Kleczynski writes, "the type of a war
song." Named the Héroïque, one hears in
it Ehlert's "ring of damascene blade and
silver spur." There is imaginative splendor
in this thrilling work, with its thunder of
horses' hoofs and fierce challengings. What
fire, what sword thrusts and smoke and
clash of mortal conflict! Here is no psychical presentation, but an objective picture of
battle, of concrete contours, and with a
cleaving brilliancy that excites the blood to
boiling pitch. That Chopin ever played it
as intended is incredible; none but the
heroes of the keyboard may grasp its dense
chordal masses, its fiery projectiles of tone.
But there is something disturbing, even
ghostly, in the strange intermezzo that sepa-
rates the trio from the polonaise. Both mist
and starlight are in it. Yet the work is
played too fast, and has been nicknamed the
"Drum" Polonaise, losing in majesty and
force because of the vanity of virtuosi. The
octaves in E major are spun out as if speed
were the sole idea of this episode. Follow
Kleczynski's advice and do not sacrifice the
Polonaise to the octaves. Karl Tausig, so

Joseffy and de Lenz assert, played this Polonaise in an unapproachable manner. Powerful battle tableau as it is, it may still be presented so as not to shock one's sense of the euphonious, of the limitations of the instrument. This work becomes vapid and unheroic when transferred to the orchestra.

The Polonaise-Fantaisie in A flat, op. 61, given to the world September, 1846, is dedicated to Madame A. Veyret. One of three great Polonaises, it is just beginning to be understood, having been derided as amorphous, febrile, of little musical moment, even Liszt declaring that "such pictures possess but little real value to art. . . . Deplorable visions which the artist should admit with extreme circumspection within the graceful circle of his charmed realm." This was written in the old-fashioned days, when art was aristocratic and excluded the "baser" and more painful emotions. For a generation accustomed to the realism of Richard Strauss, the Fantaisie-Polonaise seems vaporous and idealistic, withal new. It recalls one of those enchanted flasks of the magii from which on opening smoke exhales that gradually shapes itself into fantastic and fearsome figures. This Polonaise at no time exhibits the solidity of its two predecessors; its plasticity defies the imprint of the conventional Polonaise, though we ever feel its rhythms. It may be full of monologues, interspersed cadenzas, improvised preludes and short phrases, as Kullak suggests, yet there is unity in the composition, the units of structure and style. It was music of the future when Chopin composed; it is now music of the present, as much as Richard Wagner's. But the realism is a trifle clouded. Here is the duality of Chopin the suffering man and Chopin the prophet of Poland. Undimmed is his poetic vision — — Poland will be free! — undaunted his soul, though oppressed by a suffering body. There are in the work throes of agony blended with the trumpet notes of triumph. And what puzzled our fathers — the shifting lights and shadows, the restless tonalities — are welcome, for at the beginning of this new century the chromatic is king. The ending of this Polonaise is triumphant, recalling in key and climaxing the A flat Ballade. Chopin is still the captain of his soul — and Poland will be free! Are Celt and Slav doomed to follow ever the phosphorescent lights of patriotism? Liszt acknowledges the beauty and grandeur of this last Polonaise, which unites the characteristics of superb and original manipulation of the form, the martial and the melancholic.

Opus 71, three posthumous Polonaises, given to the world by Julius Fontana, are in D minor, published in 1827, B flat major, 1828, and F minor, 1829. They are interesting to Chopinists. The influence of Weber, a past master in this form, is felt. Of the three the last in F minor is the strongest, although if Chopin's age is taken into consideration, the first, in D minor, is a feat for a lad of eighteen. I agree with Niecks that the posthumous Polonaise, without opus number, in G sharp minor, was composed later than 1822 — the date given in the Breitkopf & Härtel edition. It is an artistic conception, and in "light winged figuration" far more mature than the Chopin of op. 71. Really a graceful and effective little composition of the florid order, but like his early music without poetic depth. The Warsaw "Echo Musicale," to commemorate the fiftieth anniversary of Chopin's death, published a special number in October, 1899, with the picture of a farmer named Krysiak, born in 1810, the year after the composer. Thereat Finck remarked that it is not a case of survival of the fittest!

A fac-simile reproduction of a hitherto un-published Polonaise in A flat, written at the age of eleven, is also included in this unique number. This tiny dance shows, it is said, the "characteristic physiognomy" of the composer. In reality this polacca is thin, a tentative groping after a form that later was mastered so magnificently by the composer. Here is the way it begins — the autograph is Chopin's:

The Alla Polacca for piano and 'cello, op. 3, was composed in 1829, while Chopin was on a visit to Prince Radziwill. It is pre-ceded by an introduction, and is dedicated to Joseph Merk, the 'cellist. Chopin him-self pronounced it a brilliant salon piece. It is now not even that, for it sounds anti-quated and threadbare. The passage work at times smacks of Chopin and Weber — a hint of the Mouvement Perpetuel — and the

'cello has the better of the bargain. Evi
dently written for my lady's chamber.

Two Polonaises remain. One, in B flat
minor, was composed in 1826, on the occasion of the composer's departure for Reinerz.
A footnote to the edition of this rather
elegiac piece tells this. Adieu to Guillaume
Kolberg, is the title, and the Trio in D flat
is accredited to an air of " Gazza Ladra," with
a sentimental Au Revoir inscribed. Kleczynski has revised the Gebethner & Wolff
edition. The little cadenza in chromatic
double notes on the last page is of a certainty Chopin. But the Polonaise in G flat
major, published by Schott, is doubtful. It
has a shallow ring, a brilliant superficiality
that warrants Niecks in stamping it as a
possible compilation. There are traces of
the master throughout, particularly in the E
flat minor Trio, but there are some vile
progressions and an air of vulgarity surely
not Chopin's. This dance form, since the
death of the great composer, has been
chiefly developed on the virtuoso side.
Beethoven, Schubert, Weber, and even Bach
— in his B minor suite for strings and flute
— also indulged in this form. Wagner, as
a student, wrote a Polonaise for four hands,
in D, and in Schumann's Papillons there

is a charming specimen. Rubinstein composed a most brilliant and dramatic example
in E flat in Le Bal. The Liszt Polonaises,
all said and done, are the most remarkable
in design and execution since Chopin.
But they are more Hungarian than Polish.

XIII

MAZURKAS :— DANCES OF THE SOUL

I

"COQUETRIES, vanities, fantasies, inclina-tions, elegies, vague emotions, passions, conquests, struggles upon which the safety or favors of others depend, all, all meet in this dance."

Thus Liszt. De Lenz further quotes him: "Of the Mazurkas, one must harness a new pianist of the first rank to each of them." Yet Liszt told Niecks he did not care much for Chopin's Mazurkas. "One often meets in them with bars which might just as well be in another place. But as Chopin puts them perhaps nobody could have put them." Liszt, despite the rhap-sodical praise of his friend, is not always to be relied upon. Capricious as Chopin, he had days when he disliked not only the Mazurkas, but all music. He confessed to Niecks that when he played a half hour for amusement it was Chopin he took up.

There is no more brilliant chapter than this Hungarian's on the dancing of the

Mazurka by the Poles. It is a companion to his equally sensational description of the Polonaise. He gives a wild, whirling, highly-colored narrative of the Mazurka, with a coda of extravagant praise of the beauty and fascination of Polish women. "Angel through love, demon through fantasy," as Balzac called her. In none of the piano rhapsodies are there such striking passages to be met as in Liszt's overwrought, cadenced prose, prose modelled after Chateaubriand. Niema iak Polki — "nothing equals the Polish women" and their "divine coquetries;" the Mazurka is their dance — it is the feminine complement to the heroic and masculine Polonaise.

An English writer describes the dancing of the Mazurka in contemporary Russia:

In the salons of St. Petersburg, for instance, the guests actually dance; they do not merely shamble to and fro in a crowd, crumpling their clothes and ruffling their tempers, and call it a set of quadrilles. They have ample space for the sweeping movements and complicated figures of all the orthodox ball dances, and are generally gifted with sufficient plastic grace to carry them out in style. They carefully cultivate dances calling for a kind of grace which is almost beyond the reach of art. The mazurka is one of the finest of these, and it is quite a favorite at balls on the banks of the Neva It needs a good deal of room, one or more spurred officers, and grace, grace and grace. The dash with which the partners rush forward, the clinking and clattering of spurs as heel clashes with heel in mid air, punctuating the staccato of the music, the loud thud of boots striking the ground, followed by their sibilant slide along the polished floor, then the swift springs and sudden bounds, the whirling gyrations and dizzy evolutions, the graceful genuflections and quick embraces, and all the other intricate and maddening movements to the accompaniment of one of Glinka's or Tschaikowsky's masterpieces, awaken and mobilize all the antique heroism, mediæval chivalry and wild romance that lie dormant in the depths of men's being. There is more genuine pleasure in being the spectator of a soul thrilling dance like that than in taking an active part in the lifeless makebelieves performed at society balls in many of the more Western countries of Europe.

Absolutely Slavonic, though a local dance of the province of Mazovia, the Mazurek or Mazurka, is written in three-four time, with the usual displaced accent in music of Eastern origin. Brodzinski is quoted as saying that in its primitive form the Mazurek is only a kind of Krakowiak, "less lively, less sautillant." At its best it is a dancing anecdote, a story told in a charming variety of steps and gestures. It is intoxicating, rude, humorous, poetic, above all melancholy. When he is happiest he sings his saddest, does the Pole. Hence his predilection for minor modes. The Mazurka is in three-four or three-eight time. Sometimes the accent is dotted, but this is by no means absolute. Here is the rhythm most frequently encountered, although Chopin employs variants and modifications. The first part of the bar has usually the quicker notes.

The scale is a mixture of major and minor —melodies are encountered that grew out of a scale shorn of a degree. Occasionally the augmented second, the Hungarian, is encountered, and skips of a third are of frequent occurrence. This, with progressions of augmented fourths and major sevenths, gives to the Mazurkas of Chopin an exotic character apart from their novel and original content. As was the case with the Polonaise, Chopin took the framework of the national dance, developed it, enlarged it and hung upon it his choicest melodies, his most piquant harmonies. He breaks and varies

343

the conventionalized rhythm in a half hun
dred ways, lifting to the plane of a poem the
heavy hoofed peasant dance. But in this
idealization he never robs it altogether of
the flavor of the soil. It is, in all its way-
ward disguises, the Polish Mazurka, and is
with the Polonaise, according to Rubinstein,
the only Polish-reflective music he has
made, although "in all of his compositions
we hear him relate rejoicingly of Poland's
vanished greatness, singing, mourning, weeping over Poland's downfall and all that, in
the most beautiful, the most musical, way."

Besides the "hard, inartistic modulations,
the startling progressions and abrupt changes
of mood" that jarred on the old-fashioned
Moscheles, and dipped in vitriol the pen of
Rellstab, there is in the Mazurkas the
greatest stumbling block of all, the much
exploited rubato. Berlioz swore that Chopin
could not play in time — which was not true
— and later we shall see that Meyerbeer
thought the same. What to the sensitive
critic is a charming wavering and swaying
in the measure — "Chopin leans about freely
within his bars," wrote an English critic
— for the classicists was a rank departure
from the time beat. According to Liszt's
description of the rubato "a wind plays in the

leaves, Life unfolds and develops beneath them, but the tree remains the same — that is the Chopin rubato." Elsewhere, "a tempo agitated, broken, interrupted, a movement flexible, yet at the same time abrupt and languishing, and vacillating as the fluctuating breath by which it is agitated." Chopin was more commonplace in his definition: "Supposing," he explained, "that a piece lasts a given number of minutes; it may take just so long to perform the whole, but in detail deviations may differ."

The tempo rubato is probably as old as music itself. It is in Bach, it was practised by the old Italian singers. Mikuli says that no matter how free Chopin was in his treatment of the right hand in melody or arabesque, the left kept strict time. Mozart and not Chopin it was who first said: "Let your left hand be your conductor and always keep time." Hallé, the pianist, once asserted that he proved Chopin to be playing four-four instead of three-four measure in a mazurka. Chopin laughingly admitted that it was a national trait. Hallé was bewildered when he first heard Chopin play, for he did not believe such music could be represented by musical signs. Still he holds that this style has been woefully ex-

aggerated by pupils and imitators. If a
Beethoven symphony or a Bach fugue be
played with metronomical rigidity it loses
its quintessential flavor. Is it not time the
ridiculous falsehoods about the Chopin rubato
be exposed? Naturally abhorring anything
that would do violence to the structural part
of his compositions, Chopin was a very
martinet with his pupils if too much license
of tempo was taken. His music needs the
greatest lucidity in presentation, and naturally a certain elasticity of phrasing.
Rhythms need not be distorted, nor need
there be absurd and vulgar haltings, silly
and explosive dynamics. Chopin sentimentalized is Chopin butchered. He loathed
false sentiment, and a man whose taste was
formed by Bach and Mozart, who was nurtured by the music of these two giants,
could never have indulged in exaggerated,
jerky tempi, in meaningless expression.
Come, let us be done with this fetish of
stolen time, of the wonderful and so seldom
comprehended rubato. If you wish to play
Chopin, play him in curves; let there be no
angularities of surface, of measure, but in
the name of the Beautiful do not deliver his
exquisitely balanced phrases with the jolt-
ing, balky eloquence of a café chantant

singer. The very balance and symmetry of the Chopin phraseology are internal; it must be delivered in a flowing, waving manner, never square or hard, yet with every accent showing like the supple muscles of an athlete beneath his skin. Without the skeleton a musical composition is flaccid, shapeless, weak and without character. Chopin's music needs a rhythmic sense that to us, fed upon the few simple forms of the West, seems almost abnormal. The Chopin rubato is rhythm liberated from its scholastic bonds, but it does not mean anarchy, disorder. What makes this popular misconception all the more singular is the freedom with which the classics are now being interpreted. A Beethoven, and even a Mozart symphony, no longer means a rigorous execution, in which the measure is ruthlessly hammered out by the conductor, but the melodic and emotional curve is followed and the tempo fluctuates. Why then is Chopin singled out as the evil and solitary representative of a vicious time-beat? Play him as you play Mendelssohn and your Chopin has evaporated. Again play him lawlessly, with his accentual life topsy-turvied, and he is no longer Chopin — his caricature only. Pianists of Slavic descent alone understand the secret of the tempo rubato.

I have read in a recently started German periodical that to make the performance of Chopin's works pleasing it is sufficient to play them with less precision of rhythm than the music of other composers. I, on the contrary, do not know a single phrase of Chopin's works — including even the freest among them — in which the balloon of inspiration, as it moves through the air, is not checked by an anchor of rhythm and symmetry. Such passages as occur in the F minor Ballade, the B flat minor Scherzo — the middle part — the F minor Prelude, and even the A flat Impromptu, are not devoid of rhythm. The most crooked recitative of the F minor Concerto, as can be easily proved, has a fundamental rhythm not at all fantastic, and which cannot be dispensed with when playing with orchestra. . . . Chopin never overdoes fantasy, and is always restrained by a pronounced æsthetical instinct. . . . Everywhere the simplicity of his poetical inspiration and his sobriety saves us from extravagance and false pathos.

Kleczynski has this in his second volume, for he enjoyed the invaluable prompting of Chopin's pupil, the late Princess Marceline Czartoryska.

Niecks quotes Mme. Friederike Streicher,

née Müller, a pupil, who wrote of her master:
"He required adherence to the strictest
rhythm, hated all lingering and lagging,
misplaced rubatos, as well as exaggerated
ritardandos. ' Je vous prie de vous asseoir,'
he said, on such an occasion, with gentle
mockery. And it is just in this respect that
people make such terrible mistakes in the
execution of his works."

And now to the Mazurkas, which de Lenz
said were Heinrich Heine's songs on the
piano. "Chopin was a phœnix of intimacy
with the piano. In his nocturnes and mazurkas he is unrivalled, downright fabulous."

No compositions are so Chopin-ish as the
Mazurkas. Ironical, sad, sweet, joyous, morbid, sour, sane and dreamy, they illustrate
what was said of their composer — "his
heart is sad, his mind is gay." That subtle
quality, for an Occidental, enigmatic, which
the Poles call Żal, is in some of them; in
others the fun is almost rough and roaring.
Żal, a poisonous word, is a baleful compound
of pain, sadness, secret rancor, revolt. It
is a Polish quality and is in the Celtic peo-
ples. Oppressed nations with a tendency
to mad lyrism develop this mental secretion
of the spleen. Liszt writes that "the Żal
colors with a reflection now argent, now

ardent the whole of Chopin's works." This sorrow is the very soil of Chopin's nature. He so confessed when questioned by Comtesse d'Agoult. Liszt further explains that the strange word includes in its meanings — for it seems packed with them — "all the tenderness, all the humility of a regret borne with resignation and without a murmur;" it also signifies "excitement, agitation, rancor, revolt full of reproach, premeditated vengeance, menace never ceasing to threaten if retaliation should ever become possible, feeding itself meanwhile with a bitter if sterile hatred."

Sterile indeed must be such a consuming passion. Even where his patriotism became a lyric cry, this Żal tainted the source of Chopin's joy. It made him irascible, and with his powers of repression, this smouldering, smothered rage must have well nigh suffocated him, and in the end proved harmful alike to his person and to his art. As in certain phases of disease it heightened the beauty of his later work, unhealthy, feverish, yet beauty without doubt. The pearl is said to be a morbid secretion, so the spiritual ferment called Żal gave to Chopin's music its morbid beauty. It is in the B minor Scherzo but not in the A flat Ballade. The F minor

Ballade overflows with it, and so does the
F sharp minor Polonaise, but not the first
Impromptu. Its dark introspection colors
many of the preludes and mazurkas, and
in the C sharp minor Scherzo it is in acrid
flowering — truly fleurs du mal. Heine and
Baudelaire, two poets far removed from the
Slavic, show traces of the terrible drowsy
Żal in their poetry. It is the collective
sorrow and tribal wrath of a down-trodden
nation, and the mazurkas for that reason
have ethnic value. As concise, even as curt
as the Preludes, they are for the most part
highly polished. They are dancing preludes, and often tiny single poems of great
poetic intensity and passionate plaint.

Chopin published during his lifetime
forty-one Mazurkas in eleven cahiers of
three, four and five numbers. Op. 6, four
Mazurkas, and op. 7, five Mazurkas, were
published December, 1832. Op. 6 is dedicated to Comtesse Pauline Plater; op. 7 to
Mr. Johns. Op. 17, four Mazurkas, May 4,
dedicated to Madame Lina Freppa; op. 24,
four Mazurkas, November, 1835, dedicated
to Comte de Perthuis; op. 30, four Mazurkas,
December, 1837, dedicated to Princesse
Czartoryska; op. 33, four Mazurkas, October, 1838, dedicated to Comtesse Mostow-

CHOPIN

ska; op. 41, four Mazurkas, December, 1840, dedicated to E. Witwicki; op. 50, three Mazurkas, November, 1841, dedicated to Léon Szmitkowski; op. 56, three Mazurkas, August, 1844, dedicated to Mlle. C. Maberly; op. 59, three Mazurkas, April, 1846, no dedication, and op. 63, three Mazurkas, September, 1847, dedicated to Comtesse Czosñowska.

Besides there are op. 67 and 68 published by Fontana after Chopin's death, consisting of eight Mazurkas, and there are a miscellaneous number, two in A minor, both in the Kullak, Klindworth and Mikuli editions, one in F sharp major, said to be written by Charles Mayer — in Klindworth's — and four others, in G, B flat, D and C major. This makes in all fifty-six to be grouped and analyzed. Niecks thinks there is a well-defined difference between the Mazurkas as far as op. 41 and those that follow. In the latter he misses "savage beauties" and spontaneity. As Chopin gripped the form, as he felt more, suffered more and knew more, his Mazurkas grew broader, revealed more Weltschmerz, became elaborate and at times impersonal, but seldom lost the racial "snap" and hue. They are sonnets in their well-rounded mécanisme, and, as Schumann says, something new is to be found in each. Toward the last, a few are blithe and jocund, but they are the exceptions. In the larger ones the universal quality is felt, but to the detriment of the intimate, Polish characteristics. These Mazurkas are just what they are called, only some dance with the heart, others with the heels. Comprising a large and original portion of Chopin's compositions, they are the least known. Perhaps when they wander from the map of Poland they lose some of their native fragrance. Like hardy, simple wild flowers, they are mostly for the open air, the only out-of-doors music Chopin ever made. But even in the open, under the moon, the note of self-torture, of sophisticated sadness is not absent. Do not accuse Chopin, for this is the sign-manual of his race. The Pole suffers in song the joy of his sorrow.

II

The F sharp minor Mazurka of op. 6 begins with the characteristic triplet that plays such a rôle in the dance. Here we find a Chopin fuller fledged than in the nocturnes and variations, and probably because of the form. This Mazurka, first in publication, is melodious, slightly mournful but of a delightful freshness. The third section with the appoggiaturas realizes a vivid vision of country couples dancing determinedly. Who plays No. 2 of this set? It, too, has the "native wood note wild," with its dominant pedal bass, its slight twang and its sweet-sad melody in C sharp minor. There is hearty delight in the major, and how natural it seems. No. 3 in E is still on the village green, and the boys and girls are romping in the dance. We hear a drone bass — a favorite device of Chopin — and the chatter of the gossips, the bustle of a rural festival. The harmonization is rich, the rhythmic life vital. But in the following one in E flat minor a different note is sounded. Its harmonies are closer and there is sorrow abroad. The incessant circling around one idea, as if obsessed by fixed grief, is used here for the first, but not for the last time, by the composer.

Opus 7 drew attention to Chopin. It was the set that brought down the thunders of Rellstab, who wrote: "If Mr. Chopin had shown this composition to a master the latter would, it is to be hoped, have torn it and thrown it at his feet, which we hereby do symbolically." Criticism had its amenities in 1833. In a later number of "The Iris," in which a caustic notice appeared of the studies, op. 10, Rellstab printed a letter, signed Chopin, the authenticity of which is extremely doubtful. In it Chopin is made to call the critic "really a very bad man." Niecks demonstrates that the Polish pianist was not the writer. It reads like the effusion of some indignant, well meaning female friend.

The B flat major Mazurka which opens op. 7 is the best known of these dances. There is an expansive swing, a laissez-aller to this piece, with its air of elegance, that are very alluring. The rubato flourishes, and at the close we hear the footing of the peasant. A jolly, reckless composition that makes one happy to be alive and dancing. The next, which begins in A minor, is as if one danced upon one's grave; a change to major does not deceive, it is too heavy-hearted. No. 3, in F minor, with its rhythmic pronouncement at the start, brings us back to earth. The triplet that sets off the phrase has great significance. Guitar-like is the bass in its snapping resolution. The section that begins on the dominant of D flat is full of vigor and imagination; the left hand is given a solo. **This Mazurka has** the true ring.

The following one, in A flat, is a sequence of moods. Its assertiveness soon melts into tenderer hues, and in an episode in A we find much to ponder. No. 5, in C, consists of three lines. It is a sort of coda to the opus and full of the echoes of lusty happiness. A silhouette with a marked profile.

Opus 17, No. 1, in B flat, is bold, chivalric, and I fancy I hear the swish of the warrior's sabre. The peasant has vanished or else gapes through the open window while his master goes through the paces of a courtlier dance. We encounter sequential chords of the seventh, and their use, rhythmically framed as they are, gives a line of sternness to the dance. Niecks thinks that the second Mazurka might be called The Request, so pathetic, playful and persuasive is it. It is in E minor and has a plaintive, appealing quality. The G major part is very pretty. In the last lines the passion mounts, but is never shrill. Kullak notes that in the fifth and sixth bars there is no slur in certain editions. Klindworth employs it, but marks the B sforzando. A slur on two notes of the same pitch with Chopin does not always mean a tie. The A flat

Mazurka, No. 3, is pessimistic, threatening and irritable. Though in the key of E major the trio displays a relentless sort of humor. The return does not mend matters. A dark page! In A minor the fourth is called by Szulc the Little Jew. Szulc, who wrote anecdotes of Chopin and collected them with the title of "Fryderyk Szopen," told the story to Kleczynski. It is this:

Chopin did not care for programme music, though more than one of his compositions, full of expression and character, may be included under that name. Who does not know the A minor Mazurka of op. 17, dedicated to Lena Freppa ? It was already known in our country as the "Little Jew" before the departure of our artist abroad. It is one of the works of Chopin which are characterized by distinct humor. A Jew in slippers and a long robe comes out of his inn, and seeing an unfortunate peasant, his customer, intoxicated, tumbling about the road and uttering complaints, exclaims from his threshold, "What is this?" Then, as if by way of contrast to this scene, the gay wedding party of a rich burgess comes along on its way from church, with shouts of various kinds, accompanied in a lively manner by violins and bagpipes. The train passes by, the tipsy peasant renews his complaints — the complaints of a man who had tried to drown his misery in the glass. The Jew returns indoors, shaking his head and again asking, "What was this?"

The story strikes one as being both child-ish and commonplace. The Mazurka is rather doleful and there is a little triplet of interrogation standing sentinel at the fourth bar. It is also the last phrase. But what of that? I, too, can build you a programme as lofty or lowly as you please, but it will not be Chopin's. Niecks, for example, finds this very dance bleak and joyless, of intimate emotional experience, and with "jarring tones that strike in and pitilessly wake the dreamer." So there is no predi-cating the content of music except in a gen-eral way; the mood key may be struck, but in Chopin's case this is by no means infal-lible. If I write with confidence it is that begot of desperation, for I know full well that my version of the story will not be yours. The A minor Mazurka for me is full of hectic despair, whatever that may mean, and its serpentining chromatics and appar-ently suspended close — on the chord of the sixth — gives an impression of morbid irreso-lution modulating into a sort of desperate gayety. Its tonality accounts for the moods evoked, being indeterminate and restless.

MAZURKAS

Opus 24 begins with the G minor Mazurka,
a favorite because of its comparative free
dom from technical difficulties. Although
in the minor mode there is mental strength
in the piece, with its exotic scale of the
augmented second, and its trio is hearty.
In the next, in C, we find, besides the
curious content, a mixture of tonalities —
Lydian and mediæval church modes. Here
the trio is occidental. The entire piece
leaves a vague impression of discontent,
and the refrain recalls the Russian barge-
men's songs utilized at various times by
Tschaikowsky. Klindworth uses variants.
There is also some editorial differences in
the metronomic markings, Mikuli being,
according to Kullak, too slow. Mention
has not been made, as in the studies and
preludes, of the tempi of the Mazurkas.
These compositions are so capricious, so
varied, that Chopin, I am sure, did not play
any one of them twice alike. They are
creatures of moods, melodic air plants,
swinging to the rhythms of any vagrant
breeze. The metronome is for the student,
but metronome and rubato are, as de Lenz
would have said, mutually exclusive.

The third Mazurka of op. 24 is in A flat.
It is pleasing, not deep, a real dance with

an ornamental coda. But the next! Ah!
here is a gem, a beautiful and exquisitely
colored poem. In B flat minor, it sends
out prehensile filaments that entwine and
draw us into the centre of a wondrous
melody, laden with rich odors, odors that
almost intoxicate. The figuration is tropical, and when the major is reached and those
glancing thirty-seconds so coyly assail us
we realize the seductive charm of Chopin.
The reprise is still more festooned, and it
is almost a relief when the little, tender
unison begins with its positive chord assertions closing the period. Then follows a
fascinating, cadenced step, with lights and
shades, sweet melancholy driving before it
joy and being routed itself, until the annun-
ciation of the first theme and the dying
away of the dance, dancers and the solid
globe itself, as if earth had committed
suicide for loss of the sun. The last two
bars could have been written only by Chopin.
They are ineffable sighs.

And now the chorus of praise begins to
mount in burning octaves. The C minor
Mazurka, op. 30, is another of those wonderful, heartfelt melodies of the master.
What can I say of the deepening feeling at
the con anima! It stabs with its pathos.

Here is the poet Chopin, the poet who
with Burns, interprets the simple strains of
the folk, who blinds us with color and rich
romanticism like Keats and lifts us Shelley-
wise to transcendental azure. And his only
apparatus a keyboard. As Schumann wrote:
"Chopin did not make his appearance by an
orchestral army, as a great genius is accustomed to do; he only possesses a small
cohort, but every soul belongs to him to the
last hero."

Eight lines is this dance, yet its meanings are almost endless. No. 2, in B
minor, is called The Cuckoo by Kleczynski.
It is sprightly and with the lilt, notwithstanding its subtle progressions, of Mazovia. No. 3 in D flat is all animation,
brightness and a determination to stay out
the dance. The alternate major-minor of
the theme is truly Polish. The graceful
trio and canorous brilliancy of this dance
make it a favored number. The ending is
epigrammatic. It comes so suddenly upon
us, our cortical cells pealing with the minor,
that its very abruptness is witty. One can
see Chopin making a mocking moue as
he wrote it. Tschaikowsky borrowed the
effect for the conclusion of the Chinoise
in a miniature orchestral suite. The fourth

of this opus is in C sharp minor. Again
I feel like letting loose the dogs of enthusiasm. The sharp rhythms and solid build
of this ample work give it a massive character. It is one of the big Mazurkas, and
the ending, raw as it is — consecutive, bare-
faced fifths and sevenths — compasses its
intended meaning.

Opus 33 is a popular set. It begins with
one in G sharp minor, which is curt and
rather depressing. The relief in B major is
less real than it seems — on paper. Moody,
withal a tender-hearted Mazurka. No. 2,
in D, is bustling, graceful and full of unrestrained vitality. Bright and not particularly profound, it was successfully arranged
for voice by Viardot-Garcia. The third of
the opus, in C, is the one described by de
Lenz as almost precipitating a violent row
between Chopin and Meyerbeer. He had
christened it the Epitaph of the Idea.

"Two-four," said Meyerbeer, after de
Lenz played it. "Three-four," answered
Chopin, flushing angrily. "Let me have it
for a ballet in my new opera and I'll show
you," retorted Meyerbeer. "It's three-
four," scolded Chopin, and played it himself. De Lenz says they parted coolly, each
holding to his opinion. Later, in St.

Petersburg, Meyerbeer met this gossip and told him that he loved Chopin. "I know no pianist, no composer for the piano like him." Meyerbeer was wrong in his idea of the tempo. Though Chopin slurs the last beat, it is there, nevertheless. This Mazurka is only four lines long and is charming, as charming as the brief specimen in the Preludes. The next Mazurka is another famous warhorse. In B minor, it is full of veiled coquetries, hazardous mood transitions, growling recitatives and smothered plaints. The continual return to the theme gives rise to all manner of fanciful programmes. One of the most characteristic is by the Polish poet Zelenski, who, so Kleczynski relates, wrote a humorous poem on this mazurka. For him it is a domestic comedy in which a drunken peasant and his much abused wife enact a little scene. Returning home the worse for wear he sings "Oj ta dana" — "Oh dear me" — and rumbles in the bass in a figure that answers the treble. His wife reproaching him, he strikes her. Here we are in B flat. She laments her fate in B major. Then her husband shouts: "Be quiet, old vixen." This is given in the octaves, a genuine dialogue, the wife tartly answering: "Sha'n't be quiet." The gruff grumbling in the bass is heard, an imitation of the above, when suddenly the man cries out, the last eight bars of the composition: "Kitty, Kitty come —do come here, I forgive you," which is decidedly masculine in its magnanimity.

If one does not care for the rather coarse realism of this reading Kleczynski offers the poem of Ujejeski, called The Dragoon. A soldier flatters a girl at the inn. She flies from him, and her lover, believing she has deceived him, despairingly drowns himself. The ending, with its "Ring, ring, ring the bell there! Horses carry me to the depths," has more poetic contour than the other. Without grafting any libretto on it, this Mazurka is a beautiful tone-piece in itself. Its theme is delicately mournful and the subject, in B major, simply entrancing in its broad, flowing melody.

In C sharp minor, op. 41, is a Mazurka that is beloved of me. Its scale is exotic, its rhythm convincing, its tune a little saddened by life, but courage never fails. This theme sounds persistently, in the middle voices, in the bass, and at the close in full harmonies, unisons, giving it a start-ling effect. Octaves take it up in profile until it vanishes. Here is the very apotheo sis of rhythm. No. 2, in E minor, is not very resolute of heart. It was composed, so Niecks avers, at Palma, when Chopin's health fully accounts for the depressed character of the piece, for it is sad to the point of tears. Of op. 41 he wrote to Fontana from Nohant in 1839, "You know I have four new Mazurkas, one from Palma, in E minor; three from here, in B major, A flat major and C sharp minor. They seem to me pretty, as the youngest children usually do when the parents grow old." No. 3 is a vigorous, sonorous dance. No. 4, over which the editors deviate on the serious matter of text, in A flat, is for the concert room, and is allied to several of his gracious Valses. Playful and decorative, but not profound in feeling.

Opus 50, the first in G major, is healthy and vivacious. Good humor predominates. Kullak notes that in some editions it closes pianissimo, which seems a little out of drawing. No. 2 is charming. In A flat, it is a perfect specimen of the aristocratic Mazurka. The D flat Trio, the answering episode in B flat minor, and the grace of the return make this one to be studied and treasured. De Lenz finds Bach-ian influences in the following, in C sharp minor: "It begins as though written for the organ, and ends in an exclusive salon; it does him credit and is worked out more fully than the others. Chopin was much pleased when I told him that in the construction of this Mazurka the passage from E major to F major was the same as that in the Agatha aria in ' Freischütz.' '' De Lenz refers to the opening Bach-like mutations. The texture of this dance is closer and finer spun than any we have encountered. Perhaps spontaneity is impaired, mais que voulez vous? Chopin was bound to develop, and his Mazurkas, fragile and constricted as is the form, were sure to show a like record of spiritual and intellectual growth.

Opus 56, in B major, is elaborate, even in its beginning. There is decoration in the ritornelle in E flat and one feels the absence of a compensating emotion, despite the display of contrapuntal skill. Very virtuoso-like, but not so intimate as some of the others. Karasowski selects No. 2 in C as an illustration. "It is as though the composer had sought for the moment to divert himself with narcotic intoxication only to fall back the more deeply into his original gloom." There is the peasant in the first bars in C, but the A minor and what follows soon dis-

turb the air of bonhomie. Theoretical ease
is in the imitative passages; Chopin is
now master of his tools. The third Mazurka
of op. 56 is in C minor. It is quite long
and does not give the impression of a whole.
With the exception of a short break in B
major, it is composed with the head, not the
heart, nor yet the heels.

Not unlike, in its sturdy affirmation, the
one in C sharp minor, op. 41, is the next
Mazurka, in A minor, op. 59. That Chopin
did not repeat himself is an artistic miracle.
A subtle turn takes us off the familiar road
to some strange glade, wherein the flowers
are rare in scent and odor. This Mazurka,
like the one that follows, has a dim resemblance to others, yet there is always a
novel point of departure, a fresh harmony, a
sudden melody or an unexpected ending.
Hadow, for example, thinks the A flat of
this opus the most beautiful of them all.
In it he finds legitimately used the repetition in various shapes of a single phrase.
To me this Mazurka seems but an amplifica-
tion, an elaboration of the lovely one in the
same key, op. 50, No. 2. The double sixths
and more complicated phraseology do not
render the later superior to the early Mazurka, yet there is no gainsaying the fact

that this is a noble composition. But the next, in F sharp minor, despite its rather saturnine gaze, is stronger in interest, if not in workmanship. While it lacks Niecks' beautés sauvages, is it not far loftier in conception and execution than op. 6, in F sharp minor? The inevitable triplet appears in the third bar, and is a hero throughout. Oh, here is charm for you! Read the close of the section in F sharp major. In the major it ends, the triplet fading away at last, a mere shadow, a turn on D sharp, but victor to the last. Chopin is at the summit of his invention. Time and tune, that wait for no man, are now his bond slaves. Pathos, delicacy, boldness, a measured melancholy and the art of euphonious presentment of all these, and many factors more, stamp this Mazurka a masterpiece.

Niecks believes there is a return of the early freshness and poetry in the last three Mazurkas, op. 63. "They are, indeed, teeming with interesting matter," he writes. "Looked at from the musician's point of view, how much do we not see novel and strange, beautiful and fascinating withal? Sharp dissonances, chromatic passing notes, suspensions and anticipations, displacement of accent, progressions of perfect fifths —

the horror of schoolmen — sudden turns and unexpected digressions that are so unaccountable, so out of the line of logical sequence, that one's following the composer is beset with difficulties. But all this is a means to an end, the expression of an individuality with its intimate experiences. The emotional content of many of these trifles — trifles if considered only by their size — is really stupendous." Spoken like a brave man and not a pedant!

Full of vitality is the first number of op. 63. In B major, it is sufficiently various in figuration and rhythmical life to single it from its fellows. The next, in F minor, has a more elegiac ring. Brief and not difficult of matter or manner is this dance. The third, of winning beauty, is in C sharp minor — surely a pendant to the C sharp minor Valse. I defy anyone to withstand the pleading, eloquent voice of this Mazurka. Slender in technical configuration, yet it impressed Louis Ehlert so much that he was impelled to write: "A more perfect canon in the octave could not have been written by one who had grown gray in the learned arts."

The four Mazurkas, published posthumously in 1855, that comprise op. 67 were

composed by Chopin at various dates. To
the first, in G, Klindworth affixes 1849 as
the year of composition. Niecks gives a
much earlier date, 1835. I fancy the latter
is correct, as the piece sounds like one of
Chopin's more youthful efforts. It is jolly
and rather superficial. The next, in G
minor, is familiar. It is very pretty, and
its date is set down by Niecks as 1849,
while Klindworth gives 1835. Here again
Niecks is correct, although I suspect that
Klindworth transposed his figures accidentally. No. 3, in C, was composed in
1835. On this both biographer and editor
agree. It is certainly an early effusion of
no great value, although a good dancing
tune. No. 4 A minor, of this opus, composed in 1846, is more mature, but in no wise
remarkable.

Opus 68, the second of the Fontana set,
was composed in 1830. The first, in C, is
commonplace; the one in A minor, composed in 1827, is much better, being lighter
and well made; the third, in F major, 1830,
weak and trivial, and the fourth, in F
minor, 1849, interesting because it is said
by Julius Fontana to be Chopin's last composition. He put it on paper a short time
before his death, but was too ill to try it at

the piano. It is certainly morbid in its sick insistence in phrase repetition, close harmonies and wild departure — in A — from the first figure. But it completes the gloomy and sardonic loop, and we wish, after playing this veritable song of the tomb, that we had parted from Chopin in health, not disease. This page is full of the premonitions of decay. Too weak and faltering to be febrile, Chopin is here a debile, prematurely exhausted young man. There are a few accents of a forced gayety, but they are swallowed up in the mists of dissolution — the dissolution of one of the most sensitive brains ever wrought by nature. Here we may echo, without any savor of Liszt's condescension or de Lenz's irony: "Pauvre Frédéric!"

Klindworth and Kullak have different ideas concerning the end of this Mazurka. Both are correct. Kullak, Klindworth and Mikuli include in their editions two Mazurkas in A minor. Neither is impressive. One, the date of composition unknown, is dedicated "à son ami Émile Gaillard;" the other first appeared in a musical publication of Schotts' about 1842 or 1843 — according to Niecks. Of this set I prefer the former; it abounds in octaves and ends with a long trill.

CHOPIN

There is in the Klindworth edition a Mazurka, the last in the set, in the key of F sharp. It is so un-Chopinish and artificial that the doubts of the pianist Ernst Pauer were aroused as to its authenticity. On inquiry — Niecks quotes from the London monthly "Musical Record," July 1, 1882 — Pauer discovered that the piece was identical with a Mazurka by Charles Mayer. Gotthard being the publisher of the alleged Chopin Mazurka, declared he bought the manuscript from a Polish countess — possibly one of the fifty in whose arms Chopin died — and that the lady parted with Chopin's autograph because of her dire poverty. It is, of course, a clear case of forgery.

Of the four early Mazurkas, in G major and B flat major — dating from 1825 — D major — composed in 1829–30, but remodelled in 1832 — and C major — of 1833 — the latter is the most characteristic. The G major is of slight worth. As Niecks remarks, it contains a harmonic error. The one in B flat starts out with a phrase that recalls the A minor Mazurka, numbered 45 in the Breitkopf & Härtel edition. This B flat Mazurka, early as it was composed, is, nevertheless, pretty. There are breadth and decision in the C major Mazurka. The recasting improves the D major Mazurka. Its trio is lifted an octave and the doubling of notes throughout gives more weight and richness.

"In the minor key laughs and cries, dances and mourns the Slav," says Dr. J. Schucht in his monograph on Chopin. Chopin here reveals not only his nationality, but his own fascinating and enigmatic individuality. Within the tremulous spaces of this immature dance is enacted the play of a human soul, a soul that voices the sorrow and revolt of a dying race, of a dying poet. They are epigrammatic, fluctuating, crazy, and tender, these Mazurkas, and some of them have a soft, melancholy light, as if shining through alabaster — true corpse light leading to a morass of doubt and terror. But a fantastic, dishevelled, debonair spirit is the guide, and to him we abandon ourselves in these precise and vertiginous dances.

XIV

CHOPIN THE CONQUEROR

THE Scherzi of Chopin are of his own creation; the type as illustrated by Beethoven and Mendelssohn had no meaning for him. Whether in earnest or serious jest, Chopin pitched on a title that is widely misleading when the content is considered. The Beethoven Scherzo is full of a robust sort of humor. In it he is seldom poetical, frequently given to gossip, and at times he hints at the mystery of life. The demoniacal element, the fierce jollity that mocks itself, the almost titanic anger of Chopin would not have been regarded by the composer of the Eroica Symphony as adapted to the form. The Pole practically built up a new musical structure, boldly called it a Scherzo, and, as in the case of the Ballades, poured into its elastic mould most disturbing and incomparable music.

Chopin seldom compasses sublimity. His arrows are tipped with fire, yet they do not fly far. But in some of his music he skirts

374

the regions where abide the gods. In at least one Scherzo, in one Ballade, in the F minor Fantaisie, in the first two movements of the B flat minor Sonata, in several of the Études, and in one of the Preludes, he compasses grandeur. Individuality of utterance, beauty of utterance, and the eloquence we call divine are his; criticism then bows its questioning brows before this anointed one. In the Scherzi Chopin is often prophet as well as poet. He fumes and frets, but upon his countenance is the precious fury of the sibyls. We see the soul that suffers from secret convulsions, but forgive the writhing for the music made. These four Scherzi are psychical records, confessions committed to paper of outpourings that never could have passed the lips. From these alone we may almost reconstruct the real Chopin, the inner Chopin, whose conventional exterior so ill prepared the world for the tragic issues of his music.

The first Scherzo is a fair model. There are a few bars of introduction — the porch, as Niecks would call it — a principal subject, a trio, a short working-out section, a skilful return to the opening theme, and an elaborate coda. This edifice, not architecturally flawless, is better adapted to the

florid beauties of Byzantine treatment than to
the severe Hellenic line. Yet Chopin gave
it dignity, largeness and a classic massive-
ness. The interior is romantic, is modern,
personal, but the façade shows gleaming
minarets, the strangely builded shapes of
the Orient. This B minor Scherzo has the
acid note of sorrow and revolt, yet the complex figuration never wavers. The walls
stand firm despite the hurricane blowing
through and around them. Ehlert finds this
Scherzo tornadic. It is gusty, and the
hurry and over-emphasis do not endear it to
the pianist. The first pages are filled with
wrathful sounds, there is much tossing of
hands and cries to heaven, calling down its
fire and brimstone. A climax mounts to a
fine frenzy until the lyric intermezzo in B is
reached. Here love chants with honeyed
tongues. The widely dispersed figure of
the melody has an entrancing tenderness.
But peace does not long prevail against the
powers of Eblis, and infernal is the Wilde
Jagd of the finale. After shrillest of dissonances, a chromatic uproar pilots the
doomed one across this desperate Styx.

What Chopin's programme was we can
but guess. He may have outlined the composition in a moment of great ebullition, a

time of soul laceration arising from a cat
scratch or a quarrel with Maurice Sand in
the garden over the possession of the goat
cart.

The Klindworth edition is preferable.
Kullak follows his example in using the
double note stems in the B major part. He
gives the A sharp in the bass six bars before
the return of the first motif. Klindworth,
and other editions, prescribe A natural,
which is not so effective. This Scherzo
might profit by being played without the
repeats. The chromatic interlocked octaves
at the close are very striking.

I find at times — as my mood changes —
something almost repellant in the B minor
Scherzo. It does not present the frank
physiognomy of the second Scherzo, op. 31,
in B flat minor. Ehlert cries that it was
composed in a blessed hour, although de
Lenz quotes Chopin as saying of the opening,
"It must be a charnel house." The defiant challenge of the beginning has no savor
of the scorn and drastic mockery of its forerunner. We are conscious that tragedy im-
pends, that after the prologue may follow fast
catastrophe. Yet it is not feared with all
the portentous thunder of its index. Nor
are we deceived. A melody of winning

distinction unrolls before us. It has a noble tone, is of a noble type. Without relaxing pace it passes and drops like a thunderbolt into the bowels of the earth. Again the story is told, and tarrying not at all we are led to a most delectable spot in the key of A major. This trio is marked by genius. Can anything be more bewitching than the episode in C sharp minor merging into E major, with the overflow at the close? The fantasy is notable for variety of tonality, freedom in rhythmical incidents and genuine power. The coda is dizzy and overwhelming. For Schumann this Scherzo is Byronic in tenderness and boldness. Karasowski speaks of its Shakespearian humor, and indeed it is a very human and lovable piece of art. It holds richer, warmer, redder blood than the other three and like the A flat Ballade, is beloved of the public. But then it is easier to understand.

Opus 39, the third Scherzo in C sharp minor, was composed or finished at Majorca and is the most dramatic of the set. I confess to see no littleness in the polished phrases, though irony lurks in its bars and there is fever in its glance — a glance full of enigmatic and luring scorn. I heartily agree with Hadow, who finds the work clear cut and of exact balance. And noting that Chopin founded whole paragraphs "either on a single phrase repeated in similar shapes or on two phrases in alternation" — a primitive practice in Polish folksongs — he asserts that "Beethoven does not attain the lucidity of his style by such parallelism of phraseology," but admits that Chopin's methods made for "clearness and precision . . . may be regarded as characteristic of the national manner." A thoroughly personal characteristic too.

There is virile clangor in the firmly struck octaves of the opening pages. No hesitating, morbid view of life, but rank, harsh assertiveness, not untinged with splenetic anger. The chorale of the trio is admirably devised and carried out. Its piety is a bit of liturgical make-believe. The contrasts here are most artistic — sonorous harmonies set off by broken chords that deliciously tinkle. There is a coda of frenetic movement and the end is in major, a surprising conclusion when considering all that has gone before. Never to become the property of the profane, the C sharp minor Scherzo, notwithstanding its marked asperities and agitated moments, is a great work of art. Without the inner freedom of its predecessor, it is more soper and self-contained than the B minor Scherzo.

The fourth Scherzo, op. 54, is in the key of E. Built up by a series of cunning touches and climaxes and without the mood depth or variety of its brethren, it is more truly a Scherzo than any of them. It has tripping lightness and there is sunshine imprisoned behind its open bars. Of it Schumann could not ask, "How is gravity to clothe itself if jest goes about in dark veils?" Here, then, is intellectual refinement and jesting of a superior sort. Niecks thinks it fragmentary. I find the fairy-like measures delightful after the doleful mutterings of some of the other Scherzi. There is the same "spirit of opposition," but of arrogance none. The C sharp minor theme is of lyric beauty, the coda with its scales, brilliant. It seems to be banned by classicists and Chopin worshippers alike. The agnostic attitude is not yet dead in the piano playing world.

Rubinstein most admired the first two Scherzi. The B minor has been criticised for being too much in the étude vein. But with all their shortcomings these compositions are without peer in the literature of the piano.

They were published and dedicated as follows: Op. 20, February, 1835, to M. T. Albrecht; op. 31, December, 1837, Comtesse de Fürstenstein; op. 39, October, 1840, Adolph Gutmann, and op. 54, December, 1843, Mlle. de Caraman. De Lenz relates that Chopin dedicated the C sharp minor Scherzo to his pupil Gutmann, because this giant, with a prize fighter's fist, could "knock a hole in the table" with a certain chord for the left hand — sixth measure from the beginning — and adds quite naïvely: "Nothing more was ever heard of this Gutmann — he was a discovery of Chopin's." Chopin died in this same Gutmann's arms, and, despite de Lenz, Gutmann was in evidence until his death as a "favorite pupil."

And now we have reached the grandest — oh, banal and abused word — of Chopin's compositions, the Fantaisie in F minor, op. 49. Robert Schumann, after remarking that the cosmopolitan must "sacrifice the small interests of the soil on which he was born," notices that Chopin's later works "begin to lose something of their especial Sarmatian physiognomy, to approach partly more nearly the universal ideal cultivated by the divine Greeks which we find again in Mozart." The F minor Fantaisie has hardly the Mozartian serenity, but parades a formal beauty — not disfigured by an excess of violence, either personal or patriotic, and its melodies, if restless by melancholy, are of surprising nobility and dramatic grandeur. Without including the Beethoven Sonatas, not strictly born of the instrument, I do not fear to maintain that this Fantaisie is one of the greatest of piano pieces. Never properly appreciated by pianists, critics, or public, it is, after more than a half century of neglect, being understood at last. It was published November, 1843, and probably composed at Nohant, as a letter of the composer indicates. The dedication is to Princesse C. de Souzzo — these interminable countesses and princesses of Chopin! For Niecks, who could not at first discern its worth, it suggests a Titan in commotion. It is Titanic; the torso of some Faust-like dream, it is Chopin's Faust. A macabre march, containing some dangerous dissonances, gravely ushers us to ascending staircases of triplets, only to precipitate us to the very abysses of the piano. That first subject, is it not almost as ethically puissant and passionate as Beethoven in his F minor Sonata? Chopin's lack of tenaciousness is visible here. Beethoven would have built a cathedral on such a foundational scheme, but Chopin, ever prodigal in his melody making, dashes impetuously to the A flat episode, that heroic love chant, erroneously marked dolce and played with the effeminacies of a salon. Three times does it resound in this strange Hall of Glancing Mirrors, yet not once should it be caressed. The bronze fingers of a Tausig are needed. Now are arching the triplets to the great, thrilling song, beginning in C minor, and then the octaves, in contrary motion, split wide asunder the very earth. After terrific chordal reverberations there is the rapid retreat of vague armies, and once again is begun the ascent of the rolling triplets to inaccessible heights, and the first theme sounds in C minor. The modulation lifts to G flat, only to drop to abysmal depths. What mighty, desperate cause is being espoused? When peace is presaged in the key of B, is this the prize for which strive these agonized hosts? Is some forlorn princess locked behind these solemn, inaccessible bars? For a few moments there is contentment beyond all price. Then the warring tribe of triplets recommence, after clamorous G flat octaves reeling from the stars to the sea of the first theme. Another rush into D flat ensues, the song of C minor reappears

in F minor, and the miracle is repeated.
Oracular octaves quake the cellarage of the
palace, the warriors hurry by, their measured
tramp is audible after they vanish, and the
triplets obscure their retreat with chromatic
vapors. Then an adagio in this fantastic
old world tale — the curtain prepares to
descend — a faint, sweet voice sings a short,
appealing cadenza, and after billowing A
flat arpeggios, soft, great hummocks of tone,
two giant chords are sounded, and the Ballade of Love and War is over. Who con-
quers? Is the Lady with the Green Eyes
and Moon White Face rescued? Or is all
this a De Quincey's Dream Fugue translated
into tone — a sonorous, awesome vision?
Like De Quincey, it suggests the apparition
of the empire of fear, the fear that is secretly
felt with dreams, wherein the spirit expands
to the drummings of infinite space.

Alas! for the validity of subjective criticism. Franz Liszt told Vladimir de Pachmann the programme of the Fantaisie, as
related to him by Chopin. At the close of
one desperate, immemorial day, the pianist
was crooning at the piano, his spirits vastly
depressed. Suddenly came a knocking at
his door, a Poe-like, sinister tapping, which
he at once rhythmically echoed upon the

keyboard, his phono-motor centre being unusually sensitive. The first two bars of the Fantaisie describe these rappings, just as the third and fourth stand for Chopin's musical invitation, entrez, entrez! This is all repeated until the doors wide open swinging admit Liszt, George Sand, Madame Camille Pleyel née Mock, and others. To the solemn measures of the march they enter, and range themselves about Chopin, who after the agitated triplets begins his complaint in the mysterious song in F minor. But Sand, with whom he has quarrelled, falls before him on her knees and pleads for pardon. Straightway the chant merges into the appealing A flat section — this sends skyward my theory of its interpretation — and from C minor the current becomes more tempestuous until the climax is reached and to the second march the intruders rapidly vanish. The remainder of the work, with the exception of the Lento Sostenuto in B — where it is to be hoped Chopin's perturbed soul finds momentary peace — is largely repetition and development. This far from ideal reading is an authoritative one, coming as it does from Chopin by way of Liszt. I console myself for its rather commonplace character with the notion that perhaps in the re-telling the story has caught some personal cadenzas of the two historians. In any case I shall cling to my own version.

The F minor Fantaisie will mean many things to many people. Chopin has never before maintained so artistically, so free from delirium, such a level of strong passion, mental power and exalted euphony. It is his largest canvas, and though there are no long-breathed periods such as in the B flat minor Scherzo, the phraseology is amply broad, without padding of paragraphs. The rapt interest is not relaxed until the final bar. This transcendental work more nearly approaches Beethoven in its unity, its formal rectitude and its brave economy of thematic material.

While few men have dared to unlock their hearts thus, Chopin is not so intimate here as in the mazurkas. But the pulse beats ardently in the tissues of this composition. As art for art, it is less perfect; the gain is on the human side. Nearing his end Chopin discerned, with ever widening, ever brighter vision, the great heart throb of the universe. Master of his material, if not of his mortal tenement, he passionately strove to shape his dreams into abiding sounds. He did not always succeed, but his victories are the precious prizes of mankind. One is loath to believe that the echo of Chopin's magic music can ever fall upon unheeding ears. He may become old-fashioned, but, like Mozart, he will remain eternally beautiful.

BIBLIOGRAPHY

BIBLIOGRAPHY

Frédéric Chopin as a Man and Musician, by Frederick Niecks. London, Novello, Ewer & Co.

Frédéric Chopin, by Franz Liszt. London, W. Reeves.

Life and Letters of Frédéric Chopin, by Moritz Karasowski, translated from the Russian by Emily Hill. London, W. Reeves.

Chopin and Other Musical Essays, by Henry T. Finck. New York, Charles Scribner's Sons.

The Works of Frédéric Chopin and their Proper Interpretation, by Jean Kleczynski, translated by A. Whittingham. London, W. Reeves.

Chopin's Greater Works, by Jean Kleczynski, translated with additions by Natalie Janotha. New York, Charles Scribner's Sons.

Frédéric François Chopin, by Charles Willeby. London, Sampson Low, Marston & Co.

Frédéric Chopin, by Joseph Bennett. Novello, Ewer & Co.

F. Chopin, la Tradicion de su Musica, por Eduardo Gariel. City of Mexico, 1894.

Frédéric Chopin, sa Vie et ses Œuvres, par Madame A. Audley. Paris, E. Plon et Cie.

F. Chopin, Essai de Critique musicale, par H. Barbedette.

CHOPIN

Friedrich Chopin und seine Werke, von Dr. J Schucht. Leipzig, C. F. Kahnt.

Friedrich Chopin's Leben und Werke, von A. Niggli. Leipzig, Breitkopf & Härtel.

Chopin, by Francis Hueffer, in Musical Studies. Edinburgh, A. & C. Black.

Frédéric Chopin, by W. H. Hadow, in Studies in Modern Music. New York, Macmillan Co.

Frédéric Chopin, by Louis Ehlert, in From the Tone World, translated by Helen D. Tretbar. New York.

Chopin, by W. de Lenz, from The Great Piano Virtuosos of our Time, translated by Madeleine R. Baker. New York, G. Schirmer.

Chopin, in Robert Schumann's Music and Musicians, translated by Fanny Raymond Ritter. New York, Schuberth & Co.

Chopin, in Anton Rubinstein's Conversation on Music, translated by Mrs. John P. Morgan. Steinway Hall: Charles F. Tretbar, publisher.

Les Musiciens Polonais, par Albert Sowinski. Paris, Le Clerc.

Les Trois Romans de Frédéric Chopin, par le Comte Wodinski. Paris, Calman Lévy.

Une Contemporaine, par M. Brault.

Histoire de ma Vie et Correspondance, par George Sand. Paris, Calman Lévy.

George Sand, by Henry James in French Poets and Novelists. New York, Macmillan Co.

G. Sand, par Stefane-Pol, from Trois Grandes Figures, preface by D'Armand Silvestre. Paris, Ernest Flammarian.

BIBLIOGRAPHY

George Sand, sa Vie et ses Œuvres, par Wladimir Karénine. Paris, Ollendorf.

Deux Élèves de Chopin, par Adolphe Brisson.

The Beautiful in Music, by Dr. Eduard Hanslick. Translated by Gustave Cohen. Novello, Ewer & Co., London and New York.

How Music Developed, by W. J. Henderson. New York, Frederick A. Stokes Co.

Wagner and His Works, by Henry T. Finck. New York, Charles Scribner's Sons.

By the Way, by William F. Apthorp. Boston, Copeland & Day.

A Study of Wagner, by Ernest Newman. New York, G. P. Putnam's Sons.

Folk-Music Studies, by H. E. Krehbiel. New York Tribune, August, 1899.

Analytical Notes to Schlesinger Edition, by Theodor Kullak.

The New Spirit, by Havelock Ellis. London, Walter Scott, Ltd.

Flaubert, par Émile Faguet. Paris, Hachette et Cie.

Reisebilder, by Heinrich Heine.

Affirmations, by Havelock Ellis. London, Walter Scott.

The Psychology of the Emotions, by Th. Ribot. New York, Charles Scribner's Sons.

The Man of Genius, by Cesare Lombroso. New York, Charles Scribner's Sons.

The Musical Courier, New York. Files from 1880 to 1900.

CHOPIN

Chopin's Works, by Rutland Boughton, in London Musical Standard.

Chopin, by Stanislas Count Tarnowski. Translated from the Polish by Natalie Janotha. 1899.

The School of Giorgione, An Essay by Walter Pater.

Chopin and the Sick Men, by John F. Runciman, in London Saturday Review, September 9, 1899.

Frederick Chopin, by Edward Dannreuther from Famous Composers and their Works. Boston, J. B. Millet Company.

Primitive Music, by Wallaschek.

Zur Psychologie des Individuums, Chopin und Nietzsche, by Stanislaw Przybyszewski. Berlin, W. Fontaine & Co., 1892.

Musical Interpretation, by Adolph Carpé. Leipzig, London and Paris, Bosworth & Co., Boston, B. F. Wood Music Co.

Pianistes Célèbres, par François Marmontel.

Frederyka Chopina, in Echo Musicale, Warsaw, Poland, October 15, 1899.

Œuvres Poétiques Complètes de Adam Miçkiewicz, Traduction du Polonais par Christien Ostrowski. Paris, Firmin Didot Frères, Fils et Cie, 1859.

The World as Will and Idea, by Arthur Schopenhauer.

The Case of Richard Wagner, by Friedrich Nietzsche. New York, Macmillan Co.

With the Immortals, by Marion Crawford. References to Chopin.

Preface to Isidor Philipp's Exercises Quotidiens tirés des Œuvres de Chopin, by Georges Mathias. Paris, J. Hamelle.

BIBLIOGRAPHY

Pianoforte Study, by Alexander McArthur.

Chopin Ein Gedenkblatt, by August Spanuth, New York Staats-Zeitung, October 15, 1899.

The Pianoforte Sonata, by J. B. Shedlock, London, Methuen & Co.

A History of Pianoforte Playing and Pianoforte Literature, by C. F. Weitzmann, translated by Dr. Th. Baker. New York, G. Schirmer.

Der Letze Virtuoso, by C. F. Weitzmann. Leipzig, Kahnt.

Chopin — and Some Others, in London Musical News, October 14, 1899.

Chopin, in A History of the Pianoforte and Pianoforte Players, by Oscar Bie. New York, E. P. Dutton & Co.

Chopin, in Rubinstein's Die Meister des Klaviers. New York, Schuberth.

Chopin, in Berliner Tageblatt, by Dr. Leopold Schmidt.

Chopin Juzgada por Schumann, in Gaceta Musical, City of Mexico.

The Chopin Rubato and so-called Chopin Fingering, by John Kautz, in The Musical Record, Boston, 1898.

Franz Liszt, by Lina Ramann. Breitkopf & Härtel.

Preface to Mikuli Edition by Carl Mikuli.

The Æsthetics of Pianoforte Playing, by Adolf Kullak. New York, G. Schirmer.

Chopin und die Frauen, by Eugen Isolani. Berliner Courier, October 17, 1899.

Chopin, by W. J. Henderson in The New York Times, October 29, 1899.

CHOPIN

A Note on Chopin, by L. A. Corbèille, and Chopin, An Irresponsibility, by "Israfel," in The Dome, October, 1899, London, Unicorn Press.

Chopin and the Romantics, by John F. Runciman in The Saturday Review (London), February 10, 1900.

Chopiniana: in the February, 1900, issue of the London Monthly Musical Record, including some new letters of Chopin's.

La maladie de Chopin (d'après des documents inédits), par Cabanes. Chronique médicale, Paris, 1899, vi., No. 21, 673-685.

Also recollections in letters and diaries of Moscheles, Hiller, Mendelssohn, Berlioz, Henselt, Schumann, Rubinstein, Mathias, Legouvé, Tarnowski, Grenier and others.

The author begs to acknowledge the kind suggestions and assistance of Rafael Joseffy, Vladimir de Pachmann, Moriz Rosenthal, Jaraslow de Zielinski, Edwin W. Morse, Edward E. Ziegler and Ignace Jan Paderewski.

INDEX

INDEX

399

INDEX

INDEX

INDEX

INDEX

INDEX

INDEX

INDEX

INDEX

INDEX

INDEX

INDEX

413

INDEX

412

413

INDEX

INDEX

BOOKS BY JAMES HUNEKER

What some distinguished writers have said of them :

Maurice Maeterlinck wrote, May 15, 1905: "Do you know that 'Iconoclasts' is the only book of high and universal critical worth that we have had for years—to be precise, since Georg Brandes. It is at once strong and fine, supple and firm, indulgent and sure."

And of "Ivory Apes and Peacocks" he said, among other things: "I have marvelled at the vigilance and clarity with which you follow and judge the new literary and artistic movements in all countries. I do not know of criticism more pure and sure than yours." (October, 1915.)

———

"The Mercure de France translated the other day from Scribner's one of the best studies which have been written on Stendhal for a long time, in which there was no evasion of the question of Stendhal's immorality. The author of that article, James Huneker, is, among foreign critics, the one best acquainted with French literature and the one who judges us with the greatest sympathy and with the most freedom. He has protested with force in numerous American journals against the campaign of defamation against France and he has easily proved that those who participate in it are ignorant and fanatical."—*"Promenades Littéraires"* (*Troisième Série*), *Remy de Gourmont.* (Translated by Burton Rascoe for the Chicago *Tribune*.)

———

Paul Bourget wrote, Lundi de Paques, 19⊂⊃, on "Egoists": "I have browsed through the pages of your book and found that you touch in a sympathetic style on diverse problems, artistic and literary. In the case of Stendhal your catholicity of treatmen. is extremely rare and courageous."

———

Dr. Georg Brandes, the versatile and profound Danish critic, wrote: "I find your breadth of view and its expression more European than American; but the essential thing is that you are an artist to your very marrow."

BOOKS BY JAMES HUNEKER

LETTERS OF JAMES GIBBONS HUNEKER

These letters have all the brilliance of his essays, but a greater spontaneity and if possible a more vivid spirit.

Among the people to whom they are written are Royal Cortissoz, Henry Cabot Lodge, Richard Aldrich, H. E. Krehbiel, Benjamin de Casseres, W. C. Brownell, Walter Pritchard Eaton, William Marion Reedy, Mrs. Gilbert, Elizabeth Jordan, Frida Ashforth, Emma Eames, the Marquise de Lanza, Henry James, Jr., Henry L. Mencken, etc.

Every page is alive with pointed comment, brilliant characterization, and vivid portraiture. Bohemian and literary New York of the last several decades is mirrored in these letters.

VARIATIONS

"Hold your breath as you go through this book—touring the universe with a man who takes all of life in its everlasting fecundity and efflorescence for his theme."
—BENJAMIN DE CASSERES, in the *New York Herald*.

STEEPLEJACK

ILLUSTRATED

"Not only interesting because of its record of Mr. Huneker's career and philosophy, but because it gives an excellent idea of the developments in art, music, and literature, both in Europe and in America, during the last forty years."
—WILLIAM LYON PHELPS, Yale University.

BEDOUINS

Mary Garden; Debussy; Chopin or the Circus; Botticelli; Poe; Brahmsody; Anatole France; Mirbeau; Caruso on Wheels; Calico Cats; the Artistic Temperament; Idols and Ambergris; With the Supreme Sin; Grindstones; A Masque of Music, and The Vision Malefic.

IVORY APES AND PEACOCKS

"His critical tact is well-nigh infallible. . . . His position among writers on æsthetics is anomalous and incredible: no merchant traffics in his heart, yet he commands a large, an eager, an affectionate public."
—LAWRENCE GILMAN, in *North American Review* (October, 1915)

BOOKS BY JAMES HUNEKER

UNICORNS

"The essays are short, full of a satisfying—and fascinating—crispness, both memorable and delightful. And they are full of fancy, too, of the gayest humor, the quickest appreciation, the gentlest sympathy, sometimes of an enchanting extravagance."
—*New York Times.*

MELOMANIACS

"It would be difficult to sum up 'Melomaniacs' in a phrase. Never did a book, in my opinion at any rate, exhibit greater contrasts, not, perhaps, of strength and weakness, but of clearness and obscurity."
—HAROLD E. GORST, in *London Saturday Review* (Dec. 8, 1906).

VISIONARIES

"In 'The Spiral Road' and in some of the other stories both fantasy and narrative may be compared with Hawthorne in his most unearthly moods. The younger man has read his Nietzsche and has cast off his heritage of simple morals. Hawthorne's Puritanism finds no echo in these modern souls, all sceptical, wavering, and unblessed. But Hawthorne's splendor of vision and his power of sympathy with a tormented mind do live again in the best of Mr. Huneker's stories."
—*London Academy* (Feb. 3, 1906).

ICONOCLASTS:
A Book of Dramatists

"His style is a little jerky, but it is one of those rare styles in which we are led to expect some significance, if not wit, in every sentence."
—G. K. CHESTERTON, in *London Daily News.*

MEZZOTINTS IN MODERN MUSIC

"Mr. Huneker is, in the best sense, a critic; he listens to the music and gives you his impressions as rapidly and in as few words as possible; or he sketches the composers in fine, broad, sweeping strokes with a magnificent disregard for unimportant details. And as Mr. Huneker is, as I have said, a powerful personality, a man of quick brain and an energetic imagination, a man of moods and temperament—a string that vibrates and sings in response to music—we get in these essays of his a distinctly original and very valuable contribution to the world's tiny musical literature."
—J. F. RUNCIMAN, in *London Saturday Review*

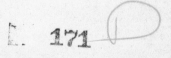

171